# Sweet Pea
# at War

# SWEET PEA AT WAR

## A HISTORY OF

## USS *PORTLAND*

## (CA-33)

WILLIAM THOMAS GENEROUS JR.

THE UNIVERSITY PRESS OF KENTUCKY

Publication of this volume was made possible in part by a grant
from the National Endowment for the Humanities.

Scholarly publisher for the Commonwealth,
serving Bellarmine University, Berea College, Centre College of Kentucky,
Eastern Kentucky University, The Filson Historical Society, Georgetown College,
Kentucky Historical Society, Kentucky State University, Morehead State University,
Murray State University, Northern Kentucky University, Transylvania University,
University of Kentucky, University of Louisville, and Western Kentucky University.
All rights reserved.

*Editorial and Sales Offices:* The University Press of Kentucky
663 South Limestone Street, Lexington, Kentucky 40508–4008
www.kentuckypress.com

07  06  05  04    5  4  3  2

*Frontispiece:* Starboard bow, underway, May 31, 1934.
(NavSource Online: Cruiser Photo Archive)

Maps by Whitney Walker

**Library of Congress Cataloging-in-Publication Data**

Generous, William T.
  Sweet Pea at war : a history of U.S.S. Portland / William T. Generous, Jr.
    p. cm.
Includes bibliographical references and index.
  ISBN 0-8131-2286-4 (Hardcover : alk. paper)
  1. Portland (Cruiser) 2. World War, 1939-1945—Naval operations,
American. 3. World War, 1939-1945—Campaigns—Pacific Area. I. Title.
  D774.P63G45 2003
  940.54'5973—dc21                                         2003008807

This book is printed on acid-free recycled paper meeting the requirements of the
American National Standard for Permanence of Paper for Printed Library Materials.

Manufactured in the United States of America

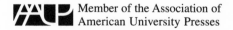 Member of the Association of
American University Presses

To the American Men and Women
of the
World War II Generation

They Had Right on Their Side

# CONTENTS

*Illustrations follow page 130*

# PREFACE

Where are all the World War II cruisers? Hardly a coastal city in the United States today does not have some World War II ship as a museum. There are battleships, aircraft carriers, destroyers, submarines, and a host of smaller craft from World War II all up and down the Atlantic, Pacific, and Gulf seaboards, proudly displayed as memorials to the gallant men who sailed in them and the resilient nation that produced and supported them in the worldwide fight against fascism.

But nowhere is there a *cruiser*. Seventy-four cruisers of all types fought in at least one battle during 1941–1945, and yet not a single one survives today. There were two large cruisers, twenty-five heavy cruisers, and forty-seven light cruisers.[1] But all have been scrapped—no wartime cruiser veteran can visit his old ship or anything like it.

Cruisers are not prominent in historical literature, either. The carriers live on in fame. Several volumes have been written about the great *Enterprise*. One *Yorktown* is the museum ship in Charleston, South Carolina, while an earlier one has recently been the subject of a famous maritime archeology expedition. *Intrepid* is visited by thousands every year at her pier in midtown Manhattan. There are several others here and there.

Many battleships are famous, too. Those sunk at Pearl Harbor, like *Arizona,* which is still officially in commission, live in honor. So do the fighters, such as *Washington, North Carolina,* and some of the Pearl Harbor victims that were refloated and did a magnificent job later. The 1945 surrender was signed on the quarterdeck of the battleship *Missouri,* and she is now a permanent monument in Pearl Harbor. "Mighty Mo" and the three other *Iowa*-class wagons have made several returns to action since 1945, each event lavishly covered by the media. Cable television's The History Channel occasionally runs a three-part series on "The Battleship," from HMS *Dreadnaught* through the placing of *Missouri* next to *Arizona*.

Several destroyers are well known, too. *Greer* and *Kearney,* which were attacked by German U-boats even before the war; the tin cans—the thin-skinned destroyers—which sailed into shallow water at Omaha Beach to help save the D-Day landing; the "Little Beavers" of "31-knot Burke" fame; the "small boys" from the 1944 Battle off Samar who were so outclassed in every way but courage—all are cherished in the nation's naval history. There's a Woodie Guthrie song about destroyer *Reuben James,* which went down with heavy loss of life when torpedoed by a German U-boat two months before Pearl Harbor.

But the cruisers? The general public knows about USS *Indianapolis* (CA-35) because of the 1945 disaster that befell her when the Navy's movement-reporting system lost track of the ship just as she was being attacked by a Japanese submarine. There have been several nonfiction best-sellers written about that tragic episode.[2] But that's *it*.

In fact, the story of the *Indianapolis* in July 1945 now seems symbolic of all the wartime cruisers: "Indy" was misplaced, forgotten, overlooked, and destroyed. All the other wartime cruisers have now suffered the same fate. They have been misplaced, forgotten, overlooked, and all are now destroyed. There are lovingly illustrated, detailed general histories of carriers, battleships, destroyers, and submarines.[3] Cruisers? One of the most useful works on American World War II cruisers was written in *German*!

The book in your hands is a history of what might have been the greatest of the World War II cruisers, USS *Portland* (CA-33). She should be well known, and not at all because she was the only sister of the ill-fated *Indianapolis*. At the end of the war, a Honolulu newspaper wrote of *Portland,* "She is known throughout the navy as the ship that remained at sea for 20 weeks without time for maintenance and repair while engaged in advanced areas with enemy air, surface and sub-surface opposition. Without adequate replenishment of stores and provisions, the PORTLAND nevertheless maintained her battle fitness during this period and participated in the Leyte landings, the Battle of Surigao Straits, the Philippine carrier air strikes, Leyte Gulf, Mindoro landings, Lingayen Patrol and Army support, Corregidor landings and [in]numberable air actions with the enemy."[4]

That paragraph does not even begin to tell the story of this great ship. As this book will show, USS *Portland*

- fought in almost every naval engagement of the Pacific War, sometimes against overwhelming odds, and always came out the victor;
- was the only American ship at all three of the battles that reversed the Japanese victory march across the Pacific;
- was nearly destroyed once by enemy attack but was saved by the skill of her Captain and crew;
- avoided being hit even once by kamikazes, the Japanese suicide aircraft, despite many attacks, again because of the skill of her CO and sailors;
- was singled out by Admiral Chester Nimitz among all the famous ships in the Pacific Fleet to accept the surrender at Truk, the great Japanese naval base in the Carolines; and
- finally was knocked out not by a human enemy, none of which ever defeated her, but by Nature's freak storm, and even then her Captain and crew got her home.

Like all other writers, I'm indebted to many people whose support was critical to the completion of this book. Foremost were the former sailors of *Portland*. The first one was Gordon Olsen, whom I met in a coffee shop in Wallingford, Connecticut, when our wives were finishing their Christmas shopping in 2000. I had never heard of USS *Portland* before that moment, but I never stopped learning about and admiring her afterward.

Every one of Olsen's former shipmates whom I asked gave me precious time on the phone, in emails, and in interviews during their 2001 reunion in Colorado Springs. Among the significant contributions were those made by, alphabetically: Joe Arbour, who was sending me things even as I finished writing; Chuck Morton, who called me again and again to make sure I was getting it right; Willie Partridge, who enthralled me with stories for hours at Colorado Springs and sent me pictures when I asked; Bill Reehl, who emailed me again and again to give me the story's outline when I was just starting; and Ted Waller, who answered uncountable questions and corrected a number of my errors along the way.

Forgive me if in naming those men I omit others who also did good things for me. Please see the bibliography for the list of all who helped out. Merle Choate was typical of them. Merle seemed to wait to finish with me before allowing himself to die just a few weeks later.

Another source I owe special thanks to is Joe Stables's two collections of the veterans' memories of their *Portland* service. Self-published, this is top-drawer, primary-source material, and I thank the stars that Joe gathered these anecdotes a decade ago. So many men have passed away since then, and their experiences would have been lost without their shipmate Stables's idea and hard work.

One work that might have deterred me but actually pressed me into the project was Heber Holbrook's self-published *The History and Times of the U.S.S.* Portland (Dixon, Calif.: Pacific Ship and Shore, 1990). The veterans all recommended it, but at bottom I was disappointed. It is mainly a replaying of the ship's log with some author's remarks on the war that had first been written for his earlier history of his own ship, USS *San Francisco* (CA-38). Then I discovered Holbrook's reluctance to give *Portland* the credit she deserved (possibly out of an understandable loyalty to *San Francisco*), obvious weariness as the work reached late 1944 (when he began simply to transcribe the ship's log), flawed analyses on some parts of the Pacific War, and skimpiness about the sailors who served in *Portland.* I came away believing that someone should do the ship's history right, and got to work hoping to be that historian.

Let me thank Dick Kohn at the University of North Carolina for encouraging me as I worked on this project and Patrick Osborne for helping me find my way through the National Archives. My debt is great to Vanessa Kubach, Alicia Mills, Michael Ward, and Stephen Wrinn for helping me get into and through the publication process. Three anonymous historians at Kentucky read and critiqued the entire manuscript, and old friends Mary Arrighi, Bob Burns, Jennifer Crumlish, Ned Gallagher, Vanessa Kubach, Alexandra Lightfoot, Dennis Mannion, Kevin McCarthy, Alicia Mills, and John Wolf, plus daughters Michelle and Suzanne and wife Diane, read parts of a revised version. All made helpful comments. I'm indebted for more than I can say to Diane, who put up with the long weeks and months I spent in front of the word processor, and then read a chapter and a half. I appreciate her love and patience.

Finally, I'm grateful to the U.S. Navy for giving me, first, an opportunity to serve for seven years, 1956–1959 and 1963–1967, during which I learned enough to be able to understand and appreciate the men who rode in Sweet Pea, and second, two remarkable opportunities to get educated, in between and after those years of active duty, so I could learn the skills it took to research and write this book.

It goes without saying that none of these people are responsible for mistakes that may occur in this book. The errors belong to me alone.

Tom Generous
Carrboro, North Carolina

**1**

# THE SHIP

USS *Portland* has few equals on the roster of naval units as an
experienced warship.

                                                    —*New York Times,* 1945

USS *Portland* was a "heavy cruiser." Battleships are bigger than
cruisers, and destroyers are smaller. The Washington Naval Treaty of
1922 defined all armored ships with gun bores of at least eight inches but
less than fourteen inches as heavy cruisers, and those with gun bores of
less than eight inches as light cruisers. The size of the ships—their
displacement—did not matter.[1]

To say *type* means "all battleships," "all cruisers," or "all
destroyers," and so on. To say *class* means, within a type, a series in
which all the ships are essentially the same. That is, there were four
virtually identical battleships in the *Iowa*-class, and two virtually
identical *North Carolina*-class battleships. The two classes, however,
were very different from each other.

In World War II, all types of ships varied from one class to another
in size. For comparison purposes, battleships were between 26,000 and
45,000 tons in weight, called displacement in the Navy.[2] Large attack
aircraft carriers ran from 20,000 to 45,000 tons, and light carriers were
11,000 to 14,000 tons.[3] Destroyers varied, too, although the most

numerous classes that came into service during the war were 2050 tons or 2200 tons.[4] USS *Portland* displaced about 9800 tons.

The United States had been building what it called "cruisers" since late in the nineteenth century, although those primitive ships were not much like the cruisers of World War II. In 1883, Congress authorized the so-called "ABCD" squadron, ships named *Atlanta, Boston, Chicago,* and *Dolphin.* As it turned out, *Dolphin* was so incompetently and corruptly done that she was not accepted by the Navy when finished. Although the other three did join the fleet, *Atlanta* and *Boston* had no armor, so they were not what was later defined as "cruisers" at all. *Chicago* was armored, to be sure, but *so* hefty that the Brooklyn Navy Yard could not install her heavy machinery, and it was years before she was commissioned. In fact, the first true cruiser to serve in the U.S. Navy was USS *New York,* commissioned in 1893.[5]

This confusion reflected what Admiral George Dewey had once testified: that the armored cruiser was "hardly a distinct type of war vessel" at all, because it was "either so slightly protected and armed as to be a doubtful cruiser or so heavily protected and armed as to be an uncertain battleship."[6] For some years bewilderment reigned, too, about how to refer to this in-between type of ship. Some of the early so-called cruisers had no type designation or hull numbers at all. Then a string of more than twenty were identified as "C-1," "C-2," and so on. Then came five ships labeled "ACR-1," and so on, for "Armored Cruiser." These five included *New York* and were named for states, although that nomenclature was later reserved for battleships.[7]

In January 1931, the U.S. Navy adopted the "heavy" and "light" distinctions mandated by the 1922 treaty. That nomenclature was maintained throughout World War II and later.[8] Heavy and light cruisers were named for cities. Light cruisers, abbreviated as "CL," were not necessarily named for smaller cities than the heavy cruisers, called "CA."

The two "large" cruisers that comprised a third type were heavily armored and carried 12-inch guns. Other navies might have called them "battle cruisers," a type big enough to destroy anything they could not run away from. Indeed their abbreviation "CB" would seem to stand for "Cruiser, Battle." But the United States had had a "battle cruiser" experience in the 1920s, when plans were made to construct six such warships. All six were cancelled because of various treaties, except for two that were converted to aircraft carriers.[9] In World War II, when the

U.S. Navy acquired two armored vessels with 12-inch main batteries, they were called "large cruisers" and named for American territories, USS *Alaska* and USS *Guam*. There were supposed to be four more, but the end of the war stopped their construction.[10]

Heavy cruiser USS *Portland* (CA-33) was built by Bethlehem Steel at its yard in Quincy, Massachusetts, and was named for the city in Maine. Begun in 1931, she was the prototype of a two-ship class.[11] *Portland*'s displacement was just under 10,000 tons, she was about 610 feet in length, 66 feet in maximum beam or width, and drew about 22 feet from keel to waterline in the forward part of the ship, a little more aft. The dimensions mean that she was twice the length of a football field, about as slim as the distance from a baseball pitcher's rubber to home plate, and her underwater depth was about two stories of a skyscraper. She was listed as being capable of almost thirty-three knots.[12] *Portland* carried nine 8-inch guns, three each in two turrets forward and one turret aft; eight 5-inch dual-purpose guns in single mounts, four to a side; and a host of smaller anti-aircraft (AA) guns that varied in caliber from time to time as the ship was repeatedly modernized.[13]

She and her sister *Indianapolis* were really modified *Northampton*-class vessels. All ships of both classes were called "treaty cruisers," because they were limited to less than ten thousand tons in displacement by the London Naval Treaty of 1930. But *Northampton* and her sisters turned out quite a bit smaller in displacement than the treaty allowed. As a result, the two *Portland*-class ships were made about ten feet longer. The difference would provide more space for crew, fuel, water, food, and ammunition. All of these cruisers were intended to counter potential enemies like the German commerce-raiders of World War I. They would do so independently or in small groups, not as members of the main fleet. As a result, *Portland* had huge fuel tanks and therefore extremely long range. But to guarantee her range and speed while keeping her displacement under the limits, she carried less protective armor than was customary for heavy cruisers. Consequently, she was thought to be particularly vulnerable to torpedo attack.[14] Her armor ranged from a high of 5.75 inches at her magazines to a mere 2.6 inches on the sides of her machinery spaces.[15] In an era when armor was supposed to be as thick as the bore of a ship's major guns, *Portland* should have been coated with 8 inches of steel belt. Her thin skin left her otherwise flimsy, as well. One time in 1944, an armed sentry on the forecastle mishandled his rifle and fired a round right through the main deck into the "head" below, where it rattled around, nearly hitting an officer in mid-shower.[16]

The weakness in armor was a major worry. During the war *Portland* was fired at by at least nine torpedoes.[17] Given her theoretical vulnerability to such attacks, one might think that she would have been left in ruins. But in fact, only one torpedo ever did any damage, a testament not only to her good luck but to the skill of her officers and men.

The cruiser was driven by a system of steam-turbine engines. Steam was generated by eight boilers, two in each of four firerooms. Using only two boilers, *Portland* could make cruising speed of about fifteen knots. To go faster she lit up additional boilers. Ordinarily the crew fired all eight when facing combat, of course.[18]

It was hot and dirty work in the boiler rooms, but it was high technology, too. Feed water going into the boilers had to be made out of the ocean's salt water, and it had to be perfect so as not to damage the delicate parts inside the boilers. Water and steam pressure were closely observed and minutely managed at several points along the process, as was both the smoke generated by the boilers and the water that was recondensed after the process was complete.[19]

*Portland*'s power plant was rated at 108,000 horsepower when all eight of her boilers were producing steam. There were two enginerooms, each of which housed two of these massive steam-turbine engines. The high-pressure steam was dumped into huge cylinders with enclosed fans, the turbines, which then spun at high speed to drive shafts that ran the length of the hull to the propellers. Each engine had large reduction gears to slow the turbine speed to a revolution rate these shafts could stand. Four propellers drove the ship through the water. The forward engines drove the two outboard screws and the after engines drove the inboard pair. In addition there were two auxiliary engines, which generated electricity. The ship used direct current (DC), by the way, except for specialty suites like the dentist's chair and the radar equipment, which had their own alternators to create alternating current (AC). The auxiliary engines were powerful enough to drive the ship at her easy cruising speed if need be, but were ordinarily used only for the auxiliary needs of the ship.[20]

Evaporators created fresh water from the limitless ocean that surrounded *Portland*. They would take in the seawater and boil it, then separate the resulting salt from the water vapor, and finally recondense the vapor into fresh water. This water was stored in four tanks, each with a ten thousand–gallon capacity.[21] Again, making fresh water, storing it, and then supplying it in the quantities needed was a matter of high technology. When fresh water was scarce—that is, most of the time—it was closely rationed. For conservation purposes, toilets were flushed by sea water. The sailors were allowed to use fresh water for personal reasons like showering and shaving only at certain hours of the day. Whenever the ship was at sea, no matter how much fresh water was available, personal hygiene required "shipboard showers." A sailor would step into the shower, then turn the water on. He would quickly wet his entire body down, then turn the shower off. With no water running, he would soap his entire body. Only when finished lathering would he turn the water on again for a quick rinse. If fresh water were very low, the sailors would have to take saltwater showers, using soap that was specifically designed for the purpose.

The fuel that powered all this machinery was Navy Standard Fuel Oil. *Portland* could carry a maximum of 900,000 gallons of the magic black stuff, stored in sixty-six tanks of various sizes throughout the ship. The largest held thirty-five thousand gallons, the smallest about five thousand. Each tank was connected to the ship's fire main—that is, the central saltwater lines—so that it could be filled with seawater as soon as it was emptied of fuel. Yet again, this was up-to-date technology for the era. Opening and closing certain valves could send oil from any tank to fuel lines running along the starboard and port sides of the four firerooms and two enginerooms. Athwartship lines would then deliver oil from these starboard and port lines to the boilers where it was needed. Sectionalizing valves could stop or divert the fuel here or there almost anywhere along all these lines of piping.[22]

The system would bewilder anyone not familiar with it. In each fireroom, there were two oil pumps that fed the two boilers and one oil transfer pump to move the fuel around. Using the right combination of pumps and valves, the petty officer known as "the Oil King" could feed fuel to each fireroom from any oil tank on the ship. To prevent the ship from listing, fuel oil was taken as evenly as possible from tanks on both sides. During wartime, each fireroom was connected to its own separate source of oil so that no single hit by a shell or bomb could knock out the fuel supply to all the boilers.[23]

Refueling at sea became a highly proficient skill in the U.S. Navy during World War II. On a given day, *Portland* would rendezvous with a fleet oiler and would maneuver to a position alongside the fueling ship, about one hundred feet away. Together the two vessels would steam at an agreed course and speed, usually into the wind at about twelve knots. Small, weighted lines would be thrown over from the oiler and hauled in on the cruiser. The small lines were attached to larger ones and they were connected to even larger ones and so on, until *Portland*'s crew and machinery could drag across huge oil hoses attached to the strongest lines at the end of the process. When the hoses were fixed into the mouth of *Portland*'s fuel system, the oiler would pump fuel at a rate of close to 300,000 gallons per hour. It might take two and a half hours to get the cruiser's tanks filled to about 95 percent capacity. While fueling proceeded, the Oil King's men on the main deck would continuously check with sounding rods to determine how much was in each tank. Since the shutoff valves were below decks, it took a lot of good judgment and teamwork to get to 95 percent correctly.[24] No one wanted an overflow, because nothing was worse than having a lot of the infinitely slippery fuel oil on the cruiser's decks. But getting as much fuel as possible without a mess was important to maximize how much steaming or fighting the ship could do.

Originally the ship sported portholes above the waterline on several decks along both sides. They helped to ventilate berthing compartments in port during those days before air-conditioning, but they were firmly closed and battle ports were swung over them when the ship was at sea. These peacetime luxury items were welded shut when World War II began, never to be opened again.[25] *Portland* also carried paravanes, devices swung out to the side of the ship's bow for minesweeping.[26] To a later Navy mind this would seem a peculiar task for a heavy cruiser, but *Portland* drilled at minesweeping in the prewar days.[27] Since her Japanese enemies laid mines everywhere, this capability proved valuable to the entire fleet.[28]

## In Commission

Although the ship was officially named by Secretary of the Navy Charles F. Adams on June 6, 1930, her namesake Maine city had been miffed that she was built at a civilian shipyard near Boston and not by the Navy's yard in Bath, near Portland. Her keel was laid by Bethlehem Steel

Company in its yard at Quincy on February 17, 1930, and she was launched there on May 21, 1932.[29]

The cruiser was the first ship named *Portland* to serve in the U.S. Navy. Her commissioning came at the depth of the Great Depression, of course, and Portland's city fathers were further put out by the fact that they could afford to send only a small group to the launching ceremonies.[30] The star of the delegation was twelve-year-old Mary Elizabeth Brooks, daughter of the chairman of the Portland city council, Ralph D. Brooks.[31] It is said that the champagne bottle Mary Elizabeth smashed across the ship's bow when christening her was filled with mere sparkling water, since this was also the Prohibition Era.[32]

The laws against alcoholic beverages generated yet more controversy at the time of the ship's commissioning. It was traditional for the namesake city to provide a silver service set for a newly commissioned cruiser. *Portland*'s included a bowl, a tray, and cups like those used for serving grog in the early days of the Republic. Because of the twin curses of economic depression and the State of Maine's long history of temperance, however, many frugal and/or prohibitionist Down-Easters thought it wrong to spend thousands of dollars on such a thing. The city council courageously voted its approval, but compromisingly authorized no funds for the purchase. Instead, the money to pay for the silver was raised by subscription from residents, business establishments, and service clubs.[33]

Commissioned at Boston in February 1933, *Portland* was supposed to be crewed by about 850 officers and enlisted men, a complement that mushroomed during the war to as many as 1,400.[34] The first Commanding Officer was Captain Herbert Fairfax Leary.[35] By tradition, Commanding Officers of all Navy ships are called "Captain" regardless of their personal rank, but *Portland* rated as CO an actual captain, that is, an officer with four stripes on his sleeve and equal to an Army colonel. Captain Leary, forty-seven at the time he took command, was the son of an admiral. A Marine who served as his orderly described him as a large man who usually sported a pipe and, more permanently, a fully rigged sailing vessel tattooed on his chest.[36] His second-in-command, which the Navy calls the Executive Officer, or "XO," was Commander G.N. Barker.[37]

The organization of the ship followed Navy routine, in that the department heads included a Navigator, a Gunnery Officer, a First

Lieutenant and Damage Control Officer, an Engineering Officer, a Supply Officer, and a Medical Officer.[38] The general responsibilities of each will not be mysterious to a modern reader, except perhaps for "First Lieutenant." The expression is not a rank—it does not exist in the Navy or Coast Guard, although it does in all the other services—it is a *job* title. The First Lieutenant is in charge of the ship's topside upkeep and maintenance. Sailors under him keep the ship's rust under control and repair breaks in the watertight integrity. Damage control was another part of that officer's job in *Portland*'s days, although the two functions were separated in more modern times and were done by two different officers on all U.S. warships.

After commissioning, *Portland* lay strangely idle alongside the pier in Boston, taking on food, ammunition, and other items.[39] The cruiser's coffers were of course empty when she went into commission, so it is not surprising that she took on so much food and other supplies in those first few weeks. But in fact, every time she stopped in port for the rest of her career, Portland loaded massive amounts of stores. Her crew was about one thousand men or more, and they consumed huge quantities of such things. One perfectly typical example was that on November 23, 1937, the ship took aboard "730 lbs of fresh tomatoes, 252 lbs grapes, 1003 lbs sweet potatoes, 650 lbs radishes, 120 lbs hard mixed candy, . . . 305 lbs egg plant, 250 lbs whole wheat meal, 30 lbs olives, 30 lbs garlic, 30 lbs paprika, 784 lbs grapefruit, 520 lbs celery, 20 lbs maringue [*sic*] whip, 869 lbs cauliflower, 732 lbs cucumbers, 20 lbs parsley, . . . 832 lbs oranges, 720 lbs sugar, 1292 lbs smoked ham, 249 lbs beef liver, . . . 200 lbs cranberries, 1006 lbs lamb."

The items came from fifteen different companies, including Swift and Company, Hall Ship Supply Company, Harbor Ship Supply Company, and others, and would endure for a week or two.[40] The invoices demonstrate how important the fleet was to local businesses that supplied the ships. For example, every day in port in November 1937, *Portland* purchased fifty or more gallons of fresh milk from Golden State Company, Ltd.[41] That was surely a big sale for Golden State.

During the first six weeks after her commissioning, the ship's crew trained in such things as fire prevention and fire fighting, and the officers dealt with the myriad disciplinary problems that beset all ships in peace and war.[42] But even before she had her customary shakedown cruise for underway training, *Portland* was thrown into emergency action, and she responded well to the challenge. On April 4, 1933, the Navy's dirigible *Akron* crashed into the Atlantic about thirty miles off the New Jersey shore. On board the airship was the chief of the Bureau of Aeronautics, Rear Admiral William A. Moffett, a vigorous proponent of lighter-than-air aviation, and seventy-six other people. *Portland* had left Boston two days earlier and was about to visit New York City at the time. Upon receiving orders from Washington, she raced to the scene, arriving before any other American vessel.[43]

As the senior officer present afloat (SOPA), Captain Leary took control of the operation. He coordinated the efforts of a host of Navy, Coast Guard, and civilian aircraft and vessels to search and rescue, and later to search and salvage. When *Portland* arrived on the scene, a merchant vessel, SS *Phoebus* from the Danzig Free State, had already picked up the three survivors who would ever be found.[44] They were transferred a few hours later to a Coast Guard cutter and taken ashore. As more and more ships arrived, Leary assigned them to areas of patrol and search, anchoring *Portland* not far from the Barnegat Light Vessel, about ten miles due south of Tom's River on the central Jersey coast.[45]

Despite the effort, the task force saved only those three lives. Admiral Moffett was among the missing, presumed killed. Ships picked up debris and brought it to *Portland* for salvage, but not a single body of any of the victims was retrieved.[46]

While *Portland* and the other ships were trying to save lives and recover victims, they tasted the unpleasant reality of Depression America. From time to time, several fishing boats came alongside the cruiser out of the fog and high seas that interfered with the efforts. The crews would yell up to the bridge that they knew where the crash had occurred and would ask what the reward was. When Leary called back that it was their *duty* to tell him where it was, the smacks would just pull away and disappear into the mist.[47]

Within a day and a half, the Captain knew that the effort was going to prove fruitless. Late in the afternoon of April 6, he requested permission to return to port, to begin again the training that his new ship and its crew needed. Permission was granted, but a heavy fog made moving too perilous, so *Portland* remained at anchor overnight.[48] The next morning seven newsmen arrived on the scene, hoping to see a little action, and came aboard the cruiser.[49] No doubt unwilling to pass up a chance at some press and movie coverage of the gallant efforts at rescue, the Navy changed *Portland*'s orders, and she stayed out there for another two weeks. But she accomplished nothing of importance. Finally, on April 19, the commodore of a destroyer squadron relieved Leary, and *Portland* left.[50] In all that time, only scraps of wreckage were discovered. Leary had been right: the operation could have been cancelled a day or two after the dirigible went down.[51]

Off the coast of New Jersey during that stormy rescue effort, *Portland* acquired a nickname: "The Rolling P."[52] Throughout World War II and for all the years since, her crew has referred to the ship as "Sweet Pea," a name lovingly pronounced "SWEE-pee." No doubt this coinage was borrowed from the baby who was a character in the *Popeye* comic strip. Almost half a century after the war, a debate raged in the pages of the ship's reunion association newsletter about which nickname came first and which one was more appropriate. Howard Jaeckle, a former sailor from Supply Division, started it off in December 1988 by rejecting the nickname "Sweet Pea," saying that he believed there would be a lot of support for "Rolling P."[53]

The ocean is a highway only in metaphor. It is so bumpy that even the calmest of seas makes a ship move in three unintended ways. A "roll" is what a ship does when she deviates from vertical by leaning over on her right or left side, starboard or port in mariner jargon. She also "pitches," when her forward section, the bow, dives into the water and then comes up out of it. And she "yaws," when her bow is driven off course to the right or the left. Pitching and yawing happen in rougher seas, usually, but all ships roll frequently. *Portland* rolled *all the time.*

Jaeckle was right about the nickname "Rolling P." *Portland* showed her susceptibility to rolls off the coast of New Jersey during the *Akron* operation, and two months later in June 1933 her rolling became so bad she had to steer a different course for safety when the crew was moving her aircraft around.[54] In the several issues of the *Newsletter* in 1988 and 1989 after Jaeckle's letter, many of those who had been aboard during the 1930s wrote about stormy trips to the Aleutians, seasickness even at anchor, how much more stable *Portland*'s sister ship *Indianapolis* was, and other tales about the "Rolling P."[55] One veteran, Eugene Bradley, recalled that the "Ripley's Believe It or Not" series referred to *Portland*'s performance in a 1933 storm, saying that no other ship had ever rolled over so far without capsizing.[56] Another, Norman Dunning, claimed to be insulted by the name "Sweet Pea," saying the ship was a *fighter,* not a *flower!*[57]

For a while in this debate, it appeared that "Rolling P" was only an early nickname, one that *Portland* outgrew, not because she rolled less but because the name dropped out of usage.[58] But then a plankowner, one of the men who were members of the crew at the time the ship was commissioned, former Marine Ezra Johnson, wrote that his diary called her "Sweet Pea" as early as July 1935.[59] Al Stauffer, who worked in the enginerooms from 1936 to 1940, chimed in that he remembered the very man who created the Sweet Pea nickname. Stauffer said it was Ray Koepp, who also served in E Division, and that Koepp confirmed the story in a 1988 telephone call with Stauffer. The editor of the paper finally said he gave up, although only "by and large."[60]

This book will call her "Sweet Pea."

**2**

# BEFORE THE WAR

Before World War II the U.S. Navy was a single fleet that was supposed to steam from one ocean to the other, depending upon where it was needed. Ships were organized by types, so that the battleships were in the Battle Force, the cruisers in the Scouting Force, and so on. When different types of ships operated together, they became a task force led by its commander. But when the mission was ended, operational control returned to the type commanders, who had stayed with the ships during the task force's mission.

The decade of the 1930s featured endless training and long periods at sea, some of it to no purpose that the crew could detect. In that era of the Great Depression, most sailors were happy to have a job that included lodging and food, but the officers and the service in general were enmeshed in the formalism of dress uniforms, brilliantly clean wooden decks, highly shined brass fittings, and so on. The sailors did all the work that achieved these results, much of it drudgery.

But if the bluejackets were mystified by the many hours and days of operational training in seamanship, gunnery, and damage control drills, they missed the point. That very training proved to be the salvation of *Portland*, and indeed the entire U.S. Navy once the Pacific War erupted. This history will show that her wartime seamanship was impressive, her gunnery drew high praise from others around her, and her ability to prevent damage from turning calamitous saved her on at least two occasions.

After the salvage operation off New Jersey, *Portland* finally began her underway training at Guantanamo Bay, Cuba. These exercises required only a week in early May 1933.[1] She then made a visit to Kingston, Jamaica, where the Captain exchanged official calls on the British government and military leaders there, and where the ship received return calls from many of the local officials.[2] The ship's logs are silent on the specifics of the honors, because they were probably ordinary for the U.S. Navy of the day. We can imagine, though, the formal uniforms and swords worn by the officers who went back and forth on these missions of courtesy. There would be sideboys, too, enlisted sailors in their dressiest uniforms, arrayed in two lines through which the visitors would pass as they came upon *Portland*'s quarterdeck.

From Kingston, Sweet Pea sailed through the Panama Canal for California. The stop in Panama featured more of the formal calls on the general and the admiral in command of American forces there and the return visits by those officers. Again, panoply prevailed at all these events.[3]

*Portland* arrived at her new home port on June 10, 1933. Over the next several years various log-writers on the ship called it "Los Angeles Harbor," "San Pedro," or "Long Beach." Later generations of sailors knew the place as Long Beach, when it was a major base and shipyard, and yet somehow only a northern appendage to the greater base at San Diego, one hundred miles to the south. In the 1930s, though, Long Beach was the U.S. Fleet's home on the Pacific coast.[4]

On arrival, there were more examples of the formality attending to warships in those days. Entering the harbor for the first time, for example, *Portland* rendered honors to the Commander-in-Chief of the U.S. Fleet, embarked in battleship *Pennsylvania,* a full seventeen-gun salute. The battleship returned the seven-gun salute due to the cruiser's Commanding Officer.[5] The entire operation must have taken many minutes. One can only imagine how disruptive it was to those who had to hear it and other gunfire salutes that were common in those days.

Herbert Leary commanded *Portland* for sixteen months. In June 1934, he was relieved in the post by Captain David M. LeBreton.[6] As if to add to what was already a colorful ship, the new Captain brought a dog with him, a German shepherd named Oofie. The animal had trouble adjusting to sea conditions, and would not tolerate sailors who tried to pet him. One time he lifted his leg to pee on a main-deck stanchion during an official inspection, embarrassing Captain LeBreton and no doubt infuriating the deck hands who had to clean up after the CO's pooch.[7]

Oofie was not the only dog to sail in *Portland* during the prewar days. In 1939, the Captain allowed some sailors in the Repair Division to keep a dog named Salvo. Salvo brought joy to the men when he would jump in the liberty boat going ashore at Long Beach. The dog would disappear for a few days, probably doing some of the same things the sailors were up to. They would then find him waiting at fleet landing for the boat ride back to the ship. The R Division men had some bad moments with the deckhands when Salvo would himself leave "calling cards" around. One day, Salvo went on liberty and never came back, to the lasting unhappiness of the crew who loved him.[8]

## Training Exercises

Sweet Pea participated in the war games and other exercises that kept the U.S. Navy busy during the 1930s as the fleet prepared for the possibility of a two-ocean war.[9] Once the ship was in the Pacific, her schedule settled into an annual pattern. In January, February, and usually March for all those years, the ship would be in Long Beach or possibly at Catalina Island or San Diego, and would go to nearby training areas to set compasses and other precision indicators, and to drill the ship's crew and fire the guns.[10]

Although this was peacetime service, the practice was serious. *Portland* was a gunship, after all, as were all the battleships and cruisers, and these warships practiced their gunnery early and often throughout the year. For example, Sweet Pea and the other ships left Long Beach for the first time in 1934 on January 5, and conducted flight operations and main battery firing *that very day*. This was a typical first-day's work in all of those training cycles. A few days later, she and the other ships in Cruiser Division Four drilled at night fighting against the destroyers who sailed in company with them, also a typical exercise in the early days of each year's program. During the days in between these events, shooting of every sort by the main battery, the secondary and anti-aircraft 5-inch guns marked most days. There were also, every year in these first months of the training cycle, tactical drills in company with the other cruisers, involving zigzagging, station-keeping, and other such things that honed the seamanship skills of the officers and crew.[11]

Beginning in the early spring, though, the ship would usually deploy with the entire fleet in waters all around the North American continent. In 1934, the fleet transited the Canal and operated in the Caribbean and up the Atlantic Coast until returning home to San Pedro in early November.[12]

In 1935, on the other hand, the ship traveled with the fleet all the way to Midway Island, about a thousand miles west of Hawaii and, well, midway across the Pacific. The island would become famous in 1942, but in 1935 it was only a cable station, and its entire population a man and his wife, their Jersey cow, and a few chickens. The sailors enjoyed nothing they would call "liberty" in such a desolate place, although a few men did somehow get ashore just to look around.[13] The fleet did not stay there long, but came back to waters near the United States for weeks of training at sea, in between calling on the ports of San Diego, Long Beach, Bremerton, and San Francisco.[14] The summer deployment in 1936 was around Hawaii after a momentary visit to Panama with only a brief transit of the Canal.[15] In the following years, Hawaii was more often than not the scene of the fleet's training operations.

All of these exercises mixed in with routine ship's duties, of course. It was hard and incessant work. But make no mistake: how well *Portland* and the rest of the fleet did in combat when the Pacific War swept over the U.S. Navy was a direct result of all this effort.

Sometimes the operations could be unpleasant. For example, a 1937 operation in Aleutian waters confirmed the nickname "Rolling P" in the minds and stomachs of its unhappy sailors. It may, moreover, have contributed to the death of one of the Commanding Officers.

It was called the Kanaga Island Expedition. The Navy wanted to establish a new base on Kanaga, a small islet in the Aleutians. On October 24, 1937, *Portland* landed three officers and twenty-one enlisted men of a variety of rates and working skills to build that base. Two days later, with the debarked detachment secure in its new home, as grim as it probably was, the ship left to go back to Long Beach.[16]

On the way north from Puget Sound to Kanaga, sea conditions were so severe that the inclinometer, a device that measures rolls, reached forty-two degrees. Since forty-five degrees was marked as the danger point, the ship was in some peril. Remember that Sweet Pea was already infamous as an unstable ship that often rolled even at anchor in a light swell. On this trip, one sailor later recalled, "Everything in the mess hall, men, dishes, food, tables and benches went sliding to starboard and back to port when she righted herself."[17] The heavy weather ripped a dozen fifty-five-gallon drums of diesel oil out of their lashings and washed them over *Portland*'s stern. For a couple of days the ship retained stability only by moving at the very slow speed of five knots, just barely enough to maintain steerageway in the heavy pounding.[18]

The Commanding Officer at the time was Captain Benjamin Dutton Jr. On taking command of *Portland* in June 1937, Dutton was already well-known in naval circles as the author of the widely used and praised book *Navigation and Nautical Astronomy*. Midshipmen at the Naval Academy learned celestial navigation from this book, which naval officers still employed until electronic navigation replaced star-shooting in the 1980s.[19] After the huge Aleutian storm struck, Dutton returned the ship to Mare Island for repairs, and then to her home port in Long Beach.[20]

There, just past midnight on Tuesday, November 30, Captain Dutton suddenly died. He seemed healthy as he carried out his duties the day before, even holding a Captain's Mast about noon. But at about 0130 on the morning of the 30th, the quarterdeck watch was informed by the Senior Patrol Officer ashore that Dutton had died at a local hospital from a thrombosis in a coronary artery.[21] The fleet created a board of investigation to look into the circumstances of the death, but it found nothing untoward.[22] The sailors, though, had little doubt about what had killed Dutton. As Dale Figgins of C Division said years later, it was "the pressure of command during the storm."[23]

A funeral service was conducted on the *Portland* quarterdeck. At 1000 on December 2, with several admirals, ship's captains, and other high-ranking officials on hand, Captain Dutton's casket was hoisted aboard the ship, anchored at Long Beach. Lieutenant Commander E.W. Davis, the cruiser division's chaplain, conducted the service, and at 1115 the casket was lowered over the side into a motor launch for transportation ashore to the burial site. As the boat departed, a seven-gun salute was fired.[24] And the fleet went back to work.

Other events in the early years included a speed run in the summer of 1934 from the Pacific to the Atlantic. The Navy wanted to see how quickly it could shift ships from one ocean to the other when it had only a single, worldwide fleet. So *Portland* was sent at high speed from Long Beach to New York.[25] In those days, Sweet Pea would have been painted light gray, so the white water at her bow might not have stood out the way it would later against the wartime darker camouflaged gray. She would, nevertheless, have "a bone in her teeth," as sailors sometimes describe the bow wave of smaller, supposedly more nimble craft than a heavy cruiser. Watching *Portland* fly through the sea might make an observer doubt that any ship could be more agile. She was a big ship, of course, but she was so slim and trim that her powerful engines drove her at speeds as high as most of the supposedly swifter destroyers could reach.

As she dashed through the ocean, the mist would spray along *Portland*'s sides the length of a football field to about where the main deck dipped down onto what the crew called the well deck. At the after edge of that area, the aircraft hangars rose up in a huge block, providing the base for an after superstructure of secondary batteries. Eight 5-inch guns lined that upper deck, four to a side, and several smaller guns were spotted here and there among them.

The forward superstructure, which held the conning bridge, was round but sleek. Just behind it, the forward stack was noticeably taller than the after one, and both stacks had a ring around their tops. *Portland*'s lines were smooth and clean then, except for the aircraft with their pudgy silhouettes apparently carelessly stuffed on the catapults amidships. No clumsy radar antennas cluttered her masts, like so many bedsprings. And her sides were lined with those evenly spaced portholes, giving her a stylish rake.

Her guns were the most noticeable features, though. She was, let us say it again, a *gunship*. The forward turret of three 8-inch guns fitted snugly on the forecastle, about seventy-five feet back from the stem. Number Two stepped up one deck right behind, with its guns so long they extended over the Number One turret when both were aligned forward. On the main deck aft, Number Three also fit tight into the main deck and right up against the after deck house, although it nevertheless seemed much more isolated than the forward two. At full speed, USS *Portland* demonstrated clearly what a cruiser was supposed to be: powerful enough to kill what it hunted, and quick enough to escape most that might hunt it.[26]

In 1936, Sweet Pea participated in a major war game in the huge Pacific triangle bounded by Hawaii, the Aleutians, and Midway.[27] When she returned to the mainland in October following that event, two of her sailors were featured on a San Francisco radio show. Al Stauffer, a relatively rookie fireman aboard only a few months, had attached himself for liberty to a second-class petty officer named Tom Marcum. Marcum was going to show Stauffer what an old salt did ashore for fun. As they made their way through the streets of the city, a man came running out of a building and invited the two sailors to his radio studio where, on the air, they could tell about their ship and the Navy in general. Stauffer was sure that the more experienced Marcum would do all the talking. When the interview began and the host asked the petty officer his name, though, Marcum froze up. After an original stammer, Stauffer jumped in and became glib in relating his story about boot camp and what *Portland* was like. For his part, Petty Officer Marcum did not open his mouth until they were off the air. Stauffer learned a lot about alleged saltiness that day.[28]

When the fleet again transited the Canal in 1937 to operate in the Atlantic, the crew was told that German dictator Adolf Hitler had noticed. The men were enjoying what they thought was very good liberty in Mobile, Alabama. But the report they got was that the Nazi Führer had become angry about the deployment and registered a complaint with American authorities. The Navy ordered *Portland* and the other ships to recall the liberty parties, and it sent the force back to the Pacific.[29]

## FDR's Fishing Trip

There were some "special" operations in the 1930s, not all of them related to getting ready for war. In October 1935, President Franklin Roosevelt, who had shown how much he loved riding warships when he was assistant secretary of the Navy in World War I, went on a three-week fishing trip aboard USS *Houston* (CA-30). *Portland* went along as shotgun.[30]

Roosevelt and his party joined the two cruisers in Long Beach on October 2. Four members of the presidential party rode in *Portland,* while the president and his other companions were in *Houston.*[31] Twenty-one-gun salutes from the rest of the fleet sent the cruisers off as they carried Mr. Roosevelt and his entourage to sea that afternoon. The ships steamed generally southeasterly at an easy fifteen knots or so for two days and then anchored in Magdalena Bay, Baja, California, for the guests to fish. A few more hours of travel brought the cruisers to a spot in the open ocean where they lay to for more fishing on October 5. It was like that for a week more, gentle steaming, stop for a few hours here or there along the Hispano-American coast for fishing, until the cruisers reached the Panama Canal.[32] After transit to the Atlantic side, it was more of the same, stopping each day to fish, until they lay to off Charleston, South Carolina. There the president and his party debarked, and Sweet Pea's log noted that she had completed her duty "as escort to HOUSTON, (S.O.P.A) President of the United States."[33]

On another occasion, just before the costly Kanaga operation, the ship is reported to have spent two weeks in 1937 searching in the Pacific for Amelia Earhart and her navigator, Fred Noonan, after their plane went down during its attempt at a round-the-world flight.[34] In a different search-and-rescue attempt about which there is no doubt, the "Rolling P" ran into yet another ferocious Pacific storm. In August 1941 as *Portland* was on her way to Pearl Harbor from California in company with USS *San Francisco* (CA-38), the two cruisers were diverted to search for a sea-going dredge named *Jefferson*, which had lost power in a storm about a thousand miles west of the southern tip of Baja, California.[35] The group drove to the site at sixteen knots in an effort that led to the rescue of the battered dredge, but *Portland* suffered damage in doing so. Shortly before midnight on August 21, her jack staff was torn away by the heavy seas. A few hours later she shipped enormous waves over the bow and damaged most of the machinery on her forecastle. Although a hasty inspection determined that her seaworthiness was not adversely affected, two of her bridge windows were smashed, injuring Ensign E.N. Smith so severely he had to be relieved from watch. Smith lost two of his front teeth and took nine stitches in his lacerated scalp.[36] Two men from *Portland* were washed over the side by huge waves, but both were dumped back on the deck by the next upswelling of the sea. Alas, one of them, a boatswain's mate named Mastrianni, was swept overboard for good by the next wave before he could be brought to safety.[37]

*Portland* sailed in the Pacific with the Scouting Force for Fleet Problem XXI in 1940. But when that exercise ended in May 1940, she did not return home to California as she had in previous years. Thereafter, until the onset of the war, the fleet was based in Pearl Harbor.[38] By moving the ships to Hawaii, the Roosevelt administration hoped to deter Japan from further misbehavior in Asia. Sweet Pea did get to go home to Long Beach in mid-November 1940, when a huge number of officers and men were granted leave. But she was back in Pearl Harbor on December 6, 1940, and California would never again be her permanent home port.[39]

## Two Long Voyages

No doubt another reason for basing the fleet in Hawaii was to reassure friendly nations in the Pacific and Asian areas that America's formidable strength had yet to be thrown into the balance of the huge war that was already rippling around the world. It was probably for that reason that *Portland* was included on a goodwill trip to Australia. In early March 1941, she joined Task Force 9, comprising three other cruisers, a fleet oiler, and a destroyer squadron.[40]

They left Pearl Harbor on March 1, 1941, but the crews were not told the destination for four more days.[41] Several days after that, *Portland* crossed the equator for the second time in her career.[42] The U.S. Navy has traditionally made a great celebration out of this event. Those who have crossed the line at least once before, the so-called shellbacks, spend a little time hazing those who have not, the pollywogs. On *Portland* in 1941, the festivities took less than an hour out of the afternoon of March 6. At 1430, "special pollywog watches" were stationed throughout the ship for the expected visit of "Davy Jones, Royal Scribe to His Majesty Neptunus Rex." The crew was then called to quarters for muster and assembled on the quarterdeck to receive Jones and his party, who came aboard at 1517, when they were greeted by the Captain, Clifford E. Van Hook, himself no doubt a shellback from long before.[43]

Davy Jones then addressed the crew, and "subpoenas" were issued to all pollywogs to appear before the Royal Court.[44] All were found guilty of this or that spurious charge and were sentenced to punishments like a haircut even shorter than normal, or enduring a "gummy slimy solution" to the head, and a "nasty medicine squirted into the mouth." All had to bow to the Royal Court in a show of abject allegiance, and then crawl through a gauntlet. There they were paddled by each of the shellbacks who wielded a canvas bag stuffed with sawdust and soaked in water. All the while the deck was being splashed with water, so the pollywogs were sent sprawling by each beating. As a man's slide slowed in the slippery mess, he was pummeled again and driven further down the line, where he was smashed yet again repeatedly until he reached the end of the line. At that point he was welcomed into the "Realm of Neptune" by none other than Davy Jones. He took his place alongside the other shellbacks, and began to apply his own canvas bag to the bottoms of those not yet finished with their initiation.[45]

Mr. Jones and his party left the ship at 1526, having been aboard only about ten minutes, and the ship secured from quarters at 1530, thus ending the festivities.[46] The initiation was brief and good-natured, but awful to the victims. All of them received certificates announcing their new shellback status. Similar wallet-sized cards were guarded as treasures by their owners because they were demanded for proof in future crossings.[47]

Incidentally, another *Portland* sailor was even more amazed when the ship crossed the international date line a few days later. He wrote home to his family that doing so was much rarer than crossing the equator.[48] It probably *was* in those days since the other side of the date line was mostly controlled by the not-friendly Japanese Empire, although it became common to U.S. sailors after 1945 when the Pacific was an American lake.[49]

On the way to Australia, the ship stopped for a few days of refueling and liberty in Pago Pago, American Samoa, then sailed three days to Sydney on Australia's southeast coast, reaching it on March 19, 1941.[50] The next nine days witnessed a round of partying no one ever forgot. In honor of Portland and her crew, Sydney put on parades, receptions, and dinners, threw open the doors of the pubs and milk bars, rarely charged the Americans for purchases of items ranging from beer to tickets, and showed Sweet Pea's sailors the joys of such establishments as "Prince's," "Ramona's," and "The 400 Club."[51]

After a week of this bacchanal, the Task Group steamed up the Pacific coast and called on Brisbane, where there were more parades, more receptions, more hospitality. And now the crew heard rumors of warlike events that were possible for not-so-far-away places as Port Darwin, Manila, Fiji, and Singapore.[52] These rumors were about ports the men were hoping to visit, but places that they knew the Japanese threatened. *Portland* called on none of them during this trip. Instead, Task Force 9 returned to the United States by way of Suva, Fiji Islands, a place no one in the crew may have liked, spoiled as the sailors were by Australia.[53] One place in Brisbane was described as especially delightful by one sailor: "[T]here were four girls to every man." But that same bluejacket thought Fiji much less charming: he would have put Suva at the top of his list of "stink hole" ports, because it "reeked of filth, decaying trash and everything else that could rot." Nor did he like the natives, who he thought looked "like real savages."[54]

Fortunately for this man and others of similar opinions, the *Portland* and her task force reached Pearl Harbor on April 10 after a thirty-eight-day cruise in which they covered more than ten thousand miles.[55]

A few months later, just prior to the Japanese surprise attack on Pearl Harbor, Sweet Pea was sent off on a reinforcement mission to Manila, a deployment that seems today to have been simply too close for comfort. She was assigned, *by herself* with no other warships, to accompany the U.S. Army Transport *Liberty,* which embarked five thousand infantry reinforcements for General Douglas MacArthur's defense of the Philippines. Cruisers were intended originally to operate alone, and those who ordered the voyage may not have thought anything of sending *Portland* off like this. To sail a safe route for the embarked troops, Sweet Pea would avoid passing through the heart of the extensive Japanese Pacific empire but instead take a voyage far to the south.[56]

On October 13, 1941, *Portland* left Pearl Harbor and plodded across the Pacific with the slow transport.[57] The two ships stopped for fuel in Linkas, Dutch East Indies, and finally reached Manila on November 12. Because the Army ship had set the standard for speed, the trip took thirty long, mostly hot, days.[58]

The voyage took *Portland* across the equator again, but since nearly all the men had just recently become shellbacks, some thought was given to not bothering with the initiation rites of Davy Jones. Then a few of the officers noticed that the newly assigned junior doctor, Lieutenant Robert Williams, who was liked and respected by all in the crew, had not been aboard during the March trip and was therefore still a pollywog.[59] The shellbacks fed Doctor Williams nightmarish stories about what lay in store for him. They promised him special attention since he would be one of the very few victims of the hazing.

But Williams could both take it and dish it out. At lunch in the wardroom on October 20, the very day before the crossing, the doctor passed out some tablets, telling the officers they were for "vitality." About fifteen of the unsuspecting men took these pills, hoping for new vigor, only to discover that almost immediately their urine became "a very bright blue." Worse, since they were all wearing the uniform of the day—dress whites—the drops produced by the blue substance began to stain the fronts of their trousers, now an indelible blue. The record is silent about whether the shellbacks laid it on extra thick after this blue event or whether they were deterred out of fear of even worse from the good Dr. Williams.[60]

On the way back from Manila, unencumbered by the transport, *Portland* took a more direct route right through the Japanese Empire, thereby making the trip three thousand miles shorter and only ten days in duration. She arrived in Pearl Harbor on November 26, 1941.[61] Too close for comfort? On that *very day,* Vice Admiral Chuichi Nagumo and his carrier task force set sail from Japan for their date with infamy.[62]

3

# PEARL HARBOR

Nagumo's *Kido Butai,* a powerful fleet of six carriers, two battleships, fleet oilers, screening cruisers, and destroyers, was headed for Hawaii to carry out Admiral Isoroku Yamamoto's great gamble.

In the 1930s, the Japanese Army acted independently of the Imperial government to bury itself in an endless war in China. There it won nearly all the battles and captured nearly all the populous cities. But the Japanese got no closer to final victory because the Chinese regime of Chiang Kai-Shek simply refused to surrender, and the extent of the invaded territory was too great for Japan's limited resources to gobble up. The United States and other Western powers protested Japan's assault on China, but without effect. Japanese generals could neither admit the embarrassment of failure nor accept the embarrassment of a forced withdrawal. Officials in the Tokyo government itself were too embarrassed to admit that they were unable to restrain the Army. Finally the generals and the government became one when General Hideki Tojo was named prime minister in mid-1941.

Tojo's government was determined to win the war in China, but the Roosevelt administration tightened the noose. Washington was by now alone in confronting Japan, because Europe had been overrun by Adolf Hitler's Wehrmacht. Even Britain was too busy defending itself to do much more than hope for the best on the Asian side of the world. On the other hand, the Americans controlled the raw materials that Japan's war machine desperately needed, particularly the scrap iron and the oil for her planes and tanks. In several stages during 1940 and 1941, the United States blocked the trade of these items and finally froze Japanese assets, thus forcing Tojo to face the dilemma: quit China or find another more reliable source of these materials.

It was an easy problem to solve: there would be no quitting. Japan's European ally Germany had conquered both Holland and France, heretofore imperial powers whose colonies in Asia possessed grand quantities of the things Tokyo needed to keep the war going in China. The Japanese looked rapaciously at the oil and iron in the Dutch East Indies, the rubber and rice in French Indo-China, and the tin in British Malaya and Borneo.

Consequently, only weeks before USS *Portland* and USS *Liberty* got underway to sail through some of these very places, the military men governing Japan decided to capture the European territories and resources in Southeast Asia. But here the Imperial Japanese Navy (IJN) stepped in. Yamamoto, the Commander of the Combined Fleet and the leading naval strategist, was certain that if the Army did grab the European holdings, the United States would intervene militarily. The Navy did not want to have to face the American Pacific Fleet on its flank while it was busy delivering and supporting armies in the southern areas.

Yamamoto was well known in American naval circles as a poker player who took risks, and he decided to make a preemptive attack on the Pacific Fleet. Based in Hawaii to deter further Japanese aggression, the U.S. Navy was about to fail in this mission. At Pearl Harbor, the U.S. Navy was only a target that Yamamoto decided he had to destroy. Because the Army needed his Combined Fleet's support in Southeast Asia, the admiral won Tojo's approval of his plan to smash the American Navy in the first hours of the war. On the same day, Japan would land its troops in Southeast Asia.

*Kido Butai*'s performance was one of the great military achievements of all time. It crossed two-thirds of the Pacific Ocean without ever being seen, it launched its aircraft from about two hundred miles north of Oahu, and they went that distance to Pearl Harbor without themselves being noticed. At about eight in the morning they began wrecking the American airbases and aircraft. They then bombed and torpedoed the battleships thought to be the muscle of the American Navy, sinking four and severely damaging the four others that were there, as well as sinking or damaging several other smaller vessels. *Kido*

*Butai* then sailed back, never seen by its enemy, to the western Pacific, where it assisted in the various invasions then taking place. The targets the Japanese did not hit at Pearl Harbor, such as the shipyard, the submarine base, and the oil storage tanks, allowed the Americans to bounce back surprisingly quickly from the disaster of December 7, but in the smoke and debris no one knew that at the time.

One of the ironies about the attack on Pearl Harbor was that the U.S. Navy's 1937 war games had been constructed around a mock air attack on Hawaii from the American carrier *Saratoga.* This simulated air raid was a great success. *Portland,* defending Hawaii as a member of the "Blue Fleet" in this exercise, was "sunk" during the action, as were all other ships in her cruiser division. Carrier aviation was a much more powerful force than anyone had reckoned beforehand.[1] But, of course, no American thought the IJN could pull off such an attack, however successful *Saratoga* might have been in a fleet exercise!

While *Portland* was a part of the 1937 simulation from which nothing important was learned by the high command, she missed the real Japanese attack on Pearl Harbor. On December 7, 1941, she was en route to Midway with the carrier *Lexington* to deliver aircraft to that American outpost.[2] Task Force 12 comprised the carrier, Sweet Pea, two other cruisers, and five destroyers. The attack struck *Portland*'s crew exactly the way it did all other Americans: the men never forgot exactly where they were or what they were doing when they first heard of it. For just one example, Ray Haldorson, who worked in the boiler rooms and probably never saw a navigation table in his life, reported almost fifty years later that Sweet Pea was at 23°30" north latitude, 170°30" west longitude when the word about the raid reached her.[3] *Life* magazine reporters were aboard *Portland* to report on what it was like to serve in a man-of-war just as war seemed to be very close, and some of the men originally thought the story was only a drill to give the reporters something to write about.[4] Americans everywhere reacted with disbelief at first, as they did on this ship.

That Sunday afternoon, a talent show was scheduled for the crew's entertainment. Chief Shipfitter Barney McAllister usually served as the master of ceremonies for such events. Al Lucas and a radioman named Lusk were supposed to do a balancing act, while another man named Flanagan was going to sing some Irish tunes.[5] But when the shocking announcement was made over the ship's PA system in mid-morning, the talent show was tossed aside.

Instead, *Portland*'s crew spent the rest of the day at hard work, stripping ship. They took down the mess deck's light globes and unnecessary flammable items, like the wooden paneling in the wardroom. They painted over the topside wooden decks, heretofore beautifully white from so much holystoning, but now made a darker color so the ship would be harder to see from the air.[6] They rigged false radar antennas and made other topside alterations to change the appearance of the ship.[7] One of the things they dumped over the side was the beautiful mahogany brow, the gangway used by the men to pass from the ship to the pier and back when *Portland* was tied up.[8] By the time Sweet Pea went to general quarters in the evening of December 7, no one in the crew thought it a drill.[9]

*Portland*'s task force actually looked for the Japanese fleet. World War II cruisers all carried aircraft. They scouted ahead of the ship for possible enemy forces, spotted the ship's gunfire to make it more accurate, searched for and rescued men in the water, ran errands to nearby ships or land, and so on. On December 7, one of the cruiser's aircraft hopped over to Midway for more news, while others went out to scout. Ensign Jay Yakely as pilot and Aviation Radioman First Class Vernon Cruise as crewman flew one of the searching planes. They were as excited and anxious as any Americans in the world that day. Out of sight of their ship and her task force, they found themselves out scouting the formidable Japanese fleet that had just laid waste to the great American naval and air bases in Hawaii. That may be the explanation for why they ran out of fuel and had to set down in the Pacific about fifty miles from the ship. The SOC "Seagull" they were flying stayed afloat, but the two men both became seasick in the nearly three hours they had to wait for *Portland* to rescue them.[10]

Yakely and Cruise's running out of fuel was no doubt due to their inexperience in what was now a real war. But air operations off the cruiser were heart-stopping in normal times. The aircraft these men flew carried about 160 gallons of aviation gasoline. At the standard rate of twenty-six gallons per hour, the fuel gave the plane about five and a half hours of flying time. The gasoline was carried in three tanks, one of one hundred gallons and two of thirty gallons each, with a gas gauge for only the largest. The crew was supposed to use the main tank for takeoff and then switch to one of the smaller tanks as soon as the plane was airborne. A policy that created a margin of safety required the crew to *remember* thirty minutes later to switch to the second smaller tank, and to *remember* thirty minutes after that to switch back to the main tank.[11] Under the new wartime situation and the anxiety it produced, it would be no wonder if Yakely and Cruise forgot some of these requirements and thereby ran dry.

The *Portland*'s aviation crew was called V Division, "V" being the Navy's abbreviation for "heavier-than-air, fixed wing" aircraft, and who knows why? There were usually four officer pilots, a chief petty officer, and about twenty-five enlisted men of various aviation ratings. These officers and men were not part of the ship's company, but comprised a separate unit that officially was merely attached to the cruiser.[12] This was no unusual arrangement: aircraft carriers were organized the same way; the airplane squadrons were in an Air Group, which was officially only temporarily assigned to any given flattop.

Sweet Pea's four Curtiss Seagulls measured thirty-one feet, eight inches in length, had wingspans of thirty-six feet, and took off with a full-load weight of 5,126 pounds. The bi-planes with wings that folded for storage had both a large pontoon under the main fuselage and two smaller floats under each wingtip.[13] The planes, officially SOCs but sometimes called "Gooney Birds" by *Portland* men, carried a crew of two, a pilot and a radioman/gunner, usually referred to as the "passenger," in the back seat. The armament was not impressive, even for those days. Each plane had a 30-caliber machine gun that the pilot could fire forward, synchronized through the propeller, and another 30-caliber machine gun fired through 360 degrees by the radioman in the rear seat. Each SOC could take aloft a couple of 100-pound bombs, one under each wing, or a 250-pound depth charge, carried centerline. Top speed was about one hundred knots.[14]

An SOC could be hoisted off the ship and set in the water, where it could then run into the wind until it got enough lift under its wings to become airborne. Or it could be launched directly from the ship by catapult. *Portland* had two of these, mounted on the amidships well-deck, unlike later cruisers, which always catapulted from the fantail. For launchings, the plane was fixed to a movable car on a track about fifty-four feet long. After a pre-flight check, the two men in the crew would climb up onto the catapult and take their seats in the plane. When all seemed in order, the pilot started the engine by means of a shotgun-shell starter. After checking out the engine and flying controls, the pilot would signal to the catapult officer, and that man would give a command to a gunner's mate. This man triggered a six-inch shell casing filled with black powder that propelled the car down the track. This explosive run into the wind took a couple of seconds in which no pilot could act or even think. He had one arm wrapped around the throttle to keep it all the way open and the other arm around the stick to keep the plane's nose up. At the end of the catapult, the plane was about forty feet above the water with enough lift to sustain flight. Even if something went wrong and there were not enough power to stay aloft, the Seagull had at least enough altitude and speed to land straight ahead into the wind.[15]

The recovery at the end of the flight was equally adventurous. There were three techniques. The most usual, when *Portland* was underway in the open sea, was called "Charlie." As the SOC made its approach, the cruiser would steam thirty degrees to sixty degrees off the wind direction at twelve knots. The aircraft would then fly down the beam in the opposite direction at five hundred feet. At a half-mile or so astern the ship, the plane would begin a 180-degree turn to bring it alongside Sweet Pea. The ship would then turn toward the windline, creating a landing slick, and the pilot would set his plane down on the smoothed-out ocean.[16]

The ship's deck force would have already put a recovery sled into the water. This was a triangular device of kapok tubes with a rope net attached to the base. It was streamed about three hundred feet from the ship and attached to a winch on the forecastle. The pilot would taxi through the water and onto the sled until he felt that the aircraft was being pulled toward Sweet Pea by a hook on the bottom of the main float that had engaged the webbing of the sled. Then he and his crewman climbed out of their seats to fasten cables from the plane to various hooks and lines that would fix the SOC to the ship's hoisting equipment. They and the plane would then be hauled aboard *Portland*.[17]

Every takeoff, mission, and landing was dangerous, so what happened to Yakely and Cruise the day of the Pearl Harbor raid was only slightly worse than normal. What befell them was nearly compounded when, as the crew was finally hoisting their SOC aboard, an American seaplane-bomber flew over and plopped a bomb down in *Portland*'s wake. No doubt recognition skills among the Navy's aviators were not very good that first day of the war. Of course, *Portland* did not look the same as she had even earlier that day, considering all the changes wrought during stripping ship. Sweet Pea's AA fired at the PBY, but fortunately did not hit it.[18] No doubt anti-aircraft batteries were not very good that first day of the war, either.

We have to be happy that the U.S. Navy did not find Nagumo's carrier task force that day. The Americans were just not ready yet for the highly skilled and experienced Imperial Japanese Navy.

## THE BOAT CREWS

During all this excitement at sea, a few of *Portland*'s personnel were with the fleet in Pearl Harbor when the Japanese raiders came. First, there were the men left in the harbor with the ship's boats. The Captain's gig, the motor whaleboat, and two motor launches were left behind with eleven sailors to take care of them.[19] The boats were beached because they were often damaged by Turret Three during gunfire practice. Since gunnery drills were scheduled for the trip to Midway, they were left ashore for their own protection.[20] By the luck of this duty, these men later qualified for membership in the Pearl Harbor Survivors' Association, while their shipmates did not.[21]

When they and their boats left the cruiser, the men reported to the officer-in-charge of boats at the coal docks.[22] Their only responsibility was to keep the boats in good condition. From *Portland,* they had taken a rifle with two clips of ammunition for sentry duty. Berthed in the Marine barracks only a few blocks from where the boats were tied up, they were instructed to observe regular liberty hours but to keep an armed watch on the boats twenty-four hours a day.[23]

Seaman 1/c Reimer went on liberty by himself on Saturday night, December 6. He had dinner at the YMCA, a few beers at a recreation center, and bought a few sandwiches that he planned to eat for breakfast. But when it was time for bed he decided that, instead of staying in the Marine barracks, he would sleep in the forward compartment of the motorboat. Robinson, also a Seaman 1/c, claimed seniority and chose to sack out in the more comfortable Captain's gig.[24]

On Sunday morning, following the ship's regular routine even though they were ashore, the men mustered at 0800 and gave the boats a quick wipedown, the last time they would be clean for some time. Watchstanders for the next twenty-four hours were assigned. The first sentry was Seaman 1/c Koine, who took up the rifle that he would not lay down again for many days.[25]

It was a beautiful morning and Reimer thought it was even more quiet than normal.[26] Once the bombing started, the *Portland* boat crews were slow to understand what was going on because they could not see the main harbor from the coal docks. There did seem to be a lot of planes flying around, but they did not know why until a Japanese fighter flew over strafing the docks! Koine, who had the only weapon, fired back but the rest just took cover from the airplane's bullets. They then assisted firefighters at a nearby building that had been hit by a crashed Japanese plane. Reimer started to eat one of the sandwiches he had brought back from Honolulu the night before, but seeing the mangled body of the enemy pilot made him stop munching.[27]

An officer told the *Portland* sailors to take their boats over to the liberty landing across the main channel, where they could ferry sailors who were trying to get back to the battlewagons moored along Ford Island. As they made their way, Reimer was nearly hit by a piece of AA shrapnel that fell out of the sky into the boat. He had no helmet, so thereafter while the firing continued he kept his head covered with a piece of the boat's floorboard.[28]

Later in the day, Reimer, his crew, and their boat were commandeered by a Navy Captain who was making a survey of the damage. This officer ordered Reimer to go slowly past the shipyard and Battleship Row and then all the way around Ford Island as he made notes on a yellow legal pad. When that mission was complete, Reimer's boat carried supplies from the shipyard to this or that ship. As dusk fell, Reimer decided he could not go directly back to the dock because battleship *Nevada,* which had attempted to get underway, now lay aground on Hospital Point and was blocking the route Sweet Pea's boat would have to take. He went all the way around Ford Island, which took much longer. As darkness fell over war-frightened Pearl Harbor, a sentry fired a rifle just in front of the boat, so Reimer had the engineer cut the power and cried out, *"Portland* motor launch, headed for the coaling docks." The reply was, "Proceed," and away they went.[29]

## The Women

Other *Portland* personnel in Pearl Harbor during the raid were the families of crew members. The bombing frightened Rita Lavely, the seven-year-old daughter of Chief Machinist's Mate Walter T. Lavely.

She could see all the devastation from her house in Pearl City. This town sat on a small peninsula that jutted down into Pearl Harbor, almost to Ford Island. Little Rita felt she was only a block or so from the bombs, the fires, the shooting, and the death.[30]

Kay Wilhelm's husband, Ralph, was called "Kaiser" by his shipmates, of course. He was one of *Portland*'s pilots who was on the ship when it left on December 5 to accompany *Lexington* to Midway. At Pearl Harbor on the morning of the 7th, the bombs knocked Kay out of bed at 0755. At first she thought it was just another practice, like the one a week before when aircraft dropping sandbags as mock bombs had knocked a lot of coconuts out of the trees. But then, with a good view from her apartment in Pearl City, she noticed that the planes were shooting Americans in the whaleboats. She also saw the former battleship *Utah* attacked and roll over.[31] Because most of *Utah*'s superstructure had been taken down and planked over so target shells would just bounce off, Japanese aviators mistook her for an aircraft carrier.[32]

Kay then wrestled with her neighbor Marie MacDonald, who had come out of her own house brandishing a rifle. Marie insisted she wasn't going to be raped by the Japanese, but Kay forcibly took the firearm away from her for reasons of general safety. Marie remained afraid, though, and talked Kay into leaving the Pearl City peninsula. Kay drove them about halfway down the road until a strafing aircraft made a run at them. Although they then tried to get home, authorities wouldn't let them back into Pearl City, so they had to stay with friends in another part of the Pearl Harbor area.[33]

Machinist's Mate First Class Ernie Booth was the senior petty officer of the men assigned to the boats. Since he and his wife Leila lived near the base, Ernie planned to spend the nights at home during this temporary duty. That Sunday, the couple had just finished breakfast when a radio announcement directed all service personnel to return to their bases because of the attack. Their neighbor, a sailor from battleship *Tennessee,* did not believe the report, but the Booths could see the bursting ack-ack over the harbor, so Ernie took off for the boats. He did not see Leila again for three days. Since they had no phone, moreover, Ernie could not report to her what he was doing.[34] For the next week, Ernie directed *Portland*'s boats as they hauled stores from the naval base and shipyard to several ships in the harbor. Every so often, the crews would look down the channel, hoping to see Sweet Pea coming back for them. When days went by without her return, they worried that she had been diverted or, worse, *lost* so that they would never see her again.[35]

Finally, though, on Saturday, December 13, *Portland* did return. She had tried for six fruitless days to find the Japanese task force, but now she went to the far side of Ford Island and anchored as usual in berth C-5.[36] On her return to the base, the crew was horrified at the extent of the damage done at Pearl Harbor by the Japanese. Passing *Oklahoma,* upside down in the muck, some thought it might be a submarine until the truth dawned on them.[37] The sights were "awful," said Boatswain's Mate Bob Dolezal. Ships were burning or capsized, and oil coated the surface of the water, some of it still burning.[38] *Nevada* was aground, making navigation around her a chore, *Arizona* was beyond description, and several other battleships were sunk in the mud. Bodies still floated in the water, and boats maneuvered around the harbor to pick them up.[39] Like nearly all other Americans, *Portland*'s crew was bitterly angry at the Japanese for the sneak attack.

Even while she was collecting her boats and their crews, Sweet Pea received new drafts of manpower. Some, like Henry Hight, had been assigned to the ship weeks or even months before but had had difficulty in catching transportation to Hawaii. Hight finally reached Pearl Harbor two days after the Japanese raid and was there when Sweet Pea pulled in after the fruitless effort to find Nagumo's carriers. *Portland* quickly got underway again to join a protective screen against a possible invasion. Because Hight had not yet been integrated into the crew, he was promptly disembarked and sent to Ford Island, where he worked with some of his shipmates and other men in a clean-up crew for almost two weeks. They looked for survivors in the wreckage, helped remove debris, and did a lot of other grim jobs until *Portland* came back to get them on December 27. It was tough duty and Hight remembered having a Spam sandwich for Christmas dinner.[40]

Another group of new men for the cruiser's crew came from some of the sunken ships. Ray Peugh and J.C. Banks had been aboard the battleship *California* when she was torpedoed during the raid. Pugh was in the engineroom when the ship was hit, but was able to escape without injury. Banks served in the *California*'s deck force and his battle station was in amidships damage control. During the attack he and another man were sent below to ensure watertight integrity. But the ship was sinking even as the two descended into her bowels. The other man's greater awareness of the interior of the complicated battleship enabled the two to escape as she went down. Pugh and Banks were among about twenty refugees from the *California* who reported to *Portland* on December 13. They went to sea on the cruiser almost immediately.[41]

The ordeal for the *Portland* women was not over, either. When "Kaiser" Wilhelm reached home, Kay was fine. But within a few days she suffered an attack of acute appendicitis, had emergency surgery on December 20, and was evacuated soon thereafter.[42] Leila Booth left Hawaii on January 22, just about the last date the Navy would move her since she was almost seven months pregnant by that time. What Ernie knew but couldn't tell her was that *Portland* had orders to return to California, and he wanted her there when the ship arrived. Since her family lived in Berkeley, it was a golden opportunity to get her, her sixteen-month old daughter, and the unborn baby out of the war zone and still enable the couple to have a little time together when Sweet Pea reached the West Coast. So Leila sailed on a troop ship and made an uneventful voyage home. Upon her arrival at her parents' home in Berkeley, she found that *Portland* was already moored in the nearby naval shipyard.[43]

The cruiser had gone to Mare Island, a few miles north of San Francisco, to make significant changes in her fighting equipment. John Reimer, one of the boat crew left behind in early December, said that when he first saw Sweet Pea as she pulled into still smoking Pearl Harbor, he "hardly recognized her. Change in paint color, no bright work showing and those holystoned decks painted gray." His was an early realization that for the U.S. Navy, including USS *Portland,* the days of peacetime training and ceremony, bright brass fittings, holystoned decks, and mahogany brows were over. From now on she would not only look like a fighting man-of-war, she would be one.

4

# EARLY DAYS

The highest commanders in Hawaii were fired after the calamity of December 7, some say as scapegoats for failures that should have been placed much higher on the chain of command. The shock of the attack and the losses it caused left American commanders in the Pacific struggling to calculate what to do next. There did not seem to be much left to fight with. By New Year's Day, General Douglas MacArthur was holed up in Malinta Tunnel on Corregidor as his army in Bataan and Corregidor began the fighting that would lead ultimately to surrender. In Hawaii, although Admiral Chester Nimitz had arrived to take command, the ceremony was on the deck of a submarine since there were so few undamaged larger vessels.

America and Britain had long before agreed to fight Germany first in case they faced a two-ocean war. Everyone in Washington and London agreed that the Nazis were much more dangerous than Japan. This "Hitler-first" strategy created a dilemma for the U.S. Navy when the German dictator declared war on America without an actual *causus belli*. American admirals still smarting from that Sunday morning sought revenge on Japan. But the resources at their disposal were limited by that basic strategic decision.

Sweet Pea missed the raid at Pearl Harbor but little else in the rest of the war, as this history will show. Officers and sailors who were on the ship for the duration ended up with sixteen battle stars and about a dozen

medals. With the exception of the campaign in the Marianas in the
summer of 1944 when she was in the shipyard for alterations, and Iwo
Jima when she was fighting in the Philippines and preparing for

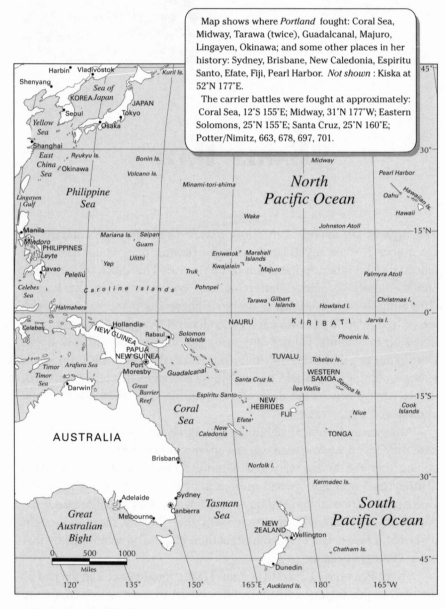

Map shows where *Portland* fought: Coral Sea,
Midway, Tarawa (twice), Guadalcanal, Majuro,
Lingayen, Okinawa; and some other places in her
history: Sydney, Brisbane, New Caledonia, Espiritu
Santo, Efate, Fiji, Pearl Harbor. *Not shown* : Kiska at
52°N 177°E.
  The carrier battles were fought at approximately:
Coral Sea, 12°S 155°E; Midway, 31°N 177°W; Eastern
Solomons, 25°N 155°E; Santa Cruz, 25°N 160°E;
Potter/Nimitz, 663, 678, 697, 701.

Map 1. The Pacific Ocean

Okinawa, *Portland* went everywhere the Pacific Fleet fought: the turning points at Coral Sea and Midway; Guadalcanal; offshore support of MacArthur's New Guinea campaign; the liberation of the Aleutians; and the island-hopping invasions across the Central Pacific.

For most of the war, *Portland* rode shotgun in the carrier task forces, lending her anti-aircraft to the umbrella of flak put up over the flattops. She was perfectly built for such duty. As the newly appointed Commander-in-Chief of the Pacific Fleet (CincPacFlt), Admiral Chester W. Nimitz decided a few weeks after Pearl Harbor that the fast carriers, cruisers, and destroyers would be David's slingshot as the crippled Pacific Fleet began to fight back against the Japanese Goliath. *Portland* became a key player in the new strategy. Nimitz dismissed to California ports the few remaining battleships that by some luck were not at Pearl Harbor on December 7. For a few weeks after the attack on Hawaii, they had been escorting convoys, but Nimitz decided they burned too much fuel for too little purpose, and in effect he beached—or *benched*—them.[1]

Because the "treaty cruisers" were not loaded down with armor, they were nearly as swift as the carriers and destroyers. The battleships sunk in 1941 were at Pearl Harbor that day because they could not keep up with the flattops on their delivery runs to outlying Midway and Wake. *Portland* and other cruisers could and did. Once the battleships were lost, the cruisers would have been outgunned in any great surface battle against the Japanese fleet that first year of the war. But *Portland* and the others had sufficient speed and could get enough AA weaponry to be eminently well qualified for the carrier task force warfare that Uncle Sam's Navy was forced to adopt.

In 1996 a *Portland* veteran, Joe Stables, listed the heavy cruisers available when Nimitz made this decision, and what happened to them during the war.[2] Fifteen ships answered the opening bell of the Pacific War. Seven of the cruisers on Stables's list were sunk in action.[3] Seven others were "heavily" or "severely" damaged, including *Portland.*[4] And the remaining one, *Salt Lake City,* was listed as merely "damaged" on two different occasions.[5] Stables's list shows how much the heavy cruisers suffered in those early days after Pearl Harbor as they stepped up to substitute for the lost battleships.

The first mission for Sweet Pea came during the raid itself, when the *Lexington* task force spent a few days looking for the Japanese who had bombed Hawaii. Shortly after that, she was at sea for a week protecting the islands from possible invasion. But the Americans began immediately to plan how to take the war to the enemy, so on December 19 a carrier task force that included *Portland* prepared to attack the Japanese-occupied Marshall Islands.[6]

Within four days this mission was cancelled, and instead the task force sailed to relieve the garrison at Wake Island. At that moment a handful of Marines had given the Americans their only victory in 1941 as they withstood the Japanese invasion of the tiny, isolated atoll. The morale of Sweet Pea's crew had been lifted by the chance to save those Leathernecks, but the euphoria did not last. All were saddened the very next day, Christmas Eve, when the task force was turned around upon receipt of the news that Wake had been overrun by the enemy.[7]

In early January 1942, the ship guarded convoys coming from California to Hawaii.[8] On New Year's Day she and two destroyers organized as Task Group 15.8 from Pearl Harbor to escort a group of cargo and passenger ships coming to Hawaii. She found them on January 3 and got them to Honolulu by the 7th. The very next day she and her task group joined another convoy, which included the passenger liner *Lurline,* going in the other direction toward San Francisco. There was at least one scare on January 16 when destroyer *Ellet* had a sound contact and made a depth charge run. But this group made its destination safely, too.[9]

The trip was enlivened by a fight that took place on one of the empty merchant ships in the convoy. As a result of the scuffle one man was severely wounded by a meat cleaver! As would happen again and again for the rest of Sweet Pea's career, her medical staff was called on to treat an injured man not in her own crew.[10]

The ship's sick bay organization, called H Division, proved repeatedly that it could do anything from giving advice on how to prevent athlete's foot to performing major surgery. The division ordinarily included two medical doctors, a dentist, one chief pharmacist's mate, and about a dozen other enlisted men.[11] Their surgical skills were shown on many occasions under various circumstances. One day in 1942, Edward Smith from the boiler division suffered severe appendicitis. The senior doctor, Lieutenant Commander Lawrence E.D. Joers, performed an emergency appendectomy while Japanese aircraft attacked Sweet Pea. Joers showed his ingenuity in this case by enlisting dentist Lieutenant R.E. Sadler as anesthesiologist.[12] Earlier the same year, Seaman George Dolezal nearly lost his leg when it was caught in the bight of a line on a turning winch. This time the junior doctor, the same Lieutenant Williams who had turned the tables on the shellbacks in October 1941, saved Dolezal's leg by emergency surgery. He took 119 skin grafts out of the injured man's other leg to restore the badly damaged skin near the injury.[13] Another time, a boatswain's mate was smashed in the eye by the lead weight attached to a line thrown from one ship to another as they began underway transfers. The sailor suffered several fractures around the socket, and the eye itself was damaged. Dr. Joers removed bone fragments from the eye socket, thus leaving the optic nerve exposed. He then cleaned and sutured the injured areas, and continued treatment of the man for days afterward.[14] Thanks to that care, the man returned to full duty.[15]

Nor did the skills of medical care belong to the doctors only. A year before the war, the ship was practicing minesweeping when one of her paravanes got caught somehow and twisted underneath the keel. The great pressure put on the boom that swung the paravane over the side snapped the deck bolt that held it in place. Seaman Walter "Red" Hall was mortally injured, and Seaman Berle "Doggie" Brents was scalped, both of them by the cable that lashed out across the deck. While the doctors worked unsuccessfully to save Hall's life, an unrated corpsman, Hospitalman 1/c James Walker, sewed Brents's scalp back on.[16] Of course, the sick bay staff also did all the things for which medical corpsmen are routinely disliked. Think "injections." For one period in 1944, when the pharmacist's mates were giving tetanus shots and typhoid boosters, members of the crew began to greet each other with a sardonic, "Hi pal, how's your arm?"[17]

The dentist kept busy as well, as the ship was a small town of about twelve hundred young men. In addition to having grown up in the pre-fluoride world, most of the crew had been Depression boys, for whom dental work was probably an unaffordable luxury. In one month, Dr. Sadler reported doing "90 extractions, 50 fillings and 150 various other types of treatment." Some of those sailors joked that they were experts on how to eat Navy food using only their gums![18]

The medical people may have deserved some of this tongue-in-cheek criticism. Chief Pharmacist's Mate Glenn Thomason almost asked for ridicule. He was described in the crew's newspaper as "the Navy's most uniquely tattooed medical corpsman." Thomason had been an embalmer in civilian life, and that experience had enabled him to direct a tattooist in portraying all over his skin and exactly in the right places most of the major internal organs, "actual size and nicely labeled." Not only that, the reporter howled, "his kneecaps had Port and Starboard running lights."[19]

On the other hand, a less colorful corpsman wrote to defend his mates in a poem that suggested that the corpsmen complained about the crew, too. In 1944, H.B. Slee wrote:

> You can talk about your bugle calls,
> Or calls upon the phone,
> But Sick Call is our private call,
> And Sick Call stands alone.
>
> There's nothing musical about our call,
> Except a cry of pain.
> But to us it holds a meaning,
> Like the "March" of Notre Dame's.
>
> A call for us to answer,
> To do the best we can.
> To ease the man that's injured,
> That is our daily plan.
>
> So why not help us out a bit?
> Come to sick call, have patience, wait.
> Instead of being a straggler,
> And coming in an hour late.[20]

Despite the joshing back and forth, at bottom *Portland*'s sick bay enjoyed the respect of the rest of the crew. Lieutenant Vince McNamara, a Communications Officer, was operated on for a hernia in the spring of 1944 when Sweet Pea was firing shore bombardment in one of the New Guinea campaigns. He wrote in his diary on the occasion, "My time in sick bay was most pleasant. . . . The people there were real, not pompous little tin soldiers, like so many of the officers."[21]

## MARE ISLAND

On January 11, 1942, the day she was in Pearl Harbor with the second convoy, *Portland* received a new Commanding Officer, Captain Robert

Rowe Thompson.[22] He led the convoy to California, and then took Sweet Pea to the naval shipyard at Mare Island where Ernie and Leila Booth were reunited.[23] Sweet Pea would stay in the shipyard only a month. Leave was granted to many sailors who had not been in the United States for more than a year, and liberty was welcomed by those who had not been off the ship in more than a month.[24]

The shipyard workers did general wartime things like permanently welding shut the portholes that had marked the ship during her peacetime deployments.[25] A cruiser that packed the heaviest punch still operational in the Pacific Fleet needed more serious work, too. Because of the destruction of so many ships at Pearl Harbor by Japanese airplanes, *Portland*'s anti-aircraft batteries were the primary goals of this modernization. Going into the yard, the ship had three types of AA guns. The eight 5-inch/25-caliber guns were dual purpose, meaning they could serve as a secondary battery against other ships, or as the biggest of the anti-aircraft weapons. In the U.S. Navy, by the way, guns described by bore diameter in inches usually list a caliber, too. When multiplied by the diameter of the bore, the caliber measured the length of the barrel. Thus the 5-inch/25-caliber gun had a barrel twenty-five times as long as five inches, or almost ten and a half feet. *Portland*'s 5-inch batteries were left unchanged by Mare Island's workers.

But the smallest AA guns, the flimsy 50-caliber machine guns, were scrapped, and the shipyard workers installed 20mm AA guns in their place. The new weapons could fire bigger rounds at a rate of 450 per minute out to 1,000 yards effective range, far outstripping the old 50-caliber guns.[26]

The intermediate AA batteries were upgraded, too. Before the war, *Portland* carried four 3-inch/50-caliber guns mounted singly around the ship. Because the old 3-inch guns had to be loaded by hand and their fuses set by hand, they were too slow for modern aircraft. After Pearl Harbor, something better was obviously needed. The 1942 answer was the 1.1-inch pom-pom, which at one hundred rounds per minute was much faster per gun than the old 3-inch. Moreover, each of the four 1.1-inch stations had quadruple mounts, so that there were sixteen guns altogether.[27] The 1.1-inch gun fired rounds 8mm larger than the 20mm gun, and was loaded in clips of five rounds each.[28]

The 20mm and 1.1-inch guns were intended as defensive weapons only. The 1.1s did not perform well in combat, though, and were

replaced a year later by quadruple 40mm mounts. The 40mm was a much
more reliable weapon that could fire 480 rounds a minute.[29] *Portland*
added 20mms up to an ultimate total of eighteen, and she finally sported
twenty-four 40mm guns in 1943.[30]

These were necessary alterations, considering the skimpy assets
the Pacific Fleet had left at its disposal. After all, in the absence of the
now sunken battleships, *Portland* was the quintessential gunboat. All
other features about the ship, her engines, her communications gear,
her radar, her food preparation crews, and so on, had only one purpose:
to get her guns where they could most effectively protect the American
aircraft carriers and do the most damage to the Imperial Japanese
enemy.

*Portland*'s main battery comprised her nine 8-inch/55-caliber guns
in triple turrets. The turrets could train, that is swing from left to right,
through about two hundred degrees. In broadside, then, all nine barrels
could fire on a target, while an enemy generally ahead could be hit only
by the forward guns, and one directly aft only by Turret Three.[31]

Each gun in a turret could be fired separately from the other two, but
they all trained and pointed, that is elevated, together. Each turret had a
trainer and a pointer, two men who controlled electrically driven motors
to move the guns in one dimension or the other. They responded to
azimuth and elevation orders given from an officer in the gun director, an
aiming device much higher than the guns and with a better view of the
combat scene. If the director were knocked out, the turrets could be
aimed and fired locally by the gun captain, who had all the same controls
as the officer in the director did. The pointer and the trainer themselves
could operate independently if necessary because they, too, had sight
ports, little windows they could look through for aiming.[32]

An 8-inch gun fired a projectile that was eight inches in diameter.
This huge shell weighed about 260 pounds, and its effective range was
about fifteen miles.[33] To propel the round toward the target, two bags of
powder, each weighing about fifty pounds, were placed in the gun's tray
just before the projectile was loaded ahead of them. The shells and bags
were hoisted into the turret by a system of lifts, but they had to be
manhandled to ensure a correct fit before they were rammed into the
chamber.[34] To get an idea of how big the ship's main battery was, one
might consider that eight inches is almost exactly 200mm. And yet, the
biggest piece the U.S. Army ordinarily carried into battle in World War

II was 155mm. What *Portland* could do to an enemy afloat or ashore with these big guns was impressive.

In addition to all the gunnery updating in February 1942, the Mare Island shipyard also installed two radar systems. The SC Air Search Radar was one. Although primitive compared to what was coming in 1943, this system was supposed to be able to detect attacking bombers out to thirty miles.[35] As an unintended sidelight, the new antenna on the foremast became handy for others to use in identifying *Portland* from other ships in the force.[36] The second system was a fire-control radar to aim the 5-inch guns, called the FD.[37]

With the shipyard work completed, on February 18, 1942, *Portland* escorted the three ships of outbound convoy #2034 part of the distance to Australia. On the way, the crew saw a U.S. destroyer with a false bow making her way to California for repairs. No one knew if the damaged ship was a survivor of December 7 or of some other mishap. But she made it clear to *Portland*'s men that a war was not far over the horizon.[38]

Indeed, *Portland* was a fast ship going in harm's way. She turned the convoy over to the British near Samoa on March 3, and steamed on to Noumea, New Caledonia, where she joined Task Force 17.[39] There Sweet Pea and some of the other cruisers and destroyers patrolled offshore for a few days while carrier *Yorktown* was making preparations. On April 20, she went into port, but a week later, in company with *Yorktown* and Task Force 17, she headed for the Coral Sea.[40]

**5**

# TURNING POINTS

In its three main theaters, World War II had turning points, moments when the tide of the war shifted. Until each theater's turning point, the Axis Powers were clearly winning, but after it the Allies were. The turning point of the Russo-German war, for example, was Stalingrad. Until that 1942–1943 battle the Nazis won most of the time, but afterward the Soviets did. In the Anglo-American war against Germany, Al Alamein in late 1942 was the turning point.

For the Allied naval war against the Japanese, however, three possible turning points are arguable. One is when the Japanese were first *stopped* after their great conquests in the Pacific and Southeast Asia. If that were the criterion, then the turning point would be the Battle of the Coral Sea, May 7–8, 1942. If the test were when Japan was first *defeated,* the turning point would have to be the Battle of Midway, June 4, 1942. Most historians indeed think that Midway was the turning point of the Pacific War. There are others who mark the turning point as the moment when the *attitudes* of the two sides changed, when the Imperial Navy began to doubt its invincibility and the American Navy began to believe it could actually win. If the appearance of new attitudes is the test, then the turning point was the Naval Battle of Guadalcanal, November 12–15, 1942.

In their various formations at these three great naval engagements, the Allies deployed sixty-seven ships, including two Royal Australian Navy cruisers at Coral Sea. Some vessels appeared in more than one of the three battles. In all, then, forty-six different American ships and the two Aussies engaged in one or another of those three arguable turning points of the Pacific War. There were four carriers, two battleships, twelve cruisers, and twenty-eight destroyers.[1]

Of all these ships, only USS *Portland* was at all three battles.

## THE BATTLE OF THE CORAL SEA

During the time of Sweet Pea's refitting at Mare Island, and while she escorted a convoy of ships headed for Australia and then joined the task force built around *Yorktown,* the Japanese pushed into the island barrier that separates Australia from the Pacific Ocean. They aimed to cut the lines between Australia and the United States. Some Japanese after the war argued that this effort was caused by a "victory disease," saying that the earlier victories had made imperial planners so arrogant that they began to reach beyond what Japan was actually capable of accomplishing. But in fact the expansion in the Southwest Pacific was a perfectly rational plan to protect one of those most important earlier victories.

Again, Admiral Yamamoto was at work. He needed to defend Rabaul, a port on the eastern tip of New Britain Island, taken from the British colonial authorities in late January 1942. The Japanese were already turning Rabaul into a great sea and air base, less than seven hundred miles from their main Pacific bastion at Truk in the Carolines. The admiral had two drives in mind, one to push into the eastern part of New Guinea, called Papua, and the other to slide down the Solomon Islands, which run easterly away from New Britain and New Guinea.[2] But American code-breaking had revealed both parts of Yamamoto's scheme. When a Japanese invasion fleet headed for Port Moresby on the southern coast of Papua, an Allied fleet that included *Portland* was sent to block it.[3]

Sweet Pea had a new CO for this fight. Captain Thompson had unfortunately sustained serious injuries in an accident only three months into his tour, in late April. The Captain had fallen headfirst down a ladder into the chain locker during a ship's inspection, chipping a vertebra in his spine.[4] Thompson, who had won a Navy Cross in World War I submarine service, was sent to a hospital ship and then back to the States for medical care. He spent the rest of the war ashore.[5] Because the ship was headed for what was known to be a major encounter with the Japanese Navy, she needed an experienced skipper. Fortunately one was at hand. The Commanding Officer of the hospital ship *Solace* where Thompson was being treated, Captain Benjamin Perlman, was pressed into service.[6] Admiral Frank Jack Fletcher, the task force commander, must have reckoned that it would be far better to have a Commander as the acting CO of the hospital ship and a Captain, Perlman, who had great experience in destroyers, leading a heavy cruiser as it went into an important battle, than the reverse.[7]

Perlman did have something like the big picture. In the daily notice for May 5, 1942, Portland's XO wrote that "Today is most likely the day we will finally see action." But when he saw that note in print, Perlman worried that should it fall into enemy hands it might reveal too much about American intelligence, so all copies were ordered turned in. Not all were, of course, because over the next few days all hands were too busy trying to stay alive.[8]

The Battle of the Coral Sea is now well known as the first time in naval history when the vessels of the contending forces never saw each other, because all the fighting was done by aircraft and the ships they attacked. It turned out to be a *tactical* Japanese victory since the Americans suffered worse losses, but a *strategic* American win since the planned Japanese invasion of Port Moresby was rebuffed. It was, then, the first time that the Japanese aggression that began in 1931 was *stopped.*[9] One should keep in mind here just how desperate the Allied cause in the Pacific was at that moment. As the two forces approached each other in the Coral Sea, some two thousand miles away the U.S. Army was suffering the greatest defeat in its history when it surrendered in the Philippines on May 6. The war looked no better anywhere else in the world, either. The Russians were reeling before the new German spring offensive, and Rommel's Afrika Korps was pushing east toward Egypt and the Suez Canal. These were not good times, and the mixed victory in the Coral Sea brightly lit an otherwise totally darkened firmament. USS *Portland* played a key role in the work of the U.S. Navy on this momentous occasion.

Sparring began on May 7, 1942, when Japanese aircraft found the American oiler *Neosho* and identified her as an aircraft carrier. A massive air attack on the woeful auxiliary oiler sank her one escorting destroyer and left *Neosho* wrecked and adrift. That night the two carrier forces came within perhaps fifty miles of each other. Both commanders considered a night surface action, but decided against it.[10] The Americans would not have done well in any such fight, so when the range between the two fleets opened before daylight, it was lucky for the U.S. Navy.

So few ships were in the U.S. Pacific Fleet at the time that on the morning of May 8, 1942, the two American carriers at Coral Sea, *Yorktown* and the larger *Lexington,* formed the center of a single formation.[11] The task force was arrayed in a rough circle in order to maximize the anti-aircraft firepower of the cruisers and smaller escorts. That morning, from *Portland*'s station about eight hundred yards to starboard of *Yorktown,* she threw up nearly four thousand rounds of AA from her 5-inch, 1.1-inch, and 20mm mounts as the Japanese attackers came in. The vigorous maneuvering of the carriers to avoid bombs and torpedoes split the task group into two parts, thus weakening the collective defensive fire. *Lexington* was hit four times by torpedo bombers and dive bombers. But officers in *Portland* could see that the volume of their own fire deterred some of the Japanese pilots from making effective torpedo runs at *Yorktown.*[12] *Yorktown* survived the onslaught to fight again at Midway, and Sweet Pea deserves some of the credit.

*Portland* did well in spite of the fact that she had trouble with her own anti-aircraft batteries. Many of the Japanese aircraft stayed too far from the cruiser for her smaller weapons to reach them. The 5-inch/25-caliber dual-purpose guns, which did have sufficient range, were slow and, because they were sited in open mounts, left their crews exposed. But that was nothing compared to what the ship endured with the new 1.1-inch guns. Installed only three months earlier and presumably top-of-the-line weapons, the 1.1s showed a tendency to jam and blow up with rounds in the barrel.[13] Radiomen who served near these guns reported how they hated them because the sound was so sharp it hurt their ears.[14] We can only imagine how it was for the men who fired them. But the gunner's mates disliked the 1.1s not for the noise but because the fragile weapons required so much work to prepare for combat and to repair afterward.[15]

Nevertheless, at first it appeared that neither *Yorktown* nor *Lexington* was seriously hurt. Partly due to *Portland*'s defense, only a single bomb struck *Yorktown* and the ship lost no immediate effectiveness. Although two torpedoes and two bombs hit *Lexington,* her engines were intact; she recovered her aircraft and maneuvered with little difficulty. But in the early afternoon a series of explosions ignited gasoline fumes below decks, disemboweling the great ship.[16]

Casualties were severe, but 1,741 officers and men from the carrier's crew successfully abandoned ship.[17] *Portland* was close enough for her sailors to see them scrambling down lines into the water. To help these survivors, Sweet Pea's men rigged rope ladders over the side and prepared to send away small boats, until destroyers with their lower freeboard actually pulled all the swimmers out of the water.[18] When the big carrier finally did go down, men on *Portland* could feel underwater explosions as *Lexington* fell toward the ocean bottom.[19]

Bill Reehl, at the time a Seaman 2/c in one of the deck divisions, served as an ammunition passer in Mess Hall #3 during general quarters. The young sailor disliked the fact that he could not see what all the topside noise was about, and he spent the next couple of weeks trying to get a new battle station in a gun mount, where the action would at least be visible if no less frightful. At the time of *Lexington*'s agony, though, he was standing a steaming watch topside, where he got an eyeful as the big ship's sailors let themselves down into the sea.[20]

It was the first time Reehl and his buddies felt real fear about the outcome of the war. Up until then the war had been an adventure and they thought their prewar training had prepared them for it. Even the devastation they saw at Pearl Harbor, while shocking in every way, had failed to affect their self-confidence. But now they were watching a disaster. Reehl was astounded that small airplanes could do such damage to a huge ship like *Lexington.* He wondered what a man would be thinking as he scrambled for his life, leaving a ship that had been his home. Witnessing *Lexington*'s death throes, Reehl also worried about how strong his own fleet was going to be after the loss of one of the two biggest carriers in the dwindling American inventory.[21] There were others not so thoughtful nor concerned, of course. One was Seaman 2/c Joseph Allen, who had successfully lied about his age to enlist in the Navy. Allen was seen happily firing his 20mm at the attacking Japanese aircraft during the fighting, although he was only fifteen years old![22]

Because Sweet Pea was the biggest ship nearby, the destroyers delivered 722 of the *Lexington* survivors to her.[23] Gunner's Mate John Geriak, the phone talker in the anti-aircraft director, had a bird's-eye view of the proceedings. The suffering of the *Lexington* sailors, many of whom were badly burned, moved him, even from his high perch.[24] Before being transferred to a naval hospital ashore, these injured men were treated by *Portland*'s medical staff, yet again distinguishing itself by the excellent care it dispensed.[25] The bodies of some dead sailors were plucked from the ocean, and one *Lexington* man, Francisco Mendiola, died after reaching Sweet Pea with extreme burns over his entire body.[26] Their remains were placed in Sweet Pea's cold storage until the battle ended and they could be properly buried.[27]

Other sailors had different worries about these rescues. From his station alongside the flag bags, Signalman Eldon Peterson watched the survivors coming aboard, some burnt, others wounded, all in shock. Besides sympathizing with the victims he could see below, what concerned Peterson was whether his ship would be able to make enough water for all these extra people.[28] Not to worry; *Portland*'s evaporators did a nice job. But the cooks did have to work overtime with so many more mouths to feed.[29] All noted a considerable drop-off in both the quantity and quality of the food served in the mess decks, as a rationing system went into effect.[30]

In one of those peculiar twists about warfare, some of *Portland*'s crew had left the ship just before the battle began. They had been transferred for transportation home to the States for further assignment, and the war should have been over for them, at least temporarily. Their ticket home had taken them aboard fleet oiler *Neosho* on May 6, the day before the battle began.[31] When the oiler was blasted the next day by Japanese aviators who misidentified her as an aircraft carrier, most of the former *Portland* men were lost.

Fifty years later, one veteran listed them as "Chief King, Flaherty and Gaylord."[32] A more recent account said the men were "Richard D. Cox, Frederick W. Fabian, Edward A. Flaherty, and William O. King."[33] In 1999, former shipmate John Fynan confirmed that Electrician's Mate 2/c Delvan C. Gaylord was indeed one of Sweet Pea's sailors lost when *Neosho* was attacked. At the same time, shipmate John Votaw wrote that "Eddy Dunn" was also among the men transferred to *Neosho*.[34] Six former *Portland* men were riding *Neosho* when she was attacked, then, and all died in the battle or during the four days the oiler stayed afloat after the bombing, except Chief Petty Officer Ed Flaherty, who reached a lifeboat and was later saved.[35]

Those men were no longer officially members of the crew, so Sweet Pea suffered no personnel casualties in the Coral Sea, officially speaking. But men on board grieved over the death of their friends. Moreover, *Portland* did endure some minor damage when a near miss caused some of her thin hull plates to buckle and one of her fuel tanks to leak oil.[36] As a result, she went with *Yorktown* to Tongatabu for repairs.[37]

## THE BATTLE OF MIDWAY

The stay at Tongatabu was brief. *Portland*'s repairs took little time, so she and another cruiser soon went to sea to protect the approaches to the island.[38] In taking up this patrol, however, Sweet Pea had yet another Commanding Officer. Temporary replacement Perlman had done such a nice job at the Coral Sea that Rear Admiral William Ward Smith, the overall commander of the cruisers and destroyers there, recommended that he be retained in permanent command of *Portland.* But Perlman expressed some misgivings about keeping the cruiser job when he visited Vice Admiral Fletcher on May 16. He told the admiral that the doctors on the hospital ship had begged him not to leave. He himself worried that he might be violating some aspect of the Geneva agreement in taking command of a combatant ship. He expressed these misgivings to Fletcher, and admitted that he was not enthusiastic about a permanent reassignment.[39]

Perlman later regretted that he passed when given the great opportunity to be Sweet Pea's Commanding Officer in the arduous months ahead, but he blamed only himself.[40] Happily for the fleet, a suitable replacement for Perlman had just arrived in the theater. Captain Laurence DuBose was slated to relieve the skipper of heavy cruiser *Astoria,* Captain Frank Scanland, who had been CO of *Nevada,* the only battleship to get underway from Battleship Row on December 7. Scanland had been ashore when his ship was attacked and did not reach her in time for that unscheduled sortie. The junior officers on *Nevada*'s bridge put her aground to keep the main channel clear and prevent her from being sunk in the deeper waters in the ocean. Since she was therefore out of commission for some time, Scanland had been sent to *Astoria* temporarily, and in May 1942 DuBose was supposed to relieve him. But since Perlman indicated to Fletcher that he was reluctant to continue with *Portland,* DuBose's orders were changed, and he went to

Sweet Pea instead, leaving Scanland to wait for another replacement. DuBose's excellent command of Sweet Pea would win him an admiral's flag, while Perlman would not advance beyond his 1942 rank.[41]

Within a few days, *Yorktown* and her task group, including *Portland* with her third Captain in four months, were ordered to rush to Pearl Harbor. Admiral Nimitz had learned from the code breakers that the Japanese were on their way to Midway, only eleven hundred miles from Hawaii. Although the U.S. fleet was badly outnumbered in every ship type, Nimitz hoped to set another ambush, this time with carriers *Enterprise* and *Hornet,* back from the Doolittle Raid. He wanted very much to have *Yorktown* there, too.[42]

*Yorktown*'s battle damage was supposed to take several months to repair, but the job was almost miraculously accomplished in a mere forty-eight hours by the Pearl Harbor shipyard. This would prove lucky for the American side, because *Yorktown*'s torpedo planes and dive-bombers would play critical roles in the great victory that lay ahead.[43] While the shipyard workers performed their heroic work on the injured carrier, *Portland*'s sailors were busy, too. They knew that something was afoot, since no liberty was granted. This time Sweet Pea's men only worked, and worked hard. The AA gunners, of course, had their hands full trying to repair those pesky 1.1-inch guns.[44] Others did the no less necessary work of loading stores, food, and ammunition around the clock for two days.[45]

The Japanese were frustrated that their attack on Pearl Harbor, though highly successful in many ways, had not knocked the U.S. Navy out of the war. As a result Admiral Yamamoto hoped to set a trap in which the American carrier groups would be destroyed. He planned to invade Midway, knowing that the Americans could not let the island fall into Japanese hands without a fight. The resulting battle would allow him to destroy their flattops. His plan was supported by the Imperial General Staff because of its embarrassment when Colonel James Doolittle's carrier-borne Army bombers had dropped a few nearly harmless bombs on Tokyo and other Japanese targets in mid-April. The high command thought that extending the Empire's perimeter as far east as Midway would make impossible any repeat of such an attack.

But Yamamoto's plan had fatal flaws that should have been seen ahead of time but were not probably because of the reverence he enjoyed. His subordinates nearly worshiped the admiral. His army contemporaries had such great respect for his strategic brilliance that they too usually concurred with him. Even the Americans gave Yamamoto great credit, to the degree that when they learned in 1943 that he was flying into Bougainville, they set a trap to kill him.[46] This extraordinary operation revealed a respect for the Japanese leader that he did not deserve. His idea to attack Pearl Harbor became only the first step on the road to a national disaster that Yamamoto did not live to see.

His supposedly equally wonderful idea about Midway was even worse. While *Yorktown* and *Portland* were scurrying back to Pearl Harbor to bring the inferior American forces together, Yamamoto scattered *his* forces all over the Pacific, in a major violation of the principle of concentration. One group made a diversionary attack on the Aleutians. A second comprised the carriers assigned to bomb Midway itself. A third would shell the island, a fourth would transport and land the troops, and a fifth included the battleships and heavy cruisers that would use their powerful gunfire to demolish the American fleet when it came up from Hawaii to fight. Yamamoto sent the carriers on ahead, thinking it would take the Americans at least two days to reach Midway, but kept the battleships and other heavies a day or so behind, from where he thought they could swoop in on the late-arriving Americans.

But the Americans were not surprised, as he was sure they would be. Their code breakers had learned so much about the scheme that they were able to predict almost exactly the bearing, range, and time when the Japanese carriers would be sighted by Midway's patrol aircraft. Yamamoto cannot be condemned for failing to realize that the enemy had broken his codes. But he certainly can be blamed for dispersing his navy all over the Pacific Ocean. The Aleutian diversion was without value, because it was scheduled for one day before the carriers struck Midway, not enough time for the Americans to react. Separating all the forces that were homing in on Midway itself approached lunacy. The Japanese Navy in mid-1942 enjoyed such superiority in all types of ships, in quality of carrier aircraft, and in experience in the crews of both that his depending on surprise was stupid. It would have been better for Japan if he had taken out an ad in the Honolulu newspapers announcing his intentions and then had his forces ready for whatever the Americans would do.

Just as bad was that Yamamoto wanted to be on hand for the death rattle of the U.S. Navy. He was, therefore, riding in one of the battleships that was a day and a half behind the carriers. As a result, he was bound by radio silence like all the other forces and could not communicate with his commanders should something unexpected take place.[47]

As it was, the American carriers were lying in wait within range when the Japanese carriers launched their first strike against Midway on June 4, 1942. Rear Admiral Raymond Spruance, in command of a task force that included carriers *Enterprise* and *Hornet* until Rear Admiral Frank Jack Fletcher in *Yorktown* could catch up, launched his air attack against the enemy flattops immediately on learning of their location. *Yorktown*'s planes were close enough to join in.

Despite a bloody morning in which everything went wrong, the American bombers luckily rolled over into their dives at the very moment when the Japanese flattops were at their most vulnerable. Dauntlesses from *Enterprise* and *Yorktown* dropped out of the clear sky to deliver crushing attacks on carriers whose flight decks were crowded with aircraft preparing to launch and therefore fully loaded with fuel and bombs. A few American hits in that melée turned the enemy aircraft themselves into lethal explosives that wrecked three of the ships that carried them.[48]

Only one of the four Japanese carriers, *Hiryu,* survived that morning attack, and she struck back before being sunk later in the day. *Yorktown* was again in a circular formation, as at the Coral Sea, but now she was the only carrier. *Portland* was one of three cruisers providing air defense, on the flattop's port quarter as the force headed easterly to launch and recover aircraft. When the bogies were first detected, *Pensacola* was on *Yorktown*'s port bow and *Vincennes* on her starboard quarter. Sweet Pea's radar detected the first batch of enemy aircraft at 1333. The Americans turned to a roughly westerly course and speeded up to thirty knots, maneuvering to evade.[49] In all the turning, sometimes by column and sometimes in formation, *Portland* was left on the side of the carrier away from the enemy attack.

The skillful Japanese pilots in *Hiryu*'s aircraft found *Yorktown* shortly after 1400. About ten minutes into the fight, the carrier was hit on the flight deck near her superstructure, perhaps twice, causing fires, lots of smoke and topside damage, and bringing her temporarily to a standstill.[50] Near misses off her stern seemed to men on Sweet Pea's bridge to lift the great carrier right out of the water.[51] Her hull still somewhat weakened by the Coral Sea damage and the quick repairs,

*Yorktown* looked doomed and the Captain ordered his crew to abandon ship. But her damage control parties did marvelous work, and the carrier rigged for *Portland* to tow. The lines were never thrown over, though, because *Yorktown* began to move again under her own power. By 1637 she was able to make nineteen knots and resume air operations.[52]

Gunner's Mate Geriak expressed the frustration many of the men in Sweet Pea felt when the raids had come in on the side away from *Portland*.[53] Faced with the difficulty of getting at the Japanese planes, Gunnery Officer Lieutenant Commander Elliott Shanklin devised a technique to achieve the most good under the circumstances. Since it was nearly impossible to hit the enemy attackers, he decided to protect their target. He had all of his anti-aircraft batteries fire at a specific point in the sky over the carrier, creating a "barrage" that he hoped would make the Japanese hesitant to fly through or under it. It seemed to work. The protecting ships, including *Portland,* claimed to shoot down twenty-four of the attacking planes. Eyewitnesses aboard Sweet Pea said that most were splashed because they flew into the barrage of flack exploding above the carrier.[54]

But at 1640, just as *Yorktown* was getting up a head of steam, another attack came on. This time the desperate Japanese hit the carrier with three torpedoes, again on the side away from *Portland*.[55] Now the flattop began circling to the left, with a noticeable port list. On this occasion her crew actually did abandon ship.[56] Many of the sailors who got off the carrier in the next hours and the next day were picked up by destroyers and transferred to *Portland*.[57] In not quite a full day, Sweet Pea took on what might have been the biggest at-sea transfer of men between ships in the history of the U.S. Navy. Destroyers *Russell, Balch, Benham, Anderson,* and *Hamman* came alongside Sweet Pea between 1835 on June 4 and 1430 on June 5. They delivered, respectively, 492, 545, 721, 203, and finally 85 survivors of the stricken *Yorktown*.[58] The total of 2,046 refugees from the carrier almost tripled the number that had come from *Lexington* after the Coral Sea, itself a figure that had stretched the cruiser's resources.

One member of the carrier's crew who was transferred from *Balch* to Sweet Pea was Chaplain Stanford E. Linzey. In his book about the battle and his survival, *God Was at Midway,* he recorded a slice of *Portland* life that ordinarily would not land in the light of history. Once aboard the cruiser, Chaplain Linzey established a Bible study and prayer group among the crew, where none had existed before. He found so many Sweet Pea sailors whose faith revived during his ministry that he used that as evidence that God was indeed at Midway.[59]

However crowded she was, Sweet Pea was an asylum for sailors from sunken ships. One of the rescued *Yorktown* sailors told his family many times afterward that, although he was picked up by a destroyer, he did not feel safe until he felt the big cruiser under his feet.[60] He could not have enjoyed the security very long, because *Portland* rushed off to the east toward Pearl Harbor to find USS *Fulton*. She was a submarine tender that had come out to the area to take the survivors from Sweet Pea so the cruiser could return to her station with the task force.[61] The two ships met shortly after noon on June 6.[62]

Pete Cole, one of Sweet Pea's most experienced enginemen, thought that sending all those sailors to *Fulton* was "one of the greatest feats of seamanship of all time."[63] When the two ships joined up, *Portland* reversed course, making nearly twenty knots, so the operation would not take her farther away from Midway. It was much faster than usual for these at-sea transfers, because the cruiser was needed back at the task force. *Fulton* came alongside to port, and as the two ships raced westerly toward where the enemy might be, six lines were rigged between them. Several large canvas bags were hung from each of the six lines, with a smaller line from each bag sent to *Fulton,* while another small line from each bag was held on *Portland*. Now the men on the tender could pull the bags across, while the cruiser's crew restrained them as needed to control the speed of the transfer.

Into each bag went three of the *Yorktown*'s survivors, all in life jackets but all frightened at the prospect. The bags were hurriedly hauled over, and the empties flew back for more human cargo. Cole and his shipmates found it "inspiring and exciting to watch the bags going back and forth with the two ships proceeding at a good speed, the water churning and foaming between them."[64] They also noticed that at first sailors from the two speeding ships did all the work, but as *Yorktown*'s survivors reached *Fulton,* they too pitched in and largely took over the task of pulling their shipmates aboard.

The most hair-raising part was yet to come: the transfer of the wounded. Each of the injured *Yorktown* men was strapped into a wire-basket stretcher. The stretcher was then hooked up and speedily though carefully pulled across. Pete Cole and other *Portland* men held their breath as they watched with hearts pounding, because they knew that if any stretcher should break loose it would mean certain death for the helpless, tied-up sailor as he plunged into what Cole called the "turbulent chasm."[65] For several hours the men on both sides completed this back-breaking and dangerous work without a single loss. *Fulton* shoved off and returned to Pearl Harbor, and *Portland* headed back to war.[66]

Meanwhile, battered *Yorktown* had another heroic moment left. On June 5, after *Portland* had gone looking for *Fulton,* Captain Elliot Buckmaster and some damage control personnel returned to the still floating *Yorktown* and tried again to save her. She was taken under tow by fleet ocean tug USS *Vireo,* and was making four knots toward Pearl Harbor when she was attacked by Japanese submarine I-168. A spread of four torpedoes fired from very close aboard immediately demolished destroyer *Hamman,* then alongside the carrier, and ripped out *Yorktown*'s bottom. She finally went down just before dawn on June 7.[67]

*Portland* returned to the main battle scene later that day and lent a hand in looking for downed aviators. Her SOCs flew search and rescue missions on June 7. Little was left to chance in this operation. One of Sweet Pea's planes was launched and recovered at night, a rare thing, because a small light had been seen in the distance and was thought to be a flare fired by an aviator. Nothing was found, though.[68]

The next day, June 8, *Portland* fell in with the carrier *Saratoga,* which had joined the fleet too late for the battle. This new task force headed for the Aleutians, where the Japanese diversionary force had taken two small islands. But two days later, the high command in Hawaii decided that the Aleutians could wait for another time, so the force returned to Pearl Harbor.[69]

Seaman Reehl, who in the space of only four weeks had now seen the destruction of two of the navy's five Pacific Fleet carriers, was afraid at that moment that the U.S. was going to lose the war. "We all wondered," he said years later, "what the hell are we going to do if we keep losing carriers like this?"[70] This anxiety was not assuaged by what historians now view as the great victories at Coral Sea and Midway. Only Guadalcanal would blot out the American fears, a fact that makes Guadalcanal the true turning point of the Pacific War.

Looking back, it is easy to see that *Portland* did excellent work in these early days when the U.S. Navy was outnumbered and outgunned.

She escorted convoys between California and Hawaii when no one knew whether they would be targets of Japanese submarines. She received a rushed augmentation of her AA batteries because everyone knew that air attacks were going to be central to the Japanese effort to conquer the Pacific. She escorted a convoy that was badly needed in Australia. She made a major contribution to the defense of the carriers that stood between Japan and victory. And when things went badly, she rescued men from sinking ships.

In light of the grim outlook prevailing in early 1942 America, that the outgunned Pacific Fleet was fighting back provided a reason for hope. And *Portland* was at the heart of that resistance. There was nothing more anyone could ask of her.

No one can be surprised to learn, though, that the U.S. Navy's bluejackets gave Sweet Pea little praise. Not always in good humor, many of them scorned the cruiser as a jinxed ship, since the two carriers it was most identified with had both been sunk by the Japanese.[71] Those who scoffed would see *Portland*'s heart and her grit just a few months ahead at Guadalcanal, then unknown. There the U.S. Navy would produce a new confident attitude that would ultimately lead the democracies to victory in this great war. *Portland* would be right in the middle of the key moments.

# 6

# GUADALCANAL

No one in the prewar U.S. Navy thought that a war against Japan would include fighting south of the equator. The strategy for fighting against the Empire was called War Plan Orange, and it imagined that the conflict would begin with an attack on the Philippines, then an American possession. The U.S. garrison there was supposed to hold out long enough for the Pacific Fleet to steam to the rescue. Somewhere in the western Pacific there would be a major naval battle along the lines of the 1916 Battle of Jutland. The United States would win, of course, and then demand Japan's surrender.[1]

But Admiral Ernest J. King, the Commander-in-Chief of the U.S. Navy, focused his attention on the Solomon Islands when the Japanese began to move down that chain in early 1942. The Solomons run southeasterly away from the Bismarck Archipelago just north of New Guinea. Historian Richard Frank described them as "footprints," as if Bougainville, Choiseul, Santa Isabel, and Malaita were the marks of the left foot, while Vella LaVella, New Georgia, the Russells, Guadalcanal, and San Cristobal were those of the right, as some giant walked away from New Guinea.[2]

Before the war, eastern New Guinea, or Papua, and most of the neighboring islands were British possessions. But during the early months of the fighting, Japanese forces easily picked up whichever among them they wanted, and turned each conquest into a base for further expansion. In late January 1942, the Japanese Navy captured

Rabaul, a town with a magnificent harbor at one end of the large island of New Britain. Rabaul was within range of support from the main Japanese base at Truk, 640 miles away.[3] In early May, another force took Tulagi, about 600 miles down the Solomons, where the British located their administrative capital of those islands. Allied reconnaissance noted these developments, but in those days there were no forces available to stop Japan's relentless forward progress.[4]

To Admiral King in Washington, though, this movement potentially threatened the American supply lines to Australia. Those routes were already long and tenuous, thus magnifying the shortage of shipping that all of the Allies were then facing. If these lines had to be moved even farther east in order to escape Japanese aircraft or ships based in the eastern Solomons, it would add to the difficulty of supporting General Douglas MacArthur. He was then in Australia, trying to build up Allied forces to defend that nation and to launch a counter-offensive that would liberate the Philippines.

The alarm bells rang from Brisbane to Capitol Hill when Australian coast watchers reported that the Japanese were building an airfield on Guadalcanal, about twenty miles from Tulagi, across a body of water soon to become famous as "Ironbottom Sound."[5] King used all of his powers to persuade the other services, the Roosevelt administration, and the British that it was wise to divert material and human resources to defend the Solomons, although the main Allied effort was supposed to be made against Hitler. Soon everyone agreed with King that the new airfield must be taken out of the enemy's hands to protect those essential supply routes to Australia.[6] On August 7, 1942, then, the First Marine Division landed at Lunga Point on Guadalcanal and that same day captured the nearly finished runways from the construction crews. For the next six months or so, Americans and Japanese fought without quarter and almost daily on that island, in the air over it, or in the sea around it in a stubborn test of wills over who would hold and therefore be able to use the airfield.[7]

Although most historians think that Midway was the turning point of the Pacific War, some who study the long and grim Guadalcanal campaign disagree. Just why is clear. Midway was only a moment in time when by great gallantry and good luck Americans smashed the carrier force of the Imperial Japanese Navy. At that time, however, no one believed that the war had changed its direction. In 1942, as the Allies were suffering such great losses in general, even tough Winston Churchill doubted whether "democratic youth could prevail in battle against the Axis."[8]

Closer to our own focus, from the landings at Guadalcanal on August 7, 1942, through the following November, few Americans thought the tide had changed and was now running in their favor. *Portland* Seaman 2/c Reehl was thinking that things were "desperate" and that America's "chances" were not "very good."[9] Enlisted sailor Reehl's anxieties were typical of those who served in the Pacific Fleet in those days, as we can see by the fact that many of the *commanders* suffered from them, too. During the preinvasion conference on his flagship *Saratoga,* Vice Admiral Frank Jack Fletcher, in overall command of the Guadalcanal operation, expressed his own fears. Fletcher had already lost carriers *Lexington* and *Yorktown,* both sunk from beneath him. After such experiences with Japanese aviators and aircraft, he was understandably skeptical when he heard of Admiral Nimitz's confidence in American superiority in personnel and equipment. Fletcher told the landing force commanders that he would keep his carriers near the beachhead to provide air support for *only two days*.[10] They were horrified and angry at Fletcher's apparent unwillingness to fight, but the admiral soon showed them even greater timidity: Fletcher was so afraid of the Japanese Navy that he withdrew before even the two days had expired.

Higher up the chain of command, Vice Admiral Robert L. Ghormley, Fletcher's superior as theater commander of the South Pacific, had gone on record in a report to Washington signed by General MacArthur and himself that the Navy's plans for the Solomons were not feasible: the Japanese were too strong. Perhaps as a way to show this disdain for what he regarded as a hopeless mission, Ghormley did not bother to attend Fletcher's conference in *Saratoga,* or even to send a representative.[11]

Fortunately, Ghormley and Fletcher were soon replaced, and under new leadership the Marines ashore and the U.S. Navy's ships and men, including *Portland,* would change the pessimism that they and their brass had once shared. By the time the sun rose on November 15, 1942, following the Naval Battle of Guadalcanal, about three months after the landings on the island, the Pacific Fleet knew it could win the war and the Imperial Japanese Navy knew that only dark days lay ahead.[12] By that time, defeatist commanders were gone and Bill Reehl's confidence was sky-high.

The effort to capture Guadalcanal was sometimes called Operation Shoe String, with good reason. The First Marine Division, which landed on August 7, was not ready for its task. It was on its way to New Zealand to conduct advanced training for an already-planned but different attack in the Solomons. But the discovery of the airfield on Guadalcanal moved up the timetable and changed the site. Some of the troops had barely landed at Wellington when they were turned around and sent to Guadalcanal.[13] None of their ships had been combat loaded. In other words, the transports were loaded so they could carry the most cargo, not so the items needed first in an invasion were most readily available. The Marines were given barely enough time in Wellington to dig out of the transports what they would need to fight with and live on. Other units of the division still at sea were steered to Guadalcanal in their civilian ships, also not combat loaded. There they had to wait for the first group to clear a beachhead so they could disembark and unscramble their equipment on the beach, trying to find what they really needed.[14] The expedition had all the earmarks of a disaster waiting to happen.

*Portland* was a member of the force that accompanied the invasion fleet.[15] This was, incidentally, one of the times when Sweet Pea was derided for the bad luck of carriers she had escorted earlier. Some men from carrier *Enterprise* let it be known they were not happy to be escorted by a cruiser with such an ominous record.[16] Perhaps the carrier sailors were comforted by the fact that their ship was not escorted by *Portland* alone, though. The task force built around *Enterprise* included the new anti-aircraft cruiser *Atlanta,* with a large number of 5-inch AA guns, and the new battleship *North Carolina.*[17] Unlike the old behemoths sunk or disabled at Pearl Harbor, *North Carolina* with her 16-inch guns and numerous AA batteries was fast enough, under most circumstances, to keep up with the carriers, cruisers, and destroyers who had been fighting for the past half-year without battleships.

The landing on Guadalcanal turned out to be an easy success. In *Portland* there was even a moment of dark humor. The cruiser was standing offshore on anti-aircraft alert when a nervous lookout reported a mass of planes approaching. But as general quarters gonged throughout the ship, Captain DuBose looked through his long glass and calmly ordered a stand-down. The "mass of planes" was merely a flock of large birds![18] In fact, the landings had caught the enemy by surprise, and the construction workers fled into the jungle to await rescue by combat forces.[19]

*Portland* was riding with *Enterprise* when Admiral Fletcher withdrew the carriers from Guadalcanal, leaving the invasion unprotected.[20] Fletcher's unwillingness to risk his ships left the Marines ashore hard-pressed. Since the withdrawal of the support led to the equally hasty departure of their transports, the Marines had little food or ammunition, and would have faced a nearly impossible job to complete the captured airfield. They were saved by the Japanese equipment they found. Tractors, automobiles, tools, and other things abandoned by the enemy workers were all put to use.[21] They were happy to have also captured a large quantity of food from the runaway enemy. The First Marine Division became quite partial in the first few days on Guadalcanal to Japanese delicacies like crabmeat, although they went on reduced rations right away.[22]

Because Sweet Pea was with the carrier and not the surface forces supporting the invasion, she missed the cruiser debacle in the Battle of Savo Island.[23] After midnight on August 9, 1942, a fast Japanese cruiser force slipped through the American screen and sank four cruisers, three American and one Australian, which were supposed to be protecting the transports. Fortunately for the Allies, the Japanese Admiral turned away and headed back to Rabaul although he could easily have destroyed much of the invasion fleet.[24] The Allies were thoroughly embarrassed by poor communications, poor command structure, and a lack of pugnacity. American naval confidence was shaken even deeper than it had been beforehand.[25] This depression in morale further belies the argument that the war had turned at Midway.

## BATTLE OF THE EASTERN SOLOMONS

Two weeks later, still in company with *Enterprise,* Sweet Pea performed singularly in an air-defense role as carrier-based Japanese aircraft swarmed over Big E. This was the Battle of the Eastern Solomons, the second of the six great naval battles in the Solomons in 1942.[26] Again the Japanese outnumbered the Americans in all types of ships, including carriers. They had three, while Task Force 16 had only two.[27]

In the afternoon of August 24, *Portland'*s task unit was arrayed in the familiar circular formation customarily employed for air defense, with *Portland* on *Enterprise'*s port quarter. When incoming bogies were reported, the force began to zigzag around base course 070, speed thirty knots. This time the Japanese aircraft flew directly over Sweet Pea, allowing her to open fire with her port batteries, and to continue firing with her starboard guns as the planes passed on their way to the carrier. All the ships in the force maneuvered radically, but even so their AA fire was able to splash about half of the attacking aircraft. Still, the skillful Japanese pilots, not so decimated by their disaster at Midway as we are sometimes asked to believe, pressed home their attack.

After several near misses, at 1834 *Enterprise* was hit. She lost steering control and for about an hour could barely make way.[28] The damage seemed severe. Observers in Sweet Pea reported that the carrier was hidden by the smoke from her own fires, by the curtain of water from the near misses, and by the smoke of a burning plane that splashed near her starboard side.[29] But then the damage control that the Americans trained at so rigorously and took justifiable pride in got the flattop repaired enough to resume steering and to make about fifteen knots.[30]

The Americans enjoyed a narrow victory in the Battle of the Eastern Solomons. The Japanese lost a light carrier and about ninety planes. American losses were less, about twenty aircraft and the damage to *Enterprise.* The most important outcome was that the convoy the Japanese warships were covering was forced back the next day and never landed the troops and equipment needed so badly by the enemy on Guadalcanal.[31] The luster was tinged badly only a few days later when carrier *Saratoga* was torpedoed by a Japanese submarine and knocked out of the war for months. The silver lining here, though, was that one of the American casualties in *Saratoga* was a slightly wounded Admiral Frank Jack Fletcher, who was sent home to recover from his injuries and never returned to a major Pacific command.[32] From now on the carriers would be led by officers who would fight.

*Portland*'s anti-aircraft fire contributed significantly to this victory at the Eastern Solomons. In the battle, Gunnery Officer Elliott Shanklin's tactic of the AA barrage was used generally and proved effective. After the action, he wrote that placing the "high volume fire barrage . . . in the path of the dive-bombers" made all of the Japanese dive at approximately the same point so that they followed in one another's wake instead of going over at the same time. Their view of the target below them, then, was obscured by planes in front of them as they dove.

Moreover, Shanklin reported that he saw some aircraft "veer from their dive rather than continue." He observed as "many released early at

high altitudes," and many others "appeared deflected to a considerable
extent from the course of their dives" by the air bursts all around them.
Shanklin thought that much of the inaccurate Japanese bombing was due
to "both the physical and psychological handicap imposed by the
barrage."[33]

Shanklin liked it that *Portland* was able to fire rapidly without regard
to getting a "slow and cumbersome" computer solution from the
director, as would be the case if she were shooting at individual aircraft.
It was much easier to aim the guns at a point in the atmosphere and divert
or distract many pilots than to aim them at a single plane. Shanklin
strongly recommended that all ships in screens should adopt the same
tactic for the protection of the carrier. He wrote that if they had all done
so in the battle just completed, they "would have almost completely
routed the attacking planes."[34]

In addition to this proposal, Shanklin also recommended a solution
to the difficult problem of how to avoid friendly aircraft who in their zeal
to defend their home carriers often came into the gunfire of friendly
ships. He urged that AA fire from the ships "must be directed against the
[enemy] planes while actually in their dive, rather than during the
approach where our fighters can handle the situation much more
effectively."[35] By this last notion, Shanklin hoped that the American
fighters would stay outside the range of the American guns. It was a
problem that was never completely solved, though, as later events
showed. And Shanklin's barrage tactic was limited to the 5-inch guns.
They were slow loading and slow firing, although they did leave a lot of
shrapnel in the sky and packed a major wallop whenever they hit an
airplane. But what would make surface AA firing truly effective would
be the development of a better rapid-fire, medium-range battery than the
miserable 1.1-inch mounts that were then state of the art.

One should see in here that not only were *Portland*'s sailors
continuing to do the great job that had been the mark of their service so
far during the war. Now her officers were making intellectual
contributions to the science of warfare, as it applied to the ship's mission.

An interesting sequel to *Portland*'s performance in this and other
carrier battles around the Solomon Islands was a letter that came to her
veteran's association some *forty-seven* years later. Remember that
*Enterprise* sailors worried when Sweet Pea joined their task force that
she meant bad luck to any carrier she escorted. But in the 1989 letter,

veterans of the great carrier wrote that at their reunions they "often mention the action and fine support" the cruiser had given them during those desperate days in 1942.[36]

At bottom then, the American effort in the Eastern Solomons had prevented Japanese reinforcements from landing, a critically important gain. But nothing so far had convinced any American that the Allied side was winning the war. That would come later, and Sweet Pea would be at the heart of the shift.

## THE LONE-SHIP RAID

In early September 1942, Sweet Pea accompanied *Enterprise* in her return to Pearl Harbor for repairs. While there, her damage-control party was called away to help fight a minor fire on board the carrier, then in the dry dock.[37] A few weeks later Sweet Pea was ordered to prepare for an unusual operation. She and light cruiser *San Juan* were directed by "Secret Operations Order 44-42" to proceed to the Gilbert Islands, British possessions captured by the Japanese in the early days of the war.[38] It would be a trip of about eighteen hundred miles, and once there they were to split up, *Portland* to attack Tarawa and *San Juan* to attack another of the atolls in the chain.[39] What was so surprising about the mission was that the cruisers would sail by themselves, without escorts of any sort, and once separated would be wholly alone in the combat zone.[40]

Cruisers were originally supposed to be raiders, and a solo raid would be perfectly compatible with the prewar theory. The *Portland*-class was created in the first place so the U.S. Navy would have a counter to the German cruiser raiders, which had done such damage during World War I. And the German *Panzerschiffen,* wrongly called "pocket battleships" by the Allied press, were cruisers not much larger than *Portland,* although with bigger main batteries. These German ships operated mainly alone in the Atlantic.[41] During prewar training exercises, the cruisers had operated with the fleet and alone, and it was only during the war, when they became the chief protectors of the carriers, that they became accustomed to operating in company with smaller vessels as escorts.

Moreover, in the desperate days of early 1942, the Pacific Fleet had sent its precious aircraft carriers on risky hit-and-run raids throughout the Japanese conquests, and even to Tokyo. Nimitz and his subordinates were therefore not shy about a single-ship cruiser raid on Tarawa. It was what *Portland* could do to show the enemy that the United States was fighting back and that no place in the new empire was safe from American retribution.

Like all other atolls, Tarawa is composed of coral, literally mountains of the living stuff that has found a home atop an extinct underwater volcano. In each atoll many islands string around the volcano's top to form a sizable lagoon. Tarawa's lagoon, while not especially large compared to some others, is nevertheless about twenty-five miles long and ten miles across at its greatest width. There are at least eight islands with names—Bairiki, Betio, Buariki, Buota, Eita, Naa, Lone Tree Islet, and in the middle of the lagoon, Bakeman Islet.[42] Atolls, and particularly Tarawa, would become painfully familiar to Americans who attacked the Japanese Empire in years to come. But right now, *Portland* was going off merely to shell this one and then get away.

The crew was informed about the mission only after leaving Pearl Harbor. Many were apprehensive, as were all Americans in those early 1942 days, about any confrontation with the Japanese. Neither *San Juan* nor *Portland* had sonar to detect submarines, or depth charges with which to attack them. Bill Reehl later recalled that he could remember no other time during the entire war when the ship was alone at sea.[43] He and probably others like him looked back on the event through their knowledge of what happened to *Portland*'s only sister ship, *Indianapolis*. In 1945, that unlucky ship was sailing alone when she was torpedoed. Many of the men who abandoned "Indy" just before she sank were lost in the water because it took so long for rescuers to find her and get to the site, a fact that Sweet Pea's crew learned after the war.[44] Talking about the single-ship raid on Tarawa, Lawrence Kotula said to a reporter that if *Portland* had trouble there, "We had just two outlooks—to be killed or taken prisoner." During the raid, Kotula was particularly worried whenever the ship stopped to retrieve her aircraft. He thought that at those moments *Portland* was a wonderfully easy target for any Japanese submarine lurking nearby.[45]

Nevertheless, with Rear Admiral Mahlon S. Tisdale embarked as Commander Task Unit 16.9.1, the single-ship unit headed for Tarawa.[46] The island would be the scene of a ferociously bloody amphibious landing a little over a year later, but on October 15, 1942, Japanese forces were just settling into their new conquest. Sweet Pea steamed at high speed during the transit, making eighteen to twenty knots for most of the trip, and cranking it up to twenty-five and even twenty-seven knots when nearing the atoll.[47]

Two of *Portland*'s SOC aircraft began the fighting at about 1410 on October 15 by dive-bombing some Japanese ships they found in the lagoon. They made no hits, although one scored a near-miss on a cargo ship. One of the SOCs was hit in the main fuel tank by AA fire but both planes returned to the ship without further trouble.[48] Sweet Pea's 8-inch main battery opened fire on a warship that was originally thought to be a light cruiser.

When the Japanese vessel returned fire, she was then thought to be only a destroyer, since her smaller guns did not reach the American cruiser. *Portland*'s bridge claimed to have hit one of the cargo vessels as well as this warship.[49] One of the officers, David Bloom, reported that the latter was hit twice and beached by her own crew.[50] Another former *Portland* man, Kenneth West, wrote differently, though, saying that Sweet Pea's own boiler smoke ruined the American aim and that the Japanese ship ran aground by accident.[51] The difficulty the Americans had in identifying the enemy vessel and what she did says something about the pressures of combat and, incidentally, why combat photography was adopted so widely as the war progressed.

Just then, according to West, *Portland*'s skipper, Captain Laurence DuBose, and Admiral Tisdale had a disagreement about what to do next.[52] The story is confirmed in the War Diary, where a typically formal and typed note says "1451 Ceased firing." Following that is an unusual statement, which appears to have been added later, saying, "in accord. orders CTU 16.9.1," namely the admiral.[53] One wonders if Captain DuBose, who would show his own pit-bull pugnacity only a month later, wanted to stay and try to do some more damage. He was outranked on this occasion, and *Portland* retrieved her damaged plane and withdrew, bringing the entire event to a close.

The day after she pulled away from Tarawa, *Portland* suffered a steering breakdown. Although no one knew it at the time, this would prove to be a harbinger of future difficulty.[54] The crew got the problem in the starboard motor repaired, so Sweet Pea was able to rejoin *San Juan* as scheduled. The two cruisers then sped toward a rendezvous with the carrier task force in the Solomons area.[55]

Sweet Pea's sailors have always been miffed that their ship was not awarded a battle star for this action.[56] And they should be: she followed an official Operations Order, got into a gunfight with an enemy warship, probably damaged that warship and another enemy cargo ship, and suffered a casualty to one of her planes. If that is not a battle, what is? Forty-five years later, one of the men, Leroy Rudder, met Marine Colonel Joseph Alexander, whose book, *Utmost Tragedy: The Three Days of Tarawa,* had just been published. Although an expert on the island and its combat history, Alexander had never heard of *Portland*'s single-ship raid.[57] It has been one of the forgotten moments of the war.

## Battle of Santa Cruz

Sweet Pea had barely rejoined *Enterprise* in the Solomons when she was in the thick of the Battle of Santa Cruz on October 24, 1942, only nine days after her attack on Tarawa. About 1012, men on the bridge could see carrier *Hornet* maneuvering some ten miles away to the southwest after her group separated from the one *Portland* was in with *Enterprise*. As they watched, *Hornet* took one bomb hit. Almost immediately two Japanese planes crashed into her flight deck near the island. The combination caused terrible fires, and the ship was ultimately abandoned.[58] This loss was something the badly strapped U.S. Navy could not afford.

Within an hour *Enterprise* herself came under heavy air attack.[59] *Portland*'s radar detected the incoming bogies at about eighty miles, far beyond its designed range, so the crew had to wait a long time for the enemy to arrive.[60] Finally, one of the attackers came streaking at the cruiser's starboard side only about twenty feet above the water. The 5-inch gun manned by *Portland*'s Marines hit the enemy plane "right on the nose," downing it only about one hundred yards from the cruiser.[61]

Lieutenant Commander Shanklin's barrage tactics failed this time. The Japanese came from a wide variety of directions, as if they had learned how dangerous the barrage could be if they came in tight formations and made their attacks from one place in the sky.[62] For the first time, *Portland* herself suffered damage and personnel injuries, though none by enemy action. One of the 1.1-inch guns blew up in firing, and a 20mm depressed too low and damaged the splinter shield, which in turn sprayed fragments around.[63] Altogether nineteen officers and men were hurt. Among them, six were burned about the face by the fire of the 5-inch battery, one suffered a possible cervical spine injury and a broken jaw from his carelessness in operating an ammunition hoist, and nine more were wounded by splinters. Although all the injuries were painful, only the spinal injury was regarded as major.[64]

The fighting was furious, because the Japanese aviators pressed home their attacks. They made a hit on *Enterprise,* a bomb that exploded on the forward part of her flight deck about 1115, setting fire to some of the planes parked there. Again, damage-control parties did a magnificent job in putting the fire out, largely by jettisoning the flaming aircraft over the side of the ship, but the carrier was temporarily out of action.[65] Brand new battleship *South Dakota,* which had just joined the task force, took a bomb hit on her forward turret at 1148. The damage to the heavily armored man-of-war was slight, although she did fly her breakdown flag for some part of the afternoon.[66] A downed bomber crashed into the forward gun mount of destroyer *Smith,* starting a serious topside fire. Her Commanding Officer ingeniously extinguished it by driving his ship through the huge waves of *South Dakota*'s wake. The water washed over *Smith*'s forecastle and pushed the fire overboard.[67] The intensity of this combat was reflected in the volume of Sweet Pea's firing as she expended about 25 percent of both her 5-inch and 20mm AA ammunition, although only about 8 percent of her 1.1-inch ammo because she used those balky guns sparingly.[68]

At least one Japanese submarine was in action that day, too. At 1101, as destroyer *Porter* stopped to pick up the crew of a downed American torpedo bomber, Sweet Pea's crew was astounded to see two F4Fs from *Enterprise* dive near *Porter* and strafe the water close to *Porter*'s port side. They were trying to hit a torpedo, but it slammed into the tin can's hull. One of the Wildcats was thrown high into the air when the warhead exploded.[69]

The most hair-raising moment for Sweet Pea herself was a torpedo incident in the middle of the air attacks. At 1153, the cruiser's bridge lost control over her steering. Battle Two, the secondary bridge farther aft where the Executive Officer was stationed, had to steer the ship, following directions sent from Captain DuBose, who remained on the bridge.[70] This was tricky business for Battle Two. Although designated as the ship's emergency control station in case the bridge were knocked out, it was preposterously ill-equipped to do any such thing. It had no steering helm or engine-order telegraph, but instead had to relay all commands from the bridge by voice over a phone or through a tube to the emergency steering station even farther aft. It was literally surrounded by guns, so the necessary voice communication was difficult at best in the noise of the firing. And on this occasion, *Portland*'s steering broke down when she was herself at flank speed in the midst of a wildly maneuvering carrier and several other escorts, each ship trying to avoid enemy air attack, and none taking much time to inform other ships of its intentions.[71] That *Portland* escaped this chaos at all was just short of a miracle.

In the moments it took to switch steering control to Battle Two, Sweet Pea found herself charging at high speed into the wreckage of a downed aircraft, still burning in a pool of its own fuel. DuBose stopped the port engines in order to swing *Portland* around the wrecked plane.[72] As she turned sharply, lookouts spotted a periscope in the debris of the downed aircraft. One of them called out that the tracks of four torpedoes were streaking for the cruiser. The range was too short for *Portland* to take any effective action, a problem magnified by the fact that the bridge, which could see the threats, did not have steering control. The ship was hit three times by the Japanese torpedoes, *none* of which detonated![73]

This event leaves one reaching for explanations. Throughout the war, Japanese torpedoes were excellent, and that three of them failed at once makes one skeptical. And yet, the story has been told from so many different angles that it must have been true. One sailor in sick bay at the time of the battle heard three thumps in the hull about sixty feet from where he was lying.[74] The ship's dentist related that he had seen a fourth torpedo duck under *Portland*'s keel at the last moment.[75] A few months later when the ship was in dry dock, bridge watch officer David Bloom, himself doubtful about the reports, went below to see what he could find. While there, he saw hard evidence in the form of "clear marks where [one] torpedo, after hitting the ship on the starboard side, had gone under the ship and clawed its way up the port side."[76]

Bloom then gave the best explanation for what happened. The distance the torpedoes had to travel to reach the *Portland,* too short for the cruiser to evade, was also too short for the torpedoes to arm.[77] Torpedoes must run for a certain length of time before they will detonate. The feature protects the vessel that launches the fish from being destroyed by it in case it comes back for some reason. It was almost as though the Fates were looking after Sweet Pea. Admiral William F. Halsey Jr. remarked wryly on reading *Portland*'s report that "it was nice to see the enemy's materiel fail, too."[78]

This intense carrier battle in late October 1942 off the Santa Cruz Islands ended up a near disaster for the U.S. Navy, since by its end the two flattops engaged were either sunk or out of action.[79] Again, though, a *near* disaster was only that, and a *draw* was a good thing for the United States since it allowed American forces on Guadalcanal to remain intact. On the same day as this sea battle was being waged, the Marines ashore fought desperately to defend Henderson Field from a huge Japanese assault in what became known as the Battle of the Matanikau River. That they did not have to face Japanese carrier aviation, too, was a victory.

7

# NIGHT CRUISER ACTION, NOVEMBER 13, 1942

As a result of the damage suffered by the carriers of both sides at Santa Cruz in October 1942, the decisive battle for Guadalcanal a month later would pit gunships against each other. *Portland* would stand out in this fight. Although she had earlier garnered suspicion as a bad omen for carriers, her good work in the early months around the Solomons had helped recover some of her reputation. In the Night Cruiser Action, a part of the Naval Battle of Guadalcanal in November 1942, *Portland* won the respect and admiration of all. It was certainly the event that all the men in Sweet Pea at the time found the most memorable, frightening, and gratifying in the entire war.[1] Out of it emerged a ship full of confidence and fight, with a spirit that would endure long after the war was over.

The Naval Battle of Guadalcanal was caused by the efforts both sides made in mid-November to send reinforcements and supplies to their ground forces on Guadalcanal. Throughout the Guadalcanal campaign, Japan and the United States were barely able to maintain and support the small number of troops fighting over who was going to hold the airfield that had fallen into the hands of the Americans almost immediately after the Marines landed.

The Japanese were as wary of committing their shipping to the area as Fletcher had been to leave his carriers there, and for the same reason: the air and waters around Guadalcanal were filled with hostile forces.

Japanese reinforcements were usually carried in Rear Admiral Raizo Tanaka's fast destroyers, which the Americans called the Tokyo Express. These ships would cram their decks and the spaces below with a few hundred troops and dash from Rabaul down "The Slot," the long waterway that divided the Solomon footprints. Tanaka would arrive in the dark and drop the soldiers off in small craft near the western end of Guadalcanal. Sometimes he would then steam several miles farther to fire into the American base at Henderson Field, hoping to kill a few people and destroy a few planes. He would then run back up The Slot before daylight exposed his ships to vengeful air attack by the "Cactus Air Force" flying out of Henderson.[2]

In early November 1942, however, Japan decided to push for a decisive victory. The Imperial Army's commanders organized and sent a division-sized element, some thirteen thousand troops. Since that number was too large for Tanaka's destroyers, the Army would also provide bigger, although much slower, transports. Admiral Gunichi Mikawa at Rabaul promised to defend these transports with the fastest and most powerful ships the Imperial Navy could provide, and he did exactly that. The entire fleet would be covered by shore-based aviation from Rabaul and a few closer places where the Japanese had established water bases for float planes.[3] It was a rare example of cooperation between the Empire's Army and Navy.

At the same time, the Americans were also mounting a major supply convoy from Noumea in New Caledonia. Sweet Pea was assigned as a part of the escort for these ships.[4] Anti-aircraft firepower for the carrier forces was not needed for the time being, since the carriers were all damaged and had been pulled out. Moreover, the sinking of all the cruisers at Savo Island in August meant that other ships had to be found somewhere in the shrunken inventory to accompany the fragile cargo ships and troop transports. *Portland* was available.

Because both sides tried to reinforce the ground troops on the island, the Japanese got their wish, a decisive battle. But it was at sea, not on the island, as they had hoped. It was actually a series of events stretching across four days, and it included daily air attacks by both sides on the enemy's shipping, a major bombardment of the American ground forces by Japanese warships, and two ferocious naval fights between contending fleets. *Portland* played a central role in the first anti-air battle and the first of the surface fights, which is sometimes called Third Savo

Island by her crew, although it is now generally known as the Night Cruiser Action.

*Portland* had steamed to Noumea with several of the ships damaged at Santa Cruz. She tried to get her steering problem fixed, but other ships needing work there included *Enterprise, South Dakota, San Juan, Smith,* and *Mahan,* so repair personnel were spread too thinly for much to be accomplished on Sweet Pea.[5] On October 30, the day after she pulled in, Admiral Tisdale left the ship, taking his flag to *Pensacola,* which could at least steer dependably. He sailed away on November 1, commanding the escort group around the still damaged *Enterprise,* which was undergoing work by a repair ship's personnel even as she stood out to sea.[6]

When Sweet Pea was ready to sail, she found herself in Task Group 67.4, comprising three other cruisers and ten destroyers. They were ordered to escort a task group of four transports carrying an Army regiment, a Marine battalion, and other badly needed reinforcements and supplies. The two groups were combined into Task Force 67, under Rear Admiral Richmond Kelly Turner, and it got underway on November 8.[7]

We now know that when these ships arrived off Lunga Point, Guadalcanal, on Thursday, November 12, 1942, and began to offload their precious goods, they were being watched by enemy eyes from ashore. Upon learning of this activity, Japanese commanders launched an air strike from farther up the Solomons. Sixteen torpedo-armed "Betty" bombers and thirty Zeroes came winging toward Guadalcanal, but both Australian coast watchers and American radar spotted them. Forewarned, Turner brilliantly maneuvered his ships to lure the two groups of planes into piecemeal attacks, so that his ships could defend themselves against one group while fighters from Henderson Field took on the other.[8]

*Portland* was at the heart of the effort that fought off the torpedo planes. The air raid alert sounded while troops and sailors were taking the material ashore. All work stopped and all ships got underway, manning their battle stations. Sweet Pea's place in the circle of warships around the transports and cargo vessels was to the northwest, and as the enemy aircraft approached from the northeast they came well within range of her guns.[9] Each of the Bettys carried two torpedoes. The vaunted Japanese torpedoes malfunctioned again, though, this time because of mistakes made by the aviators. The volume of AA fire was so great that the bombers dropped their fish too soon, that is, too high above the water. As a result, the torpedoes tumbled in the air and on hitting the water bounced in such a way that most of them ran *away* from their intended targets, to the joy of *Portland*'s crew.[10]

During this raid, Sweet Pea used her *main* battery—the 8-inch guns!—against the Japanese planes, another of Lieutenant Commander Shanklin's innovative ideas. He ordered his gunners to splash the water in front of low-flying attackers, hoping to make them crash.[11] The ship's officers were mixed on whether the tactic worked. Shanklin thought that one of the reasons the Bettys dropped their torpedoes from too high was that they were trying to avoid the huge splashes kicked up by the 8-inch projectiles.[12] But another of the officers said the big guns created such a smokey haze when they fired that after one salvo the Captain on the bridge and the personnel in the gun director could not see the targets clearly. The critics must have been right, because the 8-inch guns were never used as anti-aircraft batteries again.[13]

In this fight the Japanese airmen angered some of the *Portland* gunners. One man in the back seat thumbed his nose at Sweet Pea as his plane flew over the deck, enraging the sailors in an AA mount. The gunners were particularly joyful, therefore, when they shot the plane down before the obnoxious aviator got much farther away from the cruiser.[14]

The Japanese planes were driven off with severe losses after they had inflicted only minor damage on the American transports and cargo ships. From the time *Portland* opened fire until the withdrawal of the last enemy plane, a mere nine minutes passed.[15] In that brief interval, eleven of the sixteen Bettys were lost, as was one Zero, while American air losses were only four planes downed and one pilot killed.[16] In those few minutes, *Portland* literally filled the sky with lead, as she fired 250 rounds of 5-inch, 800 rounds of 1.1-inch, and 1,200 rounds of 20mm ammunition, not to mention the six rounds of 8-inch. She downed one plane for sure, hit another one, and contributed to the demise of a few more.[17]

Already an inveterate rescuer of survivors, *Portland* came upon a shot-down Army pilot, who was jokingly thumbing a ride from his life raft, and fished him out of the water.[18] For the first time in the war, though, Sweet Pea's sailors saw the suicidal tendencies of some Japanese. An American destroyer was sent to rescue the eight-man crew of one of the shot-down Bettys. But the airmen refused to be taken captive and began a firefight, using the only weapons they had, their sidearms. The destroyer ended the matter with her machine guns, killing all the ungrateful Japanese.[19]

During the combat, more routine but no less important matters also engaged Sweet Pea's crew. In sick bay that morning, for example, Lieutenant Commander Joers, the ship's Senior Medical Officer, began an appendectomy before the air raid sounded. Edward Smith, a petty officer from the boiler division, had come down with appendicitis the evening before.[20] Doctor Joers went right ahead with the surgery during the battle, reporting to his battle station only after Smith's procedure was complete.[21]

When the air raid ended, the cargo ships returned to the off-loading process, and one of *Portland*'s sailors noticed how much faster the work went. No one wanted to be in those waters any longer than possible, and everyone thought that the sooner the cargoes were put ashore, the sooner the convoy could get underway for safer Noumea.[22]

A few weeks earlier, Vice Admiral William F. Halsey Jr. had become Commander-in-Chief of the South Pacific Area (ComSoPac), relieving Vice Admiral Ghormley, who had shown he had no stomach for the work that was necessary in the Solomons. Halsey was determined that the Americans under his command would *fight* the Japanese, with whatever was available. Somewhat surprisingly in view of the results so far in the naval war, Halsey was confident that his forces would win when they fought. In making these points clear to all around him, Halsey immediately injected a fighting spirit into the Americans at Guadalcanal, in sharp contrast to the defeatist attitude that had permeated the South Pacific under Ghormley.

As a result, when Halsey learned that a large force of enemy warships was coming down The Slot with the Japanese transports and their thirteen thousand reinforcements, he intended to bar their way.[23] As the Americans unloaded at Guadalcanal on November 12, Halsey informed Admiral Turner of the new report, and the latter showed his own mettle by throwing what he had available in front of the enemy. This was not much, actually. The ships on hand at Guadalcanal were the ones that accompanied the transports, and the most powerful of them were the heavy cruisers *Portland* and *San Francisco*.[24]

As they sailed off at dusk on November 12 to find the Japanese fleet, the Americans were beset by a number of problems.[25] *Portland*'s steering system continued to malfunction despite the efforts at Noumea to repair it, and she endured two more breakdowns on the way to Guadalcanal. Once on November 10, the starboard steering unit failed and the bridge watch had to shift to the port unit. Later the same day she had to make emergency shifts several times since the rudder was noticed to be weaving four or five degrees from true.[26] On *San Francisco* one of the gun directors had been put out of action in the anti-air battle that afternoon, thus lessening her effectiveness. Two of the light cruisers in the force were anti-aircraft ships, virtual porcupines in the number of AA barrels that protruded from them. But the biggest gun in these two ships was only the 5-inch dual-purpose guns, which were usually secondary batteries on even a light cruiser, and they could do only minimal damage to another cruiser.[27]

Worse luck was who commanded Task Group 76. A man of great personal courage, Rear Admiral Daniel J. Callaghan was still remembered in *Portland,* where he had served as Executive Officer in 1936–1937.[28] But he was tragically not up to the job facing him. Callaghan had been Chief of Staff to Ghormley when the latter was dumped in favor of Halsey as ComSoPac on October 17. Even in that job, as historian Frank deftly put it, Callaghan "had escaped distinction."[29] Because Halsey wanted his own man as Chief of Staff, Callaghan became a rear admiral without a job. So Halsey sent him to sea in command of *Portland* and the other ships in the cruiser-destroyer screen that escorted Turner's transports to Guadalcanal.[30]

But Callaghan had never had a major sea command before, and as the great battle approached, Turner was in a tough spot because Rear Admiral Norman Scott was also present in the flotilla. Scott had defeated the Japanese at Cape Esperance in early October by successfully "capping their T," thus driving off an earlier resupply attempt. That victory gave a major lift to the morale of the hard-pressed U.S. Navy at Guadalcanal.[31]

Naval commanders since the earliest days of gunfire have eagerly sought to cap the enemy's T. If one force steams in column head-on into the enemy that lies across the route, thus forming a *T,* the force that is the cap will be able to bring *all* its guns to bear in broadside, while the other will be able to fire only its *forward* guns. Moreover, only those in the very first ship will be able to fire effectively, since the trailing ships will have to fire over or even through their friends. Thus *all* the cappers will be able to fire at the first ship in the approaching column, and once it is sunk, continue to fire at the next arriving ship, and so on until the entire enemy force is destroyed.

Some thought that Scott had been merely lucky in capping the Japanese T at Cape Esperance. Even he admitted that he made mistakes during the fighting. But his success was due not only to that lucky formation but more importantly to his willingness to train his ships' crews rigorously in gunnery and shiphandling, and to his own knowledge of how to use the advantages radar gave him.[32] And yet, Turner selected Callaghan because he was fifteen days senior to Scott. When the outgunned cruisers and destroyers steamed off to meet the Japanese battleships, then, command of the force was in the hands of the inexperienced Callaghan who had had no time to train his Captains or to learn about the magic of radar.[33]

Off they went, guided by Halsey's principle of "fight, fight, fight," which had been passed down to them by Turner. They were thirteen ships in a task force with a number whose digits added up to thirteen, going to make war on a night that was going to turn into Friday the Thirteenth. The column formation created by Callaghan showed his inexperience. In a single line, four destroyers led five cruisers, which were followed by four destroyers. It was symmetrical, but stupid. First of all, he was riding in *San Francisco,* which in addition to having a gun director out of commission did not have a surface-search radar. *Portland,* riding behind the flagship, had none either, although she did use her SC air-search radar as well as possible for surface search. Second, only destroyer *O'Bannon* ahead of the flagship had the modern SG-type surface search with PPI, but she was fourth in line.[34] Third, the other three ships with the modern radar, *Helena, Juneau,* and *Fletcher,* all trailed Callaghan's flagship. Callaghan's placement of the ships indicated that he gave no credit to the possibilities of radar in a tactical situation at night. Subsequent events confirmed his ineptitude.[35]

The Japanese force, commanded by Vice Admiral Hiroaki Abe, included the battleships *Hiei* and *Kirishima,* much larger and heavier-gunned than anything Callaghan had. They were escorted by one light cruiser and eleven destroyers. The Japanese battleships fired a 1,500-pound projectile from each of their eight guns, while the American heavy cruisers had only 260-pound shells in each of their nine guns. The 8-inch rounds fired by *Portland* and *San Francisco* could not pierce the armor of the Japanese heavies, nor of course could any of the smaller projectiles from the other American ships.[36] The Japanese had been marvelously skillful at Savo Island the previous August when a Japanese cruiser group sank four Allied cruisers in almost the same waters where this November 13 battle would be fought.[37] Torpedoes used by Japanese surface ships proved superior to what the Americans had. Although none of the IJN ships at Guadalcanal that night had radar, Japanese lookouts were especially selected for their superlative eyesight and then highly trained to take advantage of what nature had given them. They actually were more capable than the early American radar.[38]

As he steamed southeasterly along Guadalcanal's northern shore, Admiral Abe was on his way to bombard Henderson Field. His goal was to knock the airfield out of action so the troop-carrying transports could make a safe passage later the next day. Abe had his battlewagons, *Hiei* and *Kirishima,* in line in the middle of a rough circle of escorts.[39] A semi-circular screen of six destroyers led by light cruiser *Nagara* was the van, and the other destroyers trailed Abe's battlewagons both to starboard and to port. About midnight the tin cans on the starboard quarter found themselves approaching shoal water. Some of them peeled off to take up station on the port beam of the formation, while others scooted ahead to become what amounted to a skirmish line a few thousand yards ahead of *Nagara*. The formation now looked something like a bowl, headed bottom-first toward the Americans whom they did not yet see.[40]

At 0124 on November 13 the SG radar did what it was supposed to do for the U.S. ships, which were just then coming to the top of Ironbottom Sound: it gave the commander notice of the Japanese sooner than sharp-eyed enemy lookouts could discover his force. *Helena* reported a radar contact northwest of the Americans at about fourteen miles, probably light cruiser *Nagara*. A minute later, *Helena* reported another group on the same bearing but two miles farther away, probably the battleships. By 0131, *Helena* had three targets, the previously spotted two plus the skirmish-line destroyers, which although closer were smaller, so discovered later. Her radarmen had already accurately calculated the enemy's course and speed.

At this point, Admiral Callaghan gave his task force an order to turn right in column to due north, or course 000, probably hoping to duplicate Scott's maneuver of capping the T a month before.[41] But Callaghan had no good idea of what was happening. At Cape Esperance in October, the Japanese had been in a column, and their T *could* be and *was* capped. On this night, however, Callaghan's foe was in a widely dispersed formation, so there was no T. Indeed, the Americans had just sailed into chaos. The leading American ship, USS *Cushing,* a destroyer without radar, suddenly swerved to avoid a collision with one of the Japanese destroyers, and all the Americans following her had to maneuver wildly to avoid piling up on each other.[42]

Thus began what Admiral Nimitz called "a half-hour melee which for confusion and fury is scarcely paralleled in naval history. All formations

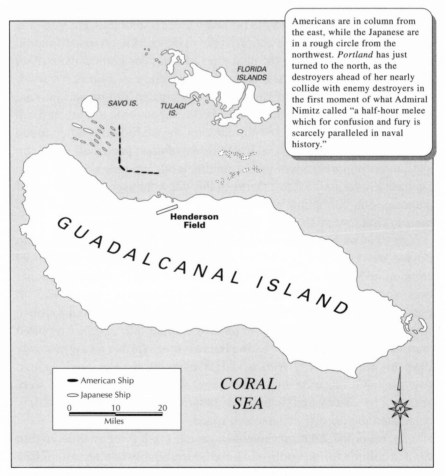

Americans are in column from the east, while the Japanese are in a rough circle from the northwest. *Portland* has just turned to the north, as the destroyers ahead of her nearly collide with enemy destroyers in the first moment of what Admiral Nimitz called "a half-hour melee which for confusion and fury is scarcely paralleled in naval history."

Map 2. Night Cruiser Action, Nov. 13, 1942, 0150 hours

broke and the engagement became a series of individual ship duels with each side at one time or another firing on its own vessels."[43]

Captain Laurence DuBose in *Portland* had been president of the Naval Academy Class of 1913, so he was not superstitious about Friday the Thirteenth. In fact, just before midnight he said to his Executive Officer, Turk Wirth, that he thought the Americans would do well if the fighting began on the thirteenth.[44] His bravery in saying so was remarkable. He and Wirth knew that the Japanese probably had battleships in the force that was approaching, and they knew that *Portland* was not without her flaws. Seventh in the American column, she was the oldest ship in the force. She had no surface-search radar, and the fire-control radar for her forward main battery was out of commission due to electrical problems.[45]

Nevertheless, Sweet Pea's after fire-control radar picked up the Japanese at a range of six or seven miles and Gunnery Officer Shanklin began plotting his targets. But Admiral Callaghan in *San Francisco* seemed frozen by the events. Without radar, he probably had no "seaman's eye" appreciation of what he was sailing into, which was indeed complex. But *Helena,* which did have radar, was almost begging to be turned loose to fire on targets she was plotting. Callaghan did nothing except give the order to turn right and, by doing so, create the nightmare that ensued.[46]

Historian Eric Hammel has argued that the cruisers were demolished by the Japanese task force in the Battle of Savo Island the previous August in large part because the Allied commanders had no battle awareness. That is, they were peacetime naval officers, very good at the drills they had to accomplish during peacetime. But when the shooting started, many of them lacked the inner fiber that would have made them tigers in fighting back tooth and claw, even when Mikawa's cruisers sneaked into their midst. As Hammel pointed out, nearly all of these officers refused to open fire on the Japanese ships that were killing them because of the chance that they "*might* be friendly."[47]

Unfortunately, in November Admiral Callaghan was like those cruisermen who had been hammered at Savo Island in August. His slow response to what happened in the next few minutes cost him his life. Except for others who were more ferocious, especially the Captain and crew of *Portland,* he might have cost the American side much more in this decisive battle.

In its attempt to avoid collisions, the American van began to come apart at 0150 just as *Portland* approached the point where she was supposed to make the right turn following the other ships. At that very moment, battleship *Hiei* and a Japanese destroyer turned on their searchlights, and hell visited the earth. Sweet Pea was in her turn, so the targets her directors had acquired were now swinging from right to left. As the Japanese lights bathed *Portland*, blinding some of her crew, Captain DuBose at first ordered "Action Starboard," but then almost immediately directed the main battery to fire on the vessels to port, because the targets had moved across his bow. Even in the chaos, the Captain of USS *Portland* did not suffer from timidity. He was going to fight.

Many in the crew were terrified by what engulfed them. Sweet Pea had gained valuable experience in the anti-aircraft fights against Japanese aircraft at the Coral Sea, Midway, Eastern Solomons, Santa Cruz, and just the day before during the offloading at Guadalcanal. But now she and her men were within a few thousand yards of Japanese ships spewing out projectile after projectile at them. It was much more intimate and ghastly than the AA fight. A few minutes before, the men in the main battery's gun director were dozing. Suddenly all were jolted awake by the Gunnery Officer's order: "Director One—Stand By."[48] Lewis Dickson on the bridge hoped the Captain would order "Let's get the hell out of here," and was amazed when DuBose instead instructed his gunners to "get the big ones."[49] Bill Ala, manning one of *Portland*'s searchlights, admits to "shaking in my boots" in the dark and cold night, thinking that at any moment he "could be blown up by enemy gunfire."[50] Harold Johnson, also topside, worried that the Japanese were firing at the muzzle-flashes of his own ship's guns.[51] But all of them overcame their fears and fought bravely.

Bill Reehl was at his new battle station at the 1.1-inch AA mount on the starboard side right behind the Number Two 8-inch turret. Captain DuBose had told the crew that there would be no anti-aircraft firing that night, and instructed those who were manning the AA guns to lie down to avoid being hit.[52] From time to time in the unfolding battle one or another battery did fire at a searchlight, but except for that these weapons were kept out of action since their muzzle flashes would give away the ship's location without doing much good even if they hit something.[53] Since Reehl and his mates expected they would have nothing to do, many of them tried to find cover wherever they could in the gun mount.[54] Others, though, wanted to see the drama all around them. Some of the AA crews climbed up as high as they could to catch the action. As storekeeper Herb Gibson said years later, "What the hell; I was twenty years old and didn't think anything could hurt me."[55]

The nearest target, only three miles away, had revealed itself by switching on its searchlight, and *Portland* commenced firing at it. *Portland* did not have to use its searchlights because the fire-control radar allowed it to find targets in the darkness.[56] The new device proved its value in this ferocious battle. When *Portland* opened fire, only the forward turrets could bear at that moment. But they made hits with their first salvo, as Shanklin saw "four bursts of flame leap from his target," the Japanese destroyer with the searchlights.[57] Sweet Pea immediately fired another salvo at the same ship, this time a nine-gun broadside since the after turret was now able to bear. As Sweet Pea raced after her own column, anti-aircraft officer Lieutenant Ken West saw the bottom of a *Hibiki*-class destroyer on the surface close aboard, probably the ship Shanklin's sharpshooters had just destroyed.[58]

But *Portland* was also hit. At 0151, as she turned to stay in column, a 14-inch shell struck her starboard hangar.[59] She was very lucky. Because the Japanese were headed for a shore bombardment mission, their guns were loaded with anti-personnel ammunition, not armor-piercing. As a result, this huge shell inflicted nothing like the fatal damage an AP projectile might have caused.[60] The hit did some incidental damage, though. It blew out a 36- by 44-inch section of hangar plating and some fragments penetrated the bulkheads enclosing the adjacent airplane crane machinery. Those fragments severed power and lighting circuits, which in turn shut down two starboard 5-inch mounts aft.[61] Flying fragments wounded several men in the area, including Executive Officer Wirth at his station in Battle Two.[62] A starshell landed on *Portland*'s forecastle and, although it did no damage, had to be extinguished before it attracted unwanted attention. A few men from an AA mount ran to push it over the side.[63]

While she was taking these hits, though, *Portland* laid some of her own on the enemy. Just after she steadied on course 000, she fired two nine-gun salvos at a second target, identified by her director crew as "definitely a cruiser, and probably a CA," scoring "many hits" and observing the enemy "burst into flames."[64] There were no Japanese heavy cruisers at Guadalcanal that night, so this ship must have been battleship *Hiei,* which was hit several times right about that moment.[65]

The noise of this sea battle would have been overwhelming. A darkened ship sailing at moderate speed through a calm, nighttime sea swishes softly as it parts the water. There are other sounds, quiet engine noises and voices of men from time to time, but in the main all is serene. That was what it was like at 0149 that night. When a gunfight begins, though, one's own batteries demolish the night and startle all the men on board with their painfully sharp and loud reports. The guns on both sides not only deafen but also blind. Men's vision adapts to the dark, but suddenly there is more light than a thousand flashbulbs, extending from one horizon to the other, and it lingers for more time than the eye can endure. That was what it was like at 0151 that night.

And when enemy rounds begin to hit, there is first a shocking thump and a head-rapping clank like a huge medieval mace hitting a knight in a suit of armor. Immediately there is an explosion as the shell detonates. A man is thrown to the deck or bounces off a bulkhead, or worse. No one can fail to be stunned in such circumstances. The apprehension is amplified by the new human sounds, of which the first are shrieks of pain. Then one hears moans from the wounded, and shouts and cries about pain and fighting the battle. "Doc, over HERE!" "Shift your rudder!" "Oh, jeezis, I'm BLEEDING!" "Bore clear!" "We got a medical kit?" "No, no, *SHIT!* Over HERE!" In the resulting chaos, everyone is afraid. But the men have to overcome their fears or they might not survive. That was what it was like at 0153 that night aboard USS *Portland,* and the way these officers and men responded was heroic.

At 0158, the American side in this melée received a strange order from Admiral Callaghan: "Cease Fire." No one in *Portland* knew why, and Captain DuBose, whose battle awareness had already taken over, leaving him way ahead of the admiral in ferocity, asked impudently, "What's the dope? Do you want a cease-fire?" The terse Callaghan answer, "Affirmative," was followed by another order for a second column turn.[66] But the admiral had long since lost control of his task force, and most ships that had targets began to fire again without his approval. That is exactly what *Portland* did. At the same moment Captain DuBose gave an order to his helmsman to comply with Callagher's turn command, he received Gunnery Officer Shanklin's report of a third target, "definitely a cruiser." The situation was nearly incomprehensible, with smoke and fires, ships moving here and there in the darkness, none clearly friend or foe, all of it diminishing DuBose's ability to calculate what was going on. But one thing was clear: his Gun Boss had a computer lock on an enemy target. Although the "cease-fire" order was only two minutes old, DuBose wasted no energy in worrying if the target *might* be friendly, nor any time in seeking permission from Callaghan. He just ordered Shanklin to fire.[67] The result was two nine-gun salvos from Sweet Pea's 8-inch battery that started several fires aboard the Japanese target.[68] Another score for *Portland.*

Callaghan was already dead by this time, probably killed at 0200 when *San Francisco* took several large-caliber hits to the bridge area, one place the enemy's bombardment rounds could do serious damage.[69] Only after the battle was over was his strange "cease-fire" order finally explained. Callaghan had seen *San Francisco*'s early salvos strike the American anti-aircraft cruiser *Atlanta.* To avoid hitting the friendly vessel again, Callaghan ordered the flagship's bridge to cease firing. But he made two important mistakes in doing so. To begin with, he gave his order too late, because *San Francisco*'s gunners had already shifted targets and were no longer crushing *Atlanta,* now dead in the water. But worse, Callaghan mistakenly sent the message out on the ultra-high-frequency radio system known as "Talk Between Ships," or "TBS," so that *all* the American ships received it over the airwaves![70] One should not be too quick to speak harshly of a man who was trying to do his best and who won a posthumous Medal of Honor for the effort, but these errors say volumes about Daniel Callaghan's incompetence in commanding a major naval force in a life-or-death struggle.

## THE TORPEDO

*Portland* was now surrounded by enemy ships of still unknown number and size, so DuBose kept his gunners firing. A few minutes after Sweet Pea's main battery hit the battleship, two destroyers passed close aboard to starboard, and *Portland*'s two forward starboard 5-inch dual-purpose mounts fired starshells to help identify the passing ships. They should have fired AP ammunition instead and asked questions later, because the targets were enemy and the Japanese did not wait to attack. In the light of the starshells, only a minute or two past 0200, Gene Howard, an ammunition handler on one of the 5-inch/25s, cried out that a torpedo wake was coming from the starboard quarter.[71] Before anyone could react, Sweet Pea was blasted. Tons of seawater blown upward by the explosion pounded down on *Portland,* smashing the ship further, while objects large and small that had ripped loose and been thrown aloft by the blast also damaged whatever they hit.[72]

The torpedo was fired by IJNS *Yudachi,* the destroyer that had nearly collided with USS *Cushing* in the first moments of the battle. *Yudachi* had veered out to port to avoid the American destroyer and was away from the fight for several minutes. Upon returning to the battle scene, *Yudachi* found a heavy cruiser in her sights. There were no Japanese heavy cruisers that night, so her Captain fired a full spread from close range and a moment later *Portland* reported being hit.[73]

Below decks the cruiser suffered considerable damage. The center of impact was on the starboard side, just forward of Turret Three, perhaps six feet below the waterline. The explosion ruptured Sweet Pea's hull for about forty-five feet in length, and destruction extended some twenty-five feet into the ship.[74] The after 8-inch turret was jammed in both train and elevation, with its guns pointing up at about 30 degrees and to starboard about 15 degrees.[75]

Glen Wolf was manning the throttles in the forward engineroom when he felt the ship lifted right out of the water by the torpedo hit. He was "jolted pretty good," but did not recall whether he fell down or lost his grip. Wolf was one of the men who had come to *Portland* from the torpedoed *California* in Pearl Harbor. Not surprisingly, some fearful memories of December 7 flashed through his brain, although no damage occurred this night in Sweet Pea's engineroom.[76] Several levels higher, radiomen misidentified the explosion, thinking it just another outgoing salvo fired by *Portland*'s own guns, although they did think it came too soon after the previous one.[77] On the searchlight platform, Electrician Willard Losh heard the warning, "Torpedo!" and grabbed a handrail and bent his knees to save them from injury. The jolt was not so bad as he had expected. But in the nearby secondary gun director men were thrown around violently, some of them suffering cuts and bruises.[78] The main battery director was located near the highest point of the ship, in the tripod mast above the bridge, and that crew was also violently banged about. One man badly cut his eye when his head smashed into the eyepiece. But he refused help and continued to train the director as Turret Two fired away.[79]

At least some men were naive during the crisis. For example, Hank Teague, a Marine manning one of the anti-aircraft guns, saw a piece of the fantail fly overhead. He was unworried because he was sure he could move out of the way if it came down near him. Years later, he laughed at how silly he had been, since the ton or more of metal was moving far too fast for him to have skipped lightly aside.[80] Whether a man were hit or not often depended on sheer luck. One great tragedy was the death of Joseph Allen, the fifteen-year-old sailor who had had such fun firing his AA guns during the battles at Coral Sea and Midway. His illegal enlistment was discovered only a few days before the battle at Guadalcanal, and the ship's officers gave him a "safe place" to stay until he could be transferred home. The place selected was the after repair station, one deck above where the torpedo hit. Everyone there, including the Allen boy, was killed in the blast.[81] On the other hand, Joe Bond of Third Division left his battle station to get a breath of fresh air just before the torpedo hit. The men he left behind were all killed or wounded, but he escaped without a scratch, an outcome that left him feeling guilty the rest of his life.[82]

There were many casualties topside in addition to Executive Officer Wirth, who had been wounded by a flying fragment during the earlier explosion of the 14-inch Japanese shell.[83] Many others were now injured by the torpedo hit.[84] In Turret Three, pointer Bill Speer was rocked by the horrible explosion and found himself flying upward, and then coming back down for a hard landing. He discovered that he too had suffered some minor eye injuries just before being launched, when the small window in the sight port that he was looking through shattered, pouring pieces of glass into his eye. They were all removed easily the next day. He was not awarded a Purple Heart because he lost no blood.[85]

Many men in compartments near the detonation were killed or mortally wounded, but there were several miraculous escapes. Signalman Eldon Peterson and Radioman Henry Hight were right above the torpedo hit in the after communications shack, an emergency station to be used in case of damage to the primary facilities sited forward. Both were thrown high off the floor, and Hight hit his head on the ceiling. Neither was badly hurt, although five or six other men in the compartment were killed.[86] Elsewhere, the blast wrapped another sailor in four-inch deck armor that curled around him. When rescued he was found to have suffered only minor cuts and bruises. The same piece of flying deck plating that Teague thought he might dodge hit three different men, killing two. The third was knocked out and had a swollen face and a black eye, but his injuries were not regarded as serious.[87]

Although carrier sailors in months past were concerned about *Portland*'s being an unlucky omen when she was around, Sweet Pea's men had begun to think her a lucky ship. Part of this feeling was based on the three torpedoes that had hit her but failed to detonate at Santa Cruz.[88] The belief was confirmed on this November night when the torpedo blasted her starboard quarter and missed by only ten feet a compartment where bombs for her planes were stored. Had they been hit the ship would surely have been destroyed.[89] Nor were any fuel tanks ruptured or fuel lost, thus minimizing the damage a major fire might have caused.[90]

Still, *Portland* was in real trouble. Damage reports coming to the bridge told the story. Turret Three had been knocked right off its track by the torpedo hit.[91] A part of the main deck was wrapped up and around the base of the turret, rather like fingers of a huge hand now holding the guns at a cockeyed angle.[92] A major section of the main deck aft had been blown away, as Teague had seen, and there was a huge hole in the starboard quarter right at the waterline. The two inboard propeller shafts had been destroyed and the steering engine knocked out. The way the after part of the ship had been twisted by the blast created the same effect as if she were using right full rudder.

The blast caused the bridge to lose steering control, not an uncommon experience recently. At Santa Cruz she could not maneuver away from the three torpedoes that hit without exploding. Immediately following that battle, when sailing to Noumea, the bridge lost control five times, thus contributing to Admiral Tisdale's decision to shift his flag to *Pensacola*. And there had been the repeated breakdowns between Noumea and Guadalcanal.[93] So *Yudachi*'s torpedo had turned a chronic failure into a serious and permanent injury. Captain DuBose found he was unable to steer by the engines, although he did not yet realize it was because the propellers had been destroyed. Sweet Pea circled helplessly to starboard.[94] Years later, Radioman Hight, who claimed to be unhurt when thrown around the emergency radio shack, insisted that the ship turned to port all night. He may have been smacked worse than he thought.[95]

In this night of bewilderment, though, Sweet Pea's sailors stood by their posts at the guns and communications stations, in the enginerooms and firerooms, and elsewhere. Many had been hurt, some severely, but some, like Henry Hight, refused to admit their injuries and just stayed where they were and did what their duty demanded.[96] A lot of the men had friends killed or wounded in the blast.[97] Others, although nowhere near the torpedo hit itself, lost all their personal items because their berthing compartments were destroyed.[98] Men of the *Portland* put these losses out of their minds and worked to fight back, to save the ship and their injured shipmates, and even to look after survivors of other ships who were bobbing around in the water nearby.[99] That this badly damaged cruiser continued to fight was a fact that decades later veterans of the ship pointed to with great pride. They sometimes quote Admiral Halsey, who wrote, "the PORTLAND'S performance was most commendable, especially as regards to ship and damage control."[100]

Heroism spread throughout *Portland* in those terrifying minutes of the fighting. Seaman 2/c Joseph Pagel, a trainer on one of the 5-inch dual-purpose guns, was hit early in the fight and suffered severe lacerations to both calves. He never mentioned his injury and stayed at his post for the rest of the engagement. Only after things quieted down a little did Pagel's gun captain notice the massive amount of blood on the deck around the man. The ship's own medical crew saved Pagel's legs in the days ahead, but it was a close call.[101] Similarly dedicated was Seaman 2/c George Weldon, a loader on a 5-inch gun who was struck in the helmet by a chunk of one of the Japanese shells. Knocked off his seat, he lay on the deck for a few moments. Regaining consciousness, he resumed his station and served the gun for the rest of the battle.[102] The torpedo opened up parts of the ship, thus exposing lights to the outside that might attract Japanese fire in the darkness after the shooting quieted down. Coxswain G.J. Metsker—his mates gave him the unlovely nickname of "Messgear"—found one light burning in the flood where the chief petty officer quarters used to be. With no apparent thought of the risk to himself, he lowered himself into the dangerous water to extinguish the offending bulb. Boatswain's Mate Thomas Johnston, the man who suffered eye injuries when he was thrown against his eyepiece in the main battery's gun director, used his own handkerchief to staunch the bleeding and stayed at his post.[103]

While the men topside were continuing the battle, sailors below decks acted with haste and expertise to keep the ship alive. Most important was the work of the damage-control parties. Scattered throughout the ship, these crews were trained to provide quick and expert repairs to battle damage even during continuing combat. Such teams repeatedly saved *Yorktown* at Coral Sea and Midway. Now it was *Portland*'s turn. The torpedo hit blew the ship open, so seawater was now flooding compartments as far forward as the mess deck. The damage-control parties nevertheless reset the ship's watertight integrity and began pumping many compartments dry, all while the ship was still under fire and was continuing to fight back.[104]

Other men helped save the ship, too. Machinist's Mate 1/c Pete Cole was the only man in the engineroom who realized that *both* inboard propellers had been torn off. He immediately shut down the steam supply to the turbines driving those props. If allowed to run without a load, they might have vibrated so badly that steam lines would have ruptured, causing unimaginable carnage and heavy flooding in the engineroom.[105] Now without an assigned function, Cole got out of the way but stayed alert. Soon, "I noticed that the Bridge was sending down a lot of speed changes on the Engine Order telegraph but I paid little attention until I walked over to the starboard side of the ER and looked down to where No. 1 propeller shaft from the Forward ER passed through down in the bilges of the After ER. I was surprised to see that the shaft was not turning."[106]

Cole began to suspect that the throttlemen on the two engines still in commission were adjusting their throttles to make power to the shafts equal. He could see that those men did not realize that, because two of the propellers were inoperable, what they were reading on their gauges was incorrect. He passed his observations on to the watch officer, who instructed the throttlemen to do their work by feel and not by the readings. The chief of the watch recommended Cole for a medal for this alert thinking, but Pete sniffed, saying, "I only did what I was trained to do." But each of his two actions taken only by itself prevented further calamity.[107]

So too did the initiative of the "Oil King," Chief Petty Officer J.E. Jones and his assistant, Water Tender 2/c Hubert Johnson. Their normal duty was to tend the oil tanks, the fuel supply to the engines, and the trim of the ship. The way they trimmed ship following the calamity of November 13 contributed significantly to saving Sweet Pea. When the torpedo slammed into her, *Portland* took on a slight starboard list that, by putting the hole further underwater, would add to the flooding. The only way to correct the list was by shifting water and fuel from starboard and aft to port and forward. Chief Jones's judgment in the complex task of shifting oil and water ballast from this tank or that to yet another one or two over the next twenty-four hours kept *Portland* from rolling over on her severely damaged starboard side. The Oil King kept the hole fairly high out of the water, thereby minimizing what was already enormous flooding.[108] An official Navy report on Sweet Pea's damage control applauded the brilliance of these decisions.[109] That same report concluded that the ship's performance in these moments of distress was "impressive and . . . a tribute to the skill of her personnel as well as the ruggedness of her design and construction."[110]

There was plenty going on topside, too. Harold Johnson reported that after the fight it was so dark one could see fires raging on many ships from both sides that had been hit in the battle. He counted twenty-two such blazes.[111] Although she too was afire, *Portland* continued to fight.

In collecting his own damage reports, Gunnery Officer Shanklin discovered that the two forward 8-inch turrets and six of the 5-inch mounts were still operating. He began to seek out new targets, but the news was mixed. The damaged Japanese battleship *Hiei* was only forty-two hundred yards away on his fire-control radar, but taking on a battleship was more than a stern chore for a heavy cruiser. Still, like Captain DuBose, Elliott Shanklin was a warrior with impressive battle awareness at his core. He asked the bridge for permission to fire at *Hiei,* and Captain DuBose told him to do so. As *Portland* continued her swing to starboard, *Hiei* finally began to bear where the forward turrets could shoot, and Sweet Pea got back into the fight. She fired four full salvos at *Hiei* before her uncontrolled swing masked her guns again.[112] Executive Officer Wirth called this shooting "rodeo gunnery," in that the ship would fire only when the involuntary swing of her head allowed it.[113] Wirth also noted with pride that after the battle Admiral Nimitz described this night gunnery by Sweet Pea, a ship out of control, as "one of the highlights of the action."[114] The Japanese fired back, of course, but the two 14-inch rounds that struck *Portland* were again not armor-piercing and therefore did only a little damage.[115]

*Hiei* soon drifted away from *Portland* and out of the fight, burning badly.[116] Another score for Sweet Pea. As things quieted down in Ironbottom Sound, Captain DuBose ceased fire because he could no longer make out friend from foe.[117] But many in his crew worked throughout the night, pulling out of the sea men from other ships now sunk, something *Portland* already had great experience with. On one occasion this terrible night, the sounds of splashing men were reported to Dubose. He asked if they were American or Japanese. "American, Captain," came the reply. DuBose called out to the men in the water:

> "I'm bringing the ship to a stop. Paddle your liferaft over to us. We have no steering control."
> "Roger, Captain," came the grateful but wry reply. "We have no liferaft, either."[118]

During those hours while she was spinning involuntarily around Ironbottom Sound, *Portland* rescued thirty-eight sailors. Some were in very bad shape, with open wounds and suffering from exposure in the oily seawater.[119] A lot of this rescue work came after sunrise when Sweet Pea was in additional jeopardy because Japanese aircraft could come after her.[120] DuBose and his men disregarded the new potential danger to carry out their work of mercy, and the cruiser's luck held. The Japanese who flew over the battle area left her alone, although she was "the next best thing to a sitting duck," as historian Hammel wrote. Invariably, the survivors were treated with kindness and hospitality.[121] One wonders whether Sweet Pea may have set records for rescuing survivors during the war. Add these men from destroyers and cruisers at Guadalcanal to the carrier sailors from *Lexington* and *Yorktown*. There would be more before she retired.

That would have been the end of the battle for *Portland,* except for a lucky break she took advantage of the next morning. At first light, although unable to control her steering, the cruiser was still picking up survivors of other American ships.[122] In the murk, her bridge watch noticed among the other drifting and sinking ships one badly damaged destroyer about six miles to the north that could be clearly identified as Japanese. No one in *Portland* knew then that it was *Yudachi,* already abandoned.[123] Nor did Sweet Pea's men know then that it was a *Yudachi* torpedo that had waylaid their own ship a few hours earlier. Because it was the only enemy target within range of her 8-inch guns when they could be brought to bear, Sweet Pea's director crews set ranges and bearings and her turrets fired when they could. On the third swing, a six-gun salvo hit the Japanese destroyer, which roared into flames, exploded, then rolled over and sank.[124] Another score for Sweet Pea.

The men on the wounded cruiser were overjoyed. Many left their stations to cheer.[125] Years later, Sweet Pea's veterans recalled it as the greatest moment of the war.[126] What happened to *Portland*'s crew in that instant stands as proof of the contention that this battle was the turning point in the *attitudes* of the contending navies.

Most of the American losses were suffered in the first ten minutes or so of the fight on November 13. As the surface of Ironbottom Sound began to lighten at dawn, nearly all the U. S. warships were out of action. Of the five cruisers, only *Helena* had escaped major damage. *Atlanta* was dead in the water, *Portland* was crippled and going in circles, *San Francisco* and *Juneau* were severely mangled and slowly fleeing the scene. Of the eight destroyers, four had been sunk or abandoned: *Barton, Cushing, Laffey,* and *Monssen.* Only *Fletcher* was unhit, and she was leading the damaged *Sterret* and *O'Bannon* away, while the badly hurt *Aaron Ward* lay dead in the water not far from Sweet Pea.[127]

On its face, this casualty list suggests that the battle was a disaster for the Americans. But the situation was nearly as grim on the Japanese side. Battleship *Kirishima* was damaged and, along with two destroyers, was then attempting to tow the severely damaged and flaming battleship *Hiei.* Light cruiser *Nagara* had been damaged and was now fleeing the battle site, taking with her five undamaged destroyers. Two destroyers, including *Yudachi,* had been sunk, and three others were damaged and limping away from the scene.[128] It was this force, so superior to the Americans at midnight a few hours earlier, that had failed to carry out its mission. The Americans had lost more but had accomplished what they set out to do.

Admiral Halsey's strategy of fighting with whatever was available and Admiral Turner's gritty courage in carrying out that new policy had won. The Imperial Navy's flotilla had come down The Slot intending to shell Henderson Field so that Tanaka's transports could land the reinforcements on Guadalcanal without fear of American air attacks. The American goal in resisting on November 13 with an undergunned force was merely to stop the Japanese, thereby keeping the airfield open. *Portland* and her sisters had succeeded by their ferocious resistance to the powerful Japanese flotilla.

Admiral Tanaka's slow transports plodded on. But because of the Night Cruiser Action and Night Battleship Action forty-eight hours later, Henderson Field remained in American hands and was still able to launch aircraft against Japanese forces ashore and afloat. Over the next few days, planes from Henderson bombed Tanaka's transports incessantly. Of the twelve transports carrying thirteen thousand fighting men so badly needed on Guadalcanal, only four with fewer than two thousand troops made it to their destination. The others were sunk and their passengers slaughtered by aircraft flying from an airfield *Portland* and her sisters had sacrificed so much to defend.[129]

The Americans achieved their mission and the Japanese did not. It was a tremendous victory for the U.S. Navy. Despite the damage to their ship, the men and officers of *Portland* were pleased with themselves and still full of fight the next morning. This was a clear indication that a great turning point in the war against Japan had indeed been reached. From now on the *Americans* believed they could win.

In Tokyo, it was different. Faced with the fact that the sea around Guadalcanal was now controlled by the Americans, as the air had been since Henderson Field became the home of the Cactus Air Force, the Imperial General Staff decided it could not reinforce Japan's forces enough to win there. A few weeks later, the emperor gave his permission to withdraw from the island.[130]

8

# Repairs

After the torpedo hit, it took Sweet Pea twenty-four hours to reach safety, but she made it thanks to the marvelous skill of her crew and others who helped. At early light on that Friday the thirteenth, American authorities at Guadalcanal and Tulagi sent assistance for the many stricken ships still afloat in the sound. Captain DuBose declined the first offer of a tow from an ocean-going tug that approached *Portland.* DuBose was now the senior officer present afloat since the two admirals and the CO of *San Francisco* were all dead. His first command was to direct the tug to help the nearby *Atlanta,* which was worse off. The anti-aircraft cruiser had been smashed several times by the first Japanese salvos and later by *San Francisco*'s 8-inch rounds, and had been torpedoed at least once by the Japanese.[1] Within a few hours, though, Captain Samuel Jenkins of *Atlanta* asked if he could scuttle the ship. DuBose gave his permission, took on some of the survivors—*more* rescued survivors for Sweet Pea— and continued trying to save his own ship.[2]

DuBose's concern for *Atlanta* was not matched by *Helena*'s Captain Gib Hoover's regard for *Portland.* When DuBose asked if *Helena* could tow Sweet Pea, Hoover replied that he would not because he feared the Japanese might catch him moving slowly while towing a huge ship that could not steer.[3]

A few days later, Captain Hoover was sacked. Halsey's headquarters blamed him for not rescuing survivors from USS *Juneau* (CL-52) later on November 13, after she was hit by a submarine-fired torpedo. A few years later a court of inquiry cleared Hoover, and later than that Admiral Halsey wrote in his memoirs that he had acted too hastily in removing *Helena*'s Captain from command. But in 1942 investigators noted mainly that *Helena* had sailed away from the five Sullivan brothers and the remaining one hundred or so who got off *Juneau,* nearly all of whom perished as a result. No one in the chain of command then would cut him any slack.[4]

Hoover had a great combat record up to then, acquitting himself well in the November 13 battle just completed. But in the cases of *Portland*'s request for a tow and *Juneau*'s disaster, *Helena*'s skipper seems to have been at least questionably eager to save his own ship, all others be damned. He may have been right, of course: U.S. Navy cruisers were getting scarcer every day and *Helena* was still relatively undamaged.[5] In making his questionable decisions, however, Hoover left himself wide open to inquiry, both contemporary and historical, something that Laurence DuBose in *Portland* did not do.

In the morning, assisted by a couple of Higgins boats from Guadalcanal that were pushing and pulling *Portland* in every possible way, DuBose tried to get her moving toward Tulagi, where he might get repairs in the port facility. But her damage was so extensive that she moved barely at all, except in the everlasting right-hand turn. In the early afternoon, YC-239 came alongside and tried to help the Higgins boats.[6] This was a yard patrol craft, a former tuna clipper intended for random chores around a navy base in an enclosed harbor. The sailors called these vessels Yippies.[7] To send one to sea, even in the close waters of Ironbottom Sound, was asking more than was planned for her. But her pre-Navy career included deep-water work, so YC-239 responded to Sweet Pea's needs. As *Portland* had done overnight, the YC did the best she could. The three small craft did help the cruiser make a little headway, but they were unable to correct the circling.[8]

At 1347, though, Commander Advance Naval Base Solomon Islands ordered USS *Bobolink* to take *Portland* in tow and proceed to Tulagi.[9] Originally a coastal minesweeper, *Bobolink* was categorized in 1942 as an "Ocean Tug–Old."[10] This was not the first time that Sweet Pea and *Bobolink* had operated together. During the cruiser's very first shakedown cruise in June 1933, *Bobolink* had towed targets for her in gunnery exercises.[11] She had provided similar services at other times, too.[12] Now the cruiser and the little ship met again in Ironbottom Sound, this time no practice exercise, but one that would determine whether *Portland* would survive or not.

*Bobolink* seems to have been pressed into every sort of miscellaneous duty during the Guadalcanal campaign, and had already been very busy that day. In the chaos that followed the battle, she had towed destroyer *Aaron Ward* into Tulagi and light cruiser *Atlanta* to an anchorage off Lunga Point. Now she was taking on her biggest load, *Portland*.[13] The Captain of the little vessel was Lieutenant James L. Foley, already well known in the Solomons as "Smilin' Jim."[14] He was resourceful and courageous. During the afternoon when an air attack was reported coming in, DuBose advised *Bobolink* that he thought she should cast off so she could maneuver independently if *Portland* were attacked. Foley called back up to DuBose, "Hell no. It took all day to hook up and I'm not about to cut loose." The crew on *Portland* cheered this feistiness. DuBose himself, ignoring the lack of the customary naval courtesy, turned to his Marine orderly and said, "There is a brave man on a brave ship."[15]

What *Bobolink* had to do about Sweet Pea on November 13, 1942, was no routine task, but a seamanship achievement requiring innovation of the first magnitude. At first one of the various small craft pushed this way while another pulled that way. Then they switched around to do something different. And then again, using one, two, three, or four of the small vessels. But *Portland,* much larger than any of the little craft trying to make her go straight, just obstinately went around in her unmerry circles. The waltz continued for several hours until finally a solution was found. Both *Bobolink* and YC-239 tied up to starboard abreast Sweet Pea's bridge and pushed together against the circling. The combined power of the two was enough to keep *Portland,* still driving on her own engines, headed in the general direction of Tulagi at two or three knots.[16]

*Bobolink* actually caused a little damage to the cruiser when sparks from her overworked engine flew up the stack and started a small fire in the flag bag on Sweet Pea's signal bridge. It was easily extinguished, but it was an uneasy moment. No one begrudged *Bobolink* that small flaw in her effort.[17] She was the hero of that day-long trip, and sailors from the cruiser recall *Bobolink* particularly fondly as a result of those long hours of creeping together across Ironbottom Sound. Three former crewmen of *Bobolink* were invited to *Portland*'s annual reunion in 1989, where they were treated as featured stars of the program.[18] Not long after that, former

Water Tender 1/c Jim Burke wrote the cruiser's association that he and his wife had just bought a new RV, which they were now towing behind their car. They called the car "Bobolink," and the trailer "Sweet Pea."[19]

For the next fourteen hours or so, *Portland* crabbed her way across the water.[20] All the while, she continued to pick up swimming Americans, many of them badly injured. Vince Pietrok, a *Portland* sailor who helped one wounded man get to Sweet Pea's sick bay, marveled at seeing only oil-soaked bones where the unfortunate survivor had lost all the flesh off his leg.[21] Some of the men that the cruiser's whaleboats picked up, even while Sweet Pea herself was in grave peril, were from the sunken destroyer *Barton*. When Petty Officer Wayne Clark climbed a cargo net, Sweet Pea's sailors helped him strip off his oil-soaked clothing, then gave him dungarees, a T-shirt, and a pair of tennis shoes from a pile of clothing donated by the cruiser crew. Another *Barton* man, Jack Slack, pulled himself up to *Portland*'s deck, wandered off, and fell asleep in some isolated topside spot. When he awoke in the morning, he found himself in a bunk obviously lent to him by one of Sweet Pea's anonymous sailors.[22]

Just before midnight November 13/14, twenty-two hours after she was torpedoed, *Portland* approached Tulagi. Awaiting her there was one more hair-raising episode before she could reach the harbor. At 2315, two American PT boats arrived and, thinking she was a Japanese warship, prepared to make a torpedo attack. When DuBose heard the PT skippers talking on their radio circuit, he got up on the frequency himself in a loud and threatening voice: "THIS IS THE AMERICAN CRUISER PORTLAND X THIS IS CAPTAIN DUBOSE SPEAKING X THERE IS A TUG STANDING OUT FROM TULAGI TO ASSIST US X THE NAME OF HER CAPTAIN IS LIEUTENANT FOLEY X WE ARE NOT REPEAT NOT A JAPANESE."

Before the PT officers were convinced, though, they launched four torpedoes at the stricken Sweet Pea. Fortunately, they overestimated her speed and missed.[23]

No doubt relieved when the torpedo boats roared away, *Portland* resumed trying to reach port. Finally, at 0118 on Saturday, November 14, she backed into the nook where Tulagi and Florida Islands come close to each other. The crew then lassoed a palm tree with a line from the cruiser's stern, and Captain DuBose sent over working parties to cut and bring back masses of foliage. These were placed over and around

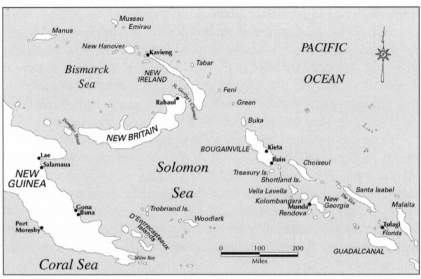

Map 3. Solomon Islands and Adjacent Area.

*Portland* to camouflage her from enemy eyes that daylight might bring.[24] Tulagi was no safe haven, though. At 1040 the next morning, Japanese planes from the carrier *Junyo* flew over and correctly reported that they had seen a *"Portland*-class" cruiser in the harbor. Happily, no one on the enemy carrier decided to do anything about the report.[25]

    The battle itself and the entire episode of the rescue of the cruiser was harrying for all. Most of the crew dealt with the two crises professionally and even heroically. There were exceptions, of course. The morning after the cruiser had moored to the palm tree, one fireroom sailor had had enough. He ran up on the main deck, dashed across the quarterdeck, and jumped right over the side into the water. At the hospital, he was diagnosed as "deranged, having been in such confinement below the waterline during the battle."[26]

    Japanese aircraft from Rabaul and nearer bases were also active in the air over Tulagi nearly every day *Portland* was there. The crew kept the ship disguised and camouflaged, and American planes from Guadalcanal flew cover over her as repair work on her damaged stern and jammed rudder progressed.[27]

    There were nevertheless some close calls. One occurred when a seaplane came by to pick up something Admiral Tisdale had left behind when he departed the ship at Noumea. As the plane was pulling in, the controller in the tower who was guiding her warned the pilot to watch out for the tied-up cruiser that was covered by foliage at the head of the bay. *Portland*'s officers worried that the message would be intercepted by the Japanese, who would then target the ship.[28] No such attack occurred, so the Japanese apparently did not hear the indiscreet message. By skill and good luck, the ship was never attacked while moored at Tulagi.

From there, though, the crew had a distant view of the later parts of the Naval Battle of Guadalcanal. Shortly after tying up to the palm tree on the 14th, *Portland* went to battle stations when medium-caliber gunfire was seen out in Ironbottom Sound, not far from where she had been wounded the night before. The firing came from a squadron of Japanese cruisers that had steamed down to shell Henderson Field. The men in *Portland* feared being discovered in such a helpless condition, moored to a palm tree.[29]

About twenty-four hours after that, they witnessed the final stage of the extended Naval Battle of Guadalcanal.[30] This engagement was the first of only two battleship-versus-battleship fights during the Pacific War. *Portland* was present for both. Again, Admiral Halsey sent everything he had to protect the Marines on Guadalcanal. It took two days for the battleships then escorting what was left of the American carriers to reach the battle scene. Once on hand, though, USS *Washington* had her moment of heroism. When her escorting destroyers and companion battleship *South Dakota* were sunk or knocked out of action, she took over the November 15 gunfight. She slipped around the battle scene unnoticed by Japanese lookouts and stealthily found her own targets on her excellent surface-search radar. In a laudable night of gunslinging, *Washington* single-handedly wrecked an enemy battleship, two heavy cruisers, and two light cruisers, knocking all of them out of action, either permanently or for many months.[31]

Without question, it is too much to say that Sweet Pea might be included in the list of American ships who *fought* in this Night Battleship Action. But she was *present* for every moment of the Naval Battle of Guadalcanal, and she and every man in her crew was in peril for every part of that four-day turning point in the war. In addition to her successful work in the air raid on November 12 and in the Night Cruiser Action of November 13, she was potentially subject to air attack all day while being pushed across the sound on November 13. She reached Tulagi in the nick of time to avoid the November 14 attack on Henderson by Japanese surface ships. She was sighted by and could have been attacked by enemy aircraft while she was moored at Tulagi. And she was within the range of the Japanese battlewagons on the 15th before they were driven off by *Washington.* No other ship in the U.S. Navy was *present* for all that. *Portland* was *there,* and everything her Captain and crew had done up to reaching Tulagi indicated that she would have fought back if attacked.

These nights of naval ferocity caught the attention of the Marines ashore. Ordinarily, sailors would not trade places with infantry, thinking of the filthy living conditions and the constant danger. But a year after the Naval Battle of Guadalcanal, Pete Cole met a Marine who had been watching the naval battles from his foxhole on Guadalcanal. He told Cole that up until then he had always thought it would be better to be a sailor with a clean bunk, good meals, and regular showers. But, he said, what he saw those nights changed his mind.[32]

Following the battle, Captain DuBose was criticized by Admiral Halsey in an endorsement on DuBose's combat action report. DuBose had written that, going into the battle, two of his fire-control radars—one for the forward main battery, and one for the starboard AA battery—did not function perfectly. Halsey was angry that, first, he had not been told beforehand, and, second, that DuBose did not find local technical support to get the radars working.[33] But ComSoPac's complaints were unreasonable. *Portland* had adequate fire-control radar even though her forward main battery's unit was out of commission, as she showed by how accurate her fire was on November 13, using only the radar on the after director. And if in the few days when DuBose might have obtained repairs he had taken his ship out of action for that work, the admiral would have had something serious to complain about. Others in the chain of command probably disagreed with Halsey because within the next few months DuBose was awarded the Navy Cross, promoted to rear admiral, and given command of a cruiser division.[34]

Accolades showered Task Force 67. Admiral Halsey praised *Portland*'s performance, as we have seen, and Admiral Turner recommended that the task force number be retired in glory.[35] "Task Force 67" was not used again in the Pacific War, but not for Turner's reasons. In 1943, the Department of the Navy changed its numbering system. Thereafter, fleets operating in the Pacific would have odd numbers, First, Third, Fifth, etc., while those in the Atlantic would be even numbered. Task forces within those fleets would all have the same first digit as the number of the fleet, so "67" would be an Atlantic Fleet number forever more.[36]

Individual heroism was also recognized. Captain DuBose, Gunnery Officer Shanklin, Boatswain's Mate Johnston, Coxswain Metsker, and Seaman 2/c Pagel each won a Navy Cross, the highest honor a warrior can be awarded by the naval service, and second only to the Medal of Honor. Executive Officer Wirth and two enlisted men were awarded the Silver Star, and three junior officers received lesser medals for their heroism under fire.[37]

The ship itself and her crew were awarded the Navy Unit Commendation Medal. Although a great honor, that decoration sticks in the craw of some *Portland* men. They point out that in the night battle of November 13, only two Japanese ships were sunk, both by *Portland,* and that their ship also got several confirmed direct hits on the two enemy battleships engaged. And yet *San Francisco,* which they think did little more than carry the admiral who made such a mess of things, received the recently created and *higher* Presidential Unit Citation.[38] *San Francisco* had an excellent career in the Pacific War other than on that awful night. But recent scholarship has determined that the main thing she achieved during the battle of November 13 was to demolish USS *Atlanta.*[39] Admiral Callaghan, Captain Cassin Young, and two others aboard *San Francisco* received Medals of Honor, too, while no one in *Portland* did.[40]

The news that Admiral Callaghan was killed in the fighting landed especially hard on Jim Young, who became a *Portland* aviator, serving aboard Sweet Pea from 1943 to 1945. When Young heard in November 1942 of the annihilation of Callaghan and his staff, he knew it was a personal near miss. In the fall of 1942, he had been an enlisted sailor working as a yeoman for the Air Officer in the ComSoPac headquarters of Admiral Ghormley. During Halsey's takeover and his reassignment of the old staff, the Air Officer was ordered with Callaghan to Task Force 67, on board the *San Francisco.* Young knew that his own orders to flight school would be arriving soon, but he liked the Air Officer. Since he did not want to switch bosses for such a short time, he asked if he could be transferred, too. The Air Officer said he would look into it, but somehow never got back to the sailor. Young instead went to flight school, where he learned that the staff had been all but wiped out in *San Francisco's* flag plot by Japanese shellfire. The one survivor was that Air Officer, who nevertheless lost a leg. For the rest of his life, Young got goose bumps whenever he thought about his close call.[41]

At Tulagi, Captain DuBose finally had time to inspect the condition of the ship. His Marine orderly remembered that the skipper thought the work of the damage-control parties during the battle was remarkable and that they no doubt had saved the ship. DuBose was nevertheless shocked by the damage, and said if he had known its extent and severity he would have considered ordering that *Portland* be abandoned.[42] To have done so, we now know, would have deprived the ship of one of its best moments in a career of greatness. The crippled ship was going to return to action, thanks to the skill and persistence of its surviving crew and the help of workers on Tulagi and two continents.

Moments of sadness marked the days after the battle, as *Portland*'s crew recovered the bodies of some who had lost their lives. It was painful, physically and psychologically, to look for, find, and remove the remains. Harold Johnson remembered how shocking it was to see a diver come up with an arm or a leg, and to realize that it had once been a shipmate.[43] Ray Anetsberger has refused over the years since 1942 to speak to his family about the Tulagi time. One reason lies in the story he *did* tell his daughter, that he had a good friend with the nickname "Freckles." When the bodies of the dead men were being retrieved from the damaged compartments, Ray saw a freckled arm fall off the gurney. He knew he had lost his buddy.[44]

The work of retrieving bodies was gruesome. Diver Frank Haskell found a body wedged between two sprung hull plates. The body was visible only from the waist up, and the head and left arm were missing, making identification extremely difficult. By standing on one of the adjoining plates, Haskell was able to loosen the body enough to get a line around it, pull it free, and guide it to the surface. It was handled reverently by the boat crew and the ship's chaplain, who had come to the scene. Taken out into Tulagi harbor, the remains were buried at sea following the old Navy ritual.[45] The body was actually misidentified as that of C.G. Parker, Electrician's Mate 2/c. The error was discovered later when Parker's actual body was found in the after-steering compartment and unquestionably identified by the contents of his wallet. A subsequent investigation determined that the decapitated sailor was more probably J.R. Gober, Machinist's Mate 1/c.[46]

Another unhappy incident regarding the remains of the men who had been killed occurred when a sailor from Georgia who was assigned to the recovery refused to touch what was left of Franklin Osborne, an African-American mess attendant. Osborne's remains were scattered all around his battle station, and the southerner, who possessed his share of the region's racist bigotry, simply refused to touch what there was of a dead black man. A Lieutenant Johnson came by and heard Bill Speer, who was in charge of the detail, trying to get the defiant Georgian to work. The officer looked the man in the eye and began to draw his pistol from his holster, saying, "Sailor, help Speer or I am shooting you." The reluctance ended abruptly and the two got to work. Years later, Speer recalled that as they were shoveling "guts, bone, and blood," he saw to it that the "stupid rebel . . . got splashed real good."[47]

The site around the wreckage was so severely damaged that not all the dead were found until a month later, when *Portland* was in dry dock in Australia.[48] Ship's officials could then certify that, in all, seventeen sailors and one Marine were killed or missing and presumed dead in the fighting on November 13, 1942.[49]

Eight of these men were discovered soon after the battle and were buried in the government cemetery at Tulagi.[50] As noted earlier, Gober and Osborne were buried at sea, and those who were found after the ship reached Australia were buried in Rookwood Cemetery in Sydney.[51] The others were never recovered. Captain DuBose guessed that they were probably blown over the side by the torpedo or some other hit on the ship.[52]

Caring for the injured was made more difficult because the ship's medical staff had been severely diminished by the torpedo. When it wrecked the chief's quarters it also caused numerous casualties in the after battle casualty station, which was located there during general quarters. Junior Medical Officer Lieutenant Robert Williams was killed, a loss severely felt by most of the sailors, who liked him very much.[53] Three corpsmen petty officers, including Chief Pharmacist's Mate Charles Compton, were also killed on station there.[54]

Several of the ship's berthing spaces were total losses. One man returning to the F Division compartment saw his collection of photos and memorabilia drifting on top of the flood, luckily without a single wet page. It had been resting on top of his locker and had just floated away.[55] The laundry was nearly destroyed and nearby crew living spaces suffered great damage. At least one of the sailors whose bunks were there went into the water to retrieve whatever he could.[56] But most of the men whose compartments were flooded lost everything. The supply department gave them enough clothing to get by, but their personal items were gone.[57]

In addition to the eighteen dead, seventeen *Portland* men were officially listed as "wounded in action."[58] Most of these men were treated by the on-board staff. Ted Waller, for example, recalled the bedside manner of *Portland* surgeon Lawrence Joers and Pharmacist's Mate Dan Hardin, who helped the nineteen-year-old seaman get through the frightening time.[59] Others received some care at Tulagi's naval facility. Executive Officer Wirth traded a sack of potatoes for an X-ray, and *not* the dehydrated types. But he too was under the primary care of Doctor Joers in *Portland*'s sick bay.[60]

All hands agreed that one disaster was the severe damage suffered by the gedunk stand. "Gedunk," sometimes spelled with two e's and always pronounced "GEE-dunk," is Navy jargon for any of the items one might buy at a soda fountain, an ice cream shop, or a candy store. The plural is gedunks, and the place where these things are sold is the gedunk stand. Every ship has such a store, more or less spectacular depending on the size of the ship and crew. As a large combatant ship, *Portland*'s gedunk stand was elaborate, and was managed by an S Division man named W.N. "Bunky" Schneider. He was a major factor in maintaining the good spirits of the men, many of whom were not much more than boys and all of whom liked the gedunks that he sold there.[61]

The stand had fixed hours of operation, and on occasion that schedule could be irritating. A cartoon strip in the ship's newspaper once showed a man waiting impatiently as the line at the gedunk stand crawled on, worried that he wouldn't get his order in before the place closed at 1600. The overhead clock said 1550 just as he got to the head of the line but, frustratingly, an officer came and cut him off. The officer got the last order filled that day.[62] *Portland* was not immune to officers who pulled rank like that, and they were roundly hated by enlisted men throughout World War II.[63]

Schneider and others who worked in the stand had some persistent trouble with the equipment that supported their operation.[64] There were mixers and freezers, refrigerators and pumps, plumbing and electricity that all required tending from time to time.[65] But virtually no other ship's work took precedence over repairs needed at the gedunk stand. Two reasons put it at the top of the priority list: (1) everyone on board wanted the place to be operating during its regular hours at the end of the work day, and (2) a sailor who fixed something broken at the gedunk stand was usually rewarded by a free treat.[66]

When the torpedo ripped into the ship, it drove metal fragments through Schneider's store. For three days at Tulagi, the electricians worked around the clock to get the equipment, particularly the refrigerator and freezer, back in working condition. No one could be sure how long *Portland* would be in Tulagi, but everyone reckoned that as long as she *was* there, no additional gedunks would arrive at the ship. So the pressure was on to keep the existing items from spoiling. It was a major question of ship's morale in an already trying time. When the mission was accomplished, all breathed easier.[67]

Perhaps more important to the fighting future of the cruiser was the emergency work done to repair the torpedo hole and the steering problem. One should keep in mind here just how badly the ship was hurt. The torpedo probably carried six hundred pounds of explosive in its warhead.[68] The official report said that damage extended for more than forty-five feet along the ship's length, for twenty-five feet into the ship from her starboard side, and from the main deck down three levels in depth.[69]

Sydney, Australia, had a shipyard that was already being used to repair combat damage endured by U.S. ships. It was decided that Sweet Pea should go there for repairs that would enable her to sail back to California for more permanent work and some needed renovations. But she could not get to Sydney with the huge hole in her starboard quarter and the steering problem created by her twisted stern. Somehow those problems had to be corrected where she was, at the palm tree in Tulagi.

The ship's own crew did the bulk of the work on temporarily sealing up the hole. Two sailors named "Chips" Weatherford and "Boats" Stimpfel discovered some I-beams the Japanese had abandoned on Florida Island.[70] One is reminded here that without enemy equipment captured at Guadalcanal, Henderson Field could not have been completed, and without Henderson Field the Marines may not have been able to hold their ground. The same was true for wounded *Portland*. Without these Japanese I-beams, the plugging of the cruiser's stern would have been much more difficult or impossible.

DuBose was able to get some help from Seabees on Guadalcanal, who provided the vehicles to lug the I-beams from Florida to the ship. When the damaged compartments were cleared, their bulkheads were shored up. Then the Seabees and *Portland* men welded the I-beams to bridge the damaged area by connecting the still-intact frames forward of the hole to the aftermost part of the ship, very close to the sternpost. Patching along the length of the I-beams was then possible. But *Portland* was not only a taker at Tulagi; she gave some helpful support, too. One example was that she became a kind of tender for the many PT boats operating around the Solomons. Her aircraft had been left ashore before the Night Cruiser Action to eliminate the fire hazard they presented.[71] As a result, she had plenty of aviation gasoline but no planes to use it. The PTs used the same fuel the SOCs did, so they came calling, and *Portland* became a service station for the torpedo boats.[72]

Clearing the flooded compartments was itself arduous and unforgettable. Vince Pietrok remembers working most of the time in water up to his waist in the messy spaces.[73] Brothers George and Bob Dolezal, normally assigned to AA guns, were put to work splicing wires for temporary repairs while they too stood waist-deep in water.[74] Frank Haskell and two other *Portland* men who were qualified as divers worked below the surface to clear away debris that might leave a trail the enemy could use to find Sweet Pea as the ship sailed to Sydney.[75]

On November 16, underwater shipfitters from Espiritu Santo, New Hebrides, arrived to help solve the steering problem. Together with the ship's own divers, these men worked around the clock. First they cut the damaged rudder arms, which were about five inches in diameter and more than ten feet long. They brought from Espiritu Santo underwater cutting torches fitted with 1/8-inch carbon rods about a foot long. Hundreds of those rods were used in cutting through the twisted steel, actually by melting it. They also brought dozens of huge bottles of oxygen, needed to keep the electric arc flowing to the rods. Once the rudder arms were cut, the ship's deck force rigged cables and chain falls from the main deck to reposition the rudder itself.[76] They were assisted by Haskell and other divers, who worked for almost three hours to set the rudder. Again, broken parts were cut away and repairs were made by workmen beneath the surface of Tulagi's harbor.[77]

The Espiritu Santo shipfitters completed their work in two days. These highly skilled men were needed all over the South Pacific, so they quickly boarded a PBY for the flight back to their home base and future assignments. To the horror of the crew of *Portland,* the plane took off and almost immediately crashed back into the water, killing all on board. Again, Sweet Pea went into action to rescue downed sailors, but this time all her crew pulled out of Ironbottom Sound were the bodies of dead men.[78]

The ship was pronounced ready to sail to Sydney on November 22, only nine days after being so severely damaged.[79] This quick work was a remarkable testament to the skill of all who worked on her, both the ship's company and others from Tulagi and Espiritu Santo. They were heroes, too. *Portland* sailors had fought the enemy, suffered losses, made good a hair-raising escape, and then worked hours without rest in deplorable conditions to keep the ship afloat to fight another day. How raw their emotions were is illustrated by what one of them wrote years later, remembering the days and nights his ship was tied to a tree, leaving him surrounded by the flora of a rain forest, "There is one odor that still nauseates me and that is the fragrance of carnations. That odor sends my hair on edge."[80]

Sweet Pea's trip away from Tulagi after all this was not without problems. Although she had been worked on around the clock for more than a week, the repairs were hurried at best. Nevertheless, everyone wanted her out of range of the Japanese, who raided Guadalcanal almost daily. So *Portland* departed for Sydney at about 1600 on November 22, 1942, escorted by destroyers *Meade* and *Zane,* and towed by USS *Navajo* (AT-64).[81] The sturdy 1,450-ton tug was powered by 3,500-horsepower diesel-electric engines and could make 16.5 knots without a load.[82] She certainly seemed capable of getting *Portland* to Sydney.

But the jury-rigged repairs to the steering system broke down just outside Tulagi. The plan had been to set the rudder at fifteen degrees left, to compensate for the twist in the ship's stern. But once the ship was moving, it was learned that the left rudder was *too* effective because the ship had only two propellers operational. Steering constantly to port was no better than steering to starboard. So *Portland* was towed back to her palm tree while further adjustments were made. The divers went down again, the deck crew re-rigged the falls, and the rudder was aligned straight amidships.[83]

About 2000 *Navajo* towed her once more out of Tulagi. As she headed southeast down Ironbottom Sound, four Japanese destroyers came roaring down The Slot to shell Henderson Field only a few miles west of her. Happily, the enemy did not see *Portland,* which went quietly on its way.[84]

Some historians have written that Sweet Pea was towed the full distance to Australia.[85] In fact, she steamed under her own power almost the entire way. On November 24, not forty-eight hours after leaving Tulagi, Captain DuBose discovered he could make better speed on *Portland*'s own engines than by being towed. He cast off the chain, and thereafter the tug merely accompanied Sweet Pea on her voyage to Australia. On the 24th, DuBose sent destroyer *Zane* back to the war.[86] *Portland* steamed for six more days to reach Sydney, perhaps thirteen hundred miles from Tulagi.[87] It was not an easy trip. The whole way, the three 8-inch guns of Turret Three were trained out to starboard, fully loaded, and almost any serious jolt might have fired them. Some moderate seas provided a stern test for the seamanship of the crew, the stability of the ammunition in the guns, and the toughness of the temporary repairs. More damage actually occurred. As the sea picked up a little, the shell of the ship opposite the torpedo hole was found to be "working and bending," and a new crack on the port side opened as a result.[88] The ocean ultimately cooperated, though, and the voyage was completed without serious damage.[89]

One sailor later recalled that from his bunk on the way to Australia he could look right out to the sea and sky because the bulkheads that normally separated him from the weather had been blasted away.[90] Others have also remarked on the *al fresco* nature of the cruise.[91] Nothing could better illustrate how thin-skinned these "treaty cruisers" were, nor how lucky and skillful *Portland* and her sailors were not to have lost the ship to *Yudachi*'s torpedo.

## SYDNEY

Sweet Pea arrived in Sydney on November 30, 1942.[92] The crew was fascinated with the names of the places they were going to. As Australian tugs took her in, *Portland* was directed by signal to "Wooloomooloo Pier #5." The Communications Officer thought it was a misprint or mistransmission, but of course it was not.[93] Sweet Pea sat there for two days, and then went alongside a repair dock at Cockatoo Island, another name that tickled the crew. For the next three weeks, temporary repairs were made to the topside areas that could be reached while the ship was still in the water. The top priority was to unload the guns in Turret Three, still elevated and trained out as the torpedo hit had left it. Some tried to imagine what the citizens of Sydney would have thought if they knew that they had been under the loaded guns of a United States heavy cruiser for several days. The entire ship went to battle stations, and gunner's mates gingerly opened the breeches one at a time. The very careful hands of some very courageous men then pulled the powder bags out and dumped them overboard. The projectiles were then also backed out and jettisoned, without mishap. All breathed a lot easier afterward.[94]

The dry dock was also located at Cockatoo Island, but *Portland* had to wait her turn, because another cruiser, USS *New Orleans* (CA-32), was still in the facility, having a temporary bow built so she could sail home for permanent reconstruction.[95] At Wooloomooloo, *Portland* had been alongside USS *Chester* (CA-27). Both of those other cruisers were light-skinned like *Portland,* and each had suffered torpedo damage.[96] *New Orleans* was a treaty cruiser, and although *Chester* was older than the 1930 treaty, her class fit the parameters allowed by the pact and suffered the weaknesses.[97] Arrayed for all to see was evidence of the price these cruisers were paying in their unexpected role as the biggest gunboats in the Pacific Fleet.

On December 24, 1942, Sweet Pea finally entered the Cockatoo dry dock, which had been ingeniously hewn out of a solid rock wall that rose about eighty feet straight up from the water. The associated machine shops were in a tunnel called "Corregidor," in obvious memory of the Malinta Tunnel that had become so famous earlier that year. Australian soldiers were posted high on the rocky island to provide security for the shipyard and the ships in it.[98]

When *Portland* finally rested high and dry, the Australians, assisted by some of the crew, resumed work again around the damaged stern. After the last remains of the dead men were removed, repairs began. Two new screws had been sent from the United States to replace the lost ones, and there was much to be done around the steering mechanism, of course. Moreover, the entire stern had to be reworked from the keel to above the main deck and from forward of the starboard hangar around the stern and almost as far forward as the port hangar. No repairs were made to the decks and bulkheads inside the hull. Since the Australians in the shipyard would accomplish most of the work, the crew spent most of its time on liberty.[99]

And what a time *that* was! Sydney was a great treat for Sweet Pea's men. At the very first glance, the city had captivated the crew. When the ship passed through a narrow opening, the harbor suddenly spread out in a huge circle. Sydney was on the left and the Harbor Bridge lay dead ahead. Everything seemed clean and tidy, with "manicured lawns right down to the water." As the damaged cruiser shut her engines down at the pier, the men thrilled to the Australian quiet and the "promise of recreation unlike anything we had experienced for months."[100]

Recreation, to be sure. Many of the sailors had been aboard *Portland* in 1941 when she visited Sydney and Brisbane in the last months of peacetime. They no doubt told wonderful stories about those happy liberty calls, so that the new hands were excited to be going there, too. And indeed, the welcome shown to the American cruiser now was almost as tumultuous as it had been then.[101] All hands remembered this stop with great joy for years thereafter. The crew had to live on board the ship, so sailors rode boats from Cockatoo over to the city. But they had overnight liberty, almost unheard of during the war.[102]

The women were mostly white and spoke English, two rare joys for a mostly white American crew fighting in the Pacific.[103] It seemed that nearly everyone met a special Aussie girl. Some, like Bill Ala and Frank Hoge, actually married Australian women they met during this visit.[104] Others nearly did. For example, Vince Pietrok met Gwen Menere as they approached each other on a sidewalk in town. Nineteen-year-old Gwen liked Vince so much she took him home to meet her family. And her grandmother liked Vince so much that she promised to set him up on a sheep station after he and Gwen were married and living in Australia. But Vince did not want to settle Down Under, and he thought that Gwen would be unhappily homesick in America, so he discouraged all such overtures and left Sydney unwed. Much later, he and the American woman he had been married to for more than thirty years visited Sydney. They looked up Gwen, who admitted to Vince that she had been only seventeen in 1942. She had had a tough life since then, but Vince thought that she looked very much the same as when he had seen her last.[105]

Even casual relationships were remembered years later because the girls had taken the boys home, or had gone on beach trips, or had spent the night with the sailors in a hotel room.[106] Harold Johnson walked by a girl on the street one day and, after passing her, turned around and saw that she, too, had turned around. They talked for a while and became friends, but nothing more. She was a *good* friend to have because she was the desk clerk in Sydney's newest hotel. Anytime Johnson needed a room, she saw to it that he got it, and anytime he needed some information about Sydney's night life, she was helpful. She too took him home to meet her family in suburban Sydney, although he insisted years later that there was no romance.[107]

*Portland* men noticed that there were few Australian men of their own age anywhere about.[108] Indeed there were few men at all, because the country's small population during World War II was less than contemporary New York City's eight million.[109] Most of the young men were in the Australian army, and the largest part of it was fighting in North Africa. Another large number had been sent to Singapore only to be surrendered almost without having had a chance to fight. Nearly all of those remaining were serving with MacArthur in New Guinea. That left very few young men at home.

Two years after this emergency stop in Sydney, *Portland* embarked a bunch of correspondents to carry to the combat zone in New Guinea. One of them was John Brennan, a reporter for the *Sydney Bulletin*. He no doubt heard a lot from the sailors about how they loved his hometown and its women. In return, Brennan was the first to tell Sweet Pea's crew what Australian *men* thought of *them* when he wrote a story in the ship's newspaper. It seems that an Australian force of about two hundred men was left behind when the Allies abandoned Timor in February 1942. For fourteen months until finally extracted, the Aussies lived in the jungle on sweet potatoes and water buffalo. *Portland* visited Sydney during the time that these troops were clinging to life under such primitive conditions. The Aussies learned about the Americans who were having such a wonderful time in their homeland, and on Timor they composed a song about their joys, hopes, and fears during their apparently endless isolation. Wrote Brennan, "One verse sung feelingly recorded their interest in the cementing of international relationships brought about by *Portland*'s visit to Sydney":

> And since the Portland's come to town
> My girl friend's name is Mrs. Brown.
> I hope the rotten bastards drown.
> The bloody, rotten bastards.[110]

There were a few sad moments for Sweet Pea's men in Australia. They had to bury not only the casualties from Guadalcanal whom they finally found in dry dock, but two other men killed after they arrived in Sydney. One was Water Tender Paul Lynch. Lynch was promoted to Chief Petty Officer about the time the ship reached Australia and had then received from his wife the thrilling news of their just-born baby. He put on his new uniform and went to walk about the city. On that walk, the stiff wind that was usual along the tops of the Sydney cliffs blew his new chief's hat off his head, and when he tried to catch it he fell to his death on the rocks below.[111] The other was youngster Irvin Faulkner, a fireman 2/c, who died on December 15, 1942, when he suffered a crushed skull and severe hemorrhaging in a truck accident on Cleveland Street in Sydney. Three days later he too was buried in the U.S. Armed Forces Cemetery at Rookwood, in a grave between an Army private and an Air Corps second lieutenant.[112]

In addition to the wonderful women, there were plenty of joys in Australia. Leroy Riehl noticed that there seemed to be no jukeboxes in Sydney. He reckoned his future right then: he would buy "a bunch of jukeboxes and make a million dollars" selling them in Australia. It may have been a good idea, but Riehl never carried it out.[113] Bill Ala recalled how happy everyone on the ship was about Sydney's good food. Up until that time, *Portland* had been serving powdered eggs, powdered potatoes, and other things that Ala condemned as "stuff like that," but almost nothing fresh. In Sydney, on the other hand, there was fresh bread, fresh milk, eggs, bacon, ham, and other things the crew had not seen "for many, many months."[114]

Even more excellent was the fact that no Australian pubkeeper ever asked for proof of age, so the young American sailors drank freely, some of them for the first time. Even better was that they often drank *for* free, since Aussies in these pubs often refused to let the Yanks pay for their beer.[115] This happy custom began almost immediately. During one of the first days the ship was in Sydney, Bill Reehl was assigned to a work crew to unload a truckload of fresh produce and bring the foodstuffs back to the ship. When the sailors got to the spot, though, the truck had not yet arrived. As they stood around, the bluejackets were invited by a bunch of passing Australians to join them in a few pints. By the time the produce arrived, Sweet Pea's men were totally zonkers and had to be sent back to the ship because they were not able to work.[116]

One problem about the "good liberty" in Sydney was that many of the crew began to come back to the ship late. Because the shipyard was doing most of the work, the sailors had little to keep them occupied on board, in contrast to how much kept them interested in town. Moreover, they were supposed to return to *Portland* at 0830, just when the ferries were at their busiest carrying workers to their jobs. Captain DuBose began meting out penalties for such lateness: loss of liberty for a week or two would be pretty painful for most of the men. As the time drew near for *Portland* to leave Sydney, though, the problem worsened. No one knew exactly when the ship would get underway for the trip back to the States, and some took it upon themselves to stay in town a few hours or a day late, betting that it was the last liberty they would have in Australia.[117]

That's the decision Reehl and one of his buddies from Fifth Division made in February 1943. They had such a good time that day that they decided to stay an additional, unauthorized one. And then a second day passed. When they finally returned to the ship they were two days and thirty-five minutes absent-over-leave, or AOL. As bad an offense as this was, they were very lucky to come back when they did, because the ship got under way later that very day. Had they missed the movement to sea, they might have been charged with desertion, a potentially capital offense. As it was, Reehl was court-martialed, convicted, and sentenced by the court to ten days in the ship's brig on bread and water and a fine of $25 a month for four months. That was pretty stiff, but DuBose must have reckoned that boys will be boys, because he cut the penalty in half on review.[118]

The ship's torpedo-damaged brig had not yet been repaired, so Reehl had to serve his time in a ten- by twenty-foot section of one of the damage-control stations, partitioned off by a cyclone fence. It was right next to Number Three mess hall, which must have been tough on a guy allowed only bread and water. He did get a full meal on the third day, and by the time he had served his sentence the ship had nearly reached the United States.[119]

*Portland* left Australia on February 12, 1943, in company with an Australian Navy destroyer, HMAS *Warramunga*.[120] The Aussie tin can left her on the 14th, after which *Portland* sailed alone, bound for the naval shipyard at Mare Island again, where permanent repairs and significant new alterations would be made to her.[121] The temporary repairs accomplished in Sydney must have been good because she routinely made 17 to 18 knots on the voyage, at least once cranking turns for 20.5 knots.[122] She stopped briefly for fuel in Pago Pago, but went directly from there to San Francisco, without stopping at Pearl Harbor.[123]

Two memorable incidents marked her approach to Pago Pago, however. The first came just as she received a warning from the harbor authorities that Japanese submarines were reported nearby. A lookout reported a torpedo wake passing under her stern. From that moment on, *Portland* zigzagged. This was the ninth torpedo known to have been fired at the ship: three at Santa Cruz that hit but did not detonate, one at Guadalcanal that killed many and did severe damage, four at Tulagi by American PTs that fortunately resulted in no hits, and this one at Samoa.[124] There would be at least two more.

The second event occurred the same day, when the cruiser came in sight of a group of ships leaving Pago Pago that included battleship USS *Mississippi. Portland*'s after main battery's guns were no longer loaded but were still trained out and elevated, and the battleship became alerted and challenged what appeared to be a hostile presentation. Sweet Pea explained the problem by a hasty flashing-light message, which *Mississippi* acknowledged, and went her way wishing the cruiser good luck.[125]

Although no liberty was granted in Samoa, Executive Officer Turk Wirth was able to produce a treat for the crew. Wirth was not liked by many of the sailors, as the XO had decided that no man would rate liberty in Sydney until he had cleaned "a square yard of barnacles" off the ship's hull, then exposed in the dry dock. Wirth claimed it was an old Navy tradition, but the crew thought it was simply a mean requirement by an officious martinet.[126] In the weeks to come, they would think him even less generous in his leave policy at Mare Island.

Before the war, Wirth had been assigned to the naval station at Pago Pago, and now he used contacts he had made in those days to create an onboard event that the crew loved. A native chief whom Wirth knew created a Polynesian show by his entire tribe, which he brought aboard. One sailor remembered that it featured "the young men performing knife and fire dances and the young maidens performing exotic dances which only uninhibited natives can do.[127] What the man meant by uninhibited was that the Samoan women danced bare-breasted. It probably does not need to be said that these dancers were "received with unmitigated joy by the crew," according to one of the officers.[128]

## MARE ISLAND

At Mare Island in March, April, and May of 1943, *Portland* received both full-scale repairs to her combat damage and a major overhaul and refitting of several of her weapons systems.[129] This visit bizarrely fulfilled the prediction made by Leslie Williams in Turret Two on the night of November 13. When the torpedo hit *Portland,* his immediate response was, "That will be State-side if we last that long."[130] Williams could not have imagined what it would take to make the ship "last that long," but Sweet Pea's crew accomplished the emergency repairs, the Sydney shipyard the temporary ones, and *Portland* pulled into the Mare Island Shipyard on March 3, 1943, as he had predicted almost four months earlier.[131]

She was greeted at the mouth of the inlet that led to the shipyard by one of the humblest of the Navy's vessels, a netminder. As the little craft swung open the anti-submarine net, a small number of men not actually at work manned the rail and saluted the cruiser sliding by. One of Sweet Pea's officers was still moved years later when he wrote that although he realized it was "probably" standard procedure, "to us it was our greeting on returning home after what had been a long and arduous cruise. We appreciated it and of course sounded 'Attention to Starboard,' the normal procedure when naval vessels passed each other."[132]

The work in the yard was extensive. Whereas a makeshift rebuilding of the stern section had been accomplished in Sydney, at Mare Island the repairs were made permanent. Turret Three, of course, was removed, rebuilt, and restored. A surface-search radar system was installed. The new system was the SC-1, an improvement on the old SC, which was designed as an air-search system, although it was often used for surface search. The new radar had been developed as an air-search device, too, but was much better at surface search than its predecessor.[133] Certainly not the least important innovation was that the shipyard ripped out the 1.1-inch guns, which in their one year of service had created about as many problems for the crew as casualties for the Japanese. In their place the immeasurably better 40mm Oerlikon guns were installed.[134]

Another change that occurred at Mare Island was in the

Commanding Officer. After a year of superlative command, Laurence T. DuBose was relieved as CO of *Portland* by Captain Arthur David Burhans on May 23, 1943. DuBose left as an admiral to become commander of the cruiser division that Sweet Pea would later serve in. That same month, Executive Officer Wirth and Gunnery Officer Shanklin also left the ship for other assignments.[135]

While *Portland* was at Mare Island, her crew moved into a converted ferry, *Calistoga,* that now served as a dormitory.[136] This was necessary for two reasons. First, several of the ship's own living spaces were so badly damaged that many of the crew had no place suitable to live. Second, the noise and general clutter created by the workers would have made living on board maddeningly difficult.[137]

The command granted a generous liberty schedule, as well. Many of the sailors got to know Vallejo, the nearby California town, pretty well. Heber Holbrook, who visited the town when in the crew of USS *San Francisco,* described Vallejo's Georgia Street as "four blocks of taverns [with] an abundance of pretty girls, the best of country music, [and] friendly bartenders whose motto was 'if he's old enough to wear his country's uniform he's old enough to drink a beer.'"[138]

But some *Portland* sailors remembered it later as no better than an archetypal fleet landing. One man said Vallejo was "all honky-tonk, all whores, and no one ever asked for an ID card. You could have $1000 in your pocket and when you got to the top of the hill, you'd be borrowing money."[139]

Early in the stay at Mare Island, before he left the ship, Executive Officer Turk Wirth, now sporting his Silver Star for the Guadalcanal action, brought on himself the anger of much of the crew. He divided the ship's company into four sections and awarded every enlisted man seventeen days of leave. The sailors were immediately incensed, because they knew that *Minneapolis,* in the yard at the same time, gave her crew thirty days leave.[140] For Sweet Pea's men headed to the East Coast, travel would take four of those days, and travel back four more, so the sailor might get a week and a half at home. Many of them were lastingly embittered at Wirth for his policy.[141]

While DuBose did not step in to make the leave policy more generous, he did intervene on another occasion in a way that endeared him to many of the sailors. His yeoman was instructed to arrange travel for the leave-takers who were going to Chicago or farther east. But the sailor returned from the station to tell the Captain that he could not buy tickets because the train was classified as "reserved-seat-only," and *Portland*'s sailors did not have reservations. DuBose complained immediately to the commandant of the Fourteenth Naval District. That officer called back only a couple of hours later to say that he had told the president of the railroad that either *Portland*'s crew got the tickets or the train would not be allowed to depart. The admiral had such power during wartime.[142]

DuBose charmed two other men, Robert McDannold and Marshall Roberts, who returned late from leave in Arizona. They had hitchhiked to Phoenix and happily noticed that they arrived before the bus did. Confidently, they hitchhiked back, but had much worse luck and stepped onto *Portland*'s quarterdeck about four hours late. At the Captain's Mast where they had to answer charges of being AOL, DuBose asked why they were late. McDannold and Roberts replied, "Sir, we got hung up in San Luis Obispo, and couldn't get out of there." DuBose howled in laughter, saying, "I've been hung up in San Luis Obispo a couple of times myself," and dismissed the case! Captains had such power, in peace or war.[143]

As many as one hundred men in the crew took advantage of the time Stateside to get married.[144] The Navy, too, took advantage of *Portland*'s return to the United States and her amazing combat experience by transferring about a third of her crew to other ships, most of them newly built.[145] These veterans were replaced in the main by freshly minted sailors who came in large batches from boot camp or some slightly saltier men from Navy schools in which they had learned one trade or another over a few months after basic training. The conditions they faced on their arrival were horrible, as Frank Stinson recalled, "[l]ines, hoses, cables, tools and all sorts of material needed for repair work. That was not the kind of Navy life that I had expected to find but I was soon told what was being done and what to do when I was put on my first Working Party."[146]

One group that arrived from the San Diego basic training center lined up on a walkway between *Portland* and another cruiser. As these sailors wondered what would happen to them, a petty officer began to walk down the line giving each successive man a flip to the right or a flip to the left. When two rows were formed, he sent one bunch to *Portland* and the other to the ship across the way. It might not have been a rational system, but the men who went to *Portland* were always happy they had been sent that way. The other cruiser was ill-fated *Indianapolis*.[147]

9

# CENTRAL PACIFIC

The campaign across the Central Pacific in 1943, 1944, and 1945 followed almost exactly what War Plan Orange had called for. Warfare in the Solomons, south of the equator and not anticipated in the war plan, had become the first step in the Allied counteroffensive against Japan. But the going there was so slow and the waters so constricted that Admiral Nimitz and his colleagues in the Pacific Fleet wanted to get the Navy out on the open seas of the great Pacific basin. All senior American commanders had played war games at the Naval War College involving the expected war against Japan. Those exercises had familiarized them with the islands of the Cental Pacific so well that at the end of the war Nimitz exaggerated very little in saying "nothing that happened in the Pacific War was strange or unexpected."[1]

In early 1944, Papua and the entire Solomons chain were finally either in American hands or had been neutralized and bypassed. *Portland* was in on none of these campaigns while she underwent repairs from November 1942 through May 1943. Her absence meant she missed little of real importance, though, because MacArthur and Halsey finally decided to bypass Rabaul, which had been the target of all this action. In a strategic sense, then, all of the intense and bloody work in the western Solomons and eastern New Guinea after Guadalcanal amounted to little more than mopping up.

At Pearl Harbor, on the other hand, Admiral Nimitz and his commanders in the Central Pacific theater were beginning to receive important new reinforcements, mainly in the form of the large *Essex*-class and smaller *Independence*-class fast carriers. They wanted to use these new flattops to redeem at long last the debacle of December 7. The obvious strategy to follow was War Plan Orange, which all of them knew well: recapture the Gilberts, use them as bases to capture the Marshalls, use them as bases to go even farther west, always looking for the decisive major fleet engagement against the Imperial Japanese Navy.

Over the next year, as the great fleet and its land and air forces drove into the heart of the Japanese Empire, Sweet Pea would assist in the recapture of the Aleutians and the invasions of the Gilberts in 1943 and the Marshalls in early 1944. She would sail south again in the spring of 1944 to support MacArthur, when he would finally tear himself away from the tedious slogging in Papua and take his most important leapfrog in the New Guinea campaign. She would miss the Marianas operations in the summer of 1944 while being refitted again in California, but she would be in on the Peleliu invasion in the fall, all the major assaults in the Philippines, and the Okinawa bloodbath in the spring of 1945.

When she left Mare Island in 1943, *Portland* was assigned to refresher training in the waters around San Diego. This program gave her new sailors a chance to be integrated with the veterans, and her new and old material systems a trial under simulated combat conditions.[2] Some in the crew had received specialized individual training on the new systems, and in the sessions off San Diego they had the opportunity to see how the ship's equipment worked in practice.[3]

The veterans, of course, knew the kinds of deprivations they would have to survive in the months and maybe years to come. Some of them therefore took care to make *special* preparations. In San Diego, for example, a few radarmen were sent ashore to get some spare cathode ray tubes for the new radar repeaters. The tubes came in large and bulky containers, and were so fragile they had to be braced in such a way that there was empty space around them. The radarmen used that extra space to smuggle aboard twenty-eight fifths of scotch by carefully taping a bottle into each of the four corners of the seven bulky containers. When the working party arrived at the quarterdeck with its cargo, the Officer of the Deck moved to inspect the cartons. The petty officer in charge quickly diverted the lieutenant by advising him that there was a great danger of imploding the tubes because of the way they were constructed. The officer cautiously stepped back and let the men, their tubes, and their *booze* go.[4]

The training and smuggling completed, *Portland* went back to sea for further combat action. She looked very different now. The 1943 changes were more than the cosmetic ones John Reimer had noted when she came into Pearl Harbor after the raid in December 1941. Aloft there were now innumerable radar and radio antennas, all cluttering what had once been clean lines above the superstructure. The after mast, once mounted on the after deck house near Turret Three, had been moved about sixty-five feet forward so that it now hovered over the hangars. It lent a symmetry to the ship: the forward mast still stood just forward of the well deck, while the after mast was now just aft of it. The forward stack had been cut down about twenty feet in height and now was only a few feet taller than its after mate. The change gave the ship a decidedly attractive rake.[5]

*Portland* was still a *gun*ship, only more so. The barrels of many more anti-aircraft batteries poked out here and there, as did the snouts of the various types of directors that aimed them. Gun platforms were everywhere. Four single 20mm guns were posted in the bow. The two forward triple 8-inch turrets covered most of the forecastle. Tucked in under the wings of the bridge on each side lay a 40mm quad and a 20mm single mount. On a "flying platform" just aft of the stacks, eight single 20mm guns were sprinkled in among two quadruple 40mm mounts, two twin 40mm mounts, and four 5-inch dual-purpose guns. The huge 8-inch guns of Turret Three extended well over the fantail, and two twin 40mm mounts guarded the sternpost. Even more than ever before, *Portland* looked as if she would do serious damage to any enemy that came her way.[6]

## THE ALEUTIAN CAMPAIGN

Up the coast a hundred miles this tiger of a warship went to Long Beach to pick up cold-weather gear and clothing for the crew. For a ship that had been in the South Pacific most of the war so far, this seemed a strange requisition. But it made sense when Sweet Pea joined a task force built around battleship *Tennessee* and headed for Adak in the Aleutian Islands.[7] The Japanese had captured two of the outlying Aleutians during the Midway operation a year earlier, and the United States decided to drive them out of the only North American soil they occupied during the entire war.

Just as the weather deteriorated on the way to the Gulf of Alaska, one of the sailors broke down with appendicitis. Dr. Joers, the Senior Medical Officer, had recently been promoted to commander and now faced his second emergency appendectomy under less-than-ideal conditions. This time, though, the task force commander selected a course so that the ship rode as smoothly as possible. Captain Burhans laughed that the doctor seemed to have more influence over the admiral than he did.[8]

The Battle of the Komandorski Islands in March 1943 probably convinced the Japanese that they could not hold the Aleutians.[9] It was fought while *Portland* was still in the yard at Mare Island, so she did not qualify for a battle star for the campaign, another slight than rankled her veterans after the war.[10] They pointed out that even though she arrived late *Portland* did plenty of fighting in the Aleutians campaign. She bombarded Japanese-held Kiska on July 26, 1943, and in mid-August carried out gunfire missions in support of reconnaissance landings on the same island.[11] This latter shooting was in preparation for a major landing on Kiska, although the Americans discovered when they landed that the Japanese had successfully evacuated the island earlier.

Because of the conditions in the Aleutians, it is hard to imagine why either side thought a war could be fought there. On a map, an American might say the islands seem to point right at Japan, and a Japanese would think they aim at North America. Raw geography, then, might suggest that these islands would provide a good route for an attack in one direction or the other. But the climate in that part of the world is so awful that better thinking should have concluded that military forces could not be sustained in the area.

The main feature of Aleutian weather was the fog; it blanketed everything. Nearly every day that *Portland* was in Alaskan waters the logs referred to the fog and to commanders who slowed their entire formations in times of reduced visibility.[12] Refueling at sea was treacherously dangerous, since men on *Portland*'s bridge usually could see the oiler only about the time the cruiser's prow came alongside her stern.[13] At least once, a boat crew lost its way in heavy fog and rain on short-distance errands around a harbor.[14] On another occasion, when Teofilo Ramos was having a cigarette on the *Portland*'s quarterdeck just before going on watch, he was horrified to find another large ship come out of the fog and head right for him and Sweet Pea's newly repaired stern. The weather was so bad that men on one ship could rarely see anything except their own ship. Ramos reported that the other vessel, a "heavy cruiser . . . would have cut us in half if the man at the wheel had not thrown his weight into the wheel" to avoid collision.[15]

The embarrassingly comical "Battle of the Kiska Pips" in late July 1943 was mainly caused by the strange Aleutian climate.[16] The new search radar that Mare Island had installed in *Portland* was so sensitive and so *different* that in the bitterly cold waters of the north Pacific her operators saw things on the scopes they had never seen before. Some of *Portland*'s veterans remembered that if you got a radar target at Guadalcanal and did not immediately fire on it, you were likely to get smashed when the enemy lookouts picked you up in their glasses.[17] These factors both had a bearing on what happened that night.

About midnight on July 26, 1943, battleship *Mississippi* reported radar contacts about fifteen miles distant to the northeast, and only minutes later *Portland* confirmed the contacts and lit off all eight boilers to get ready for combat. At 0113 Admiral R.C. Giffin ordered his two battlewagons and five cruisers to "commence fire," and for the next twenty-seven minutes Sweet Pea and the six other ships poured hundreds of rounds on the "enemy force." The contacts disappeared at 0140, so Giffin ordered "cease fire." But a few minutes later *Portland* alone detected new radar targets roughly in the same area. The new blips tracked at high speed, closing range. More heavy gunfire ensued. *Portland* got new contacts a few minutes after that, and fired illumination rounds to try to make the enemy visible. An air attack was picked up on Sweet Pea's radar at 0213 and reported closing fast, but nothing materialized. At 0455, yet another surface contact was found, roughly in the same area, but this one tracked erratically and was not evaluated as an enemy.[18]

In fact, there were no ships or planes out there, enemy or otherwise. Every contact was false, and all the shells splashed into an empty sea.[19] One salvo from *Portland*'s main battery was fired because she had to "unload through the muzzle." Her crew had so quickly reloaded the main battery that her guns were still loaded when the cease fire reached her. The safest thing was just to fire them.[20] But the rest was an embarrassing 276 rounds from her main 8-inch battery. More than half of all the 8-inch shells expended that night by all the cruisers in the force, plus seventy-nine 5-inch illumination rounds to see an enemy that showed up clearly on radar but not in the human eye, came from *Portland,* and all were fired at nothing.[21]

In Sweet Pea's radar room, the men on watch had grown increasingly suspicious during all the shooting. The contacts looked fuzzy on the new scopes, not the solid echoes that the radarmen expected. They asked the AA director crews to see what the contacts looked like on the fire-control radar, and they looked strange there, too. A report to that effect was made to the bridge with the suggestion that the ship might be firing at "ionized clouds," and the nonsense began to halt.[22]

In Pearl Harbor after the campaign was over, sailors from the other ships began calling *Portland* men the "radar heroes," as if the only enemy they fought were those they imagined on their radar screens.[23] Captain Burhans wrote quite guardedly—and *sheepishly,* one might think from its tone—in a confidential letter to Nimitz to explain the anomaly. Although the War Diary gives slightly later times, Burhans reported that *Portland* had radar contacts as early as 2350, only two minutes after *Mississippi* reported hers in the same place. He said the contacts tracked reasonably and consistently, so that it was "hard to understand why" they were false.[24] Although dated the same as the official action report, and virtually identical to it, this letter would reach Nimitz's headquarters sooner than a report that traveled up the chain of command. It demonstrated Burhans's own nervousness about his ship's performance that night.

*Portland*'s bridge finally became suspicious when the illumination rounds revealed nothing where the targets should have been. Later, in the fog of the Alaskan midnight sun, Burhans was more skeptical of targets that appeared authentic at first but soon thereafter tracked erratically. He pointed out in both his official report and the letter to Nimitz that all the newly installed equipment had worked well, and that all the personnel, including men who had joined the crew recently, performed their duties efficiently. Even the firing, he said, "was conducted without confusion on what appeared to be a very good radar target."[25]

Captain Burhans thought this laughable event might best be considered a continuation of the ship's refresher training when he said that "the advantages of opening fire first on radar targets, which may later prove to be doubtful, outweigh the disadvantages." The Captain thought that, armed with such experiences, radar personnel would soon gain the skill to be to be able to distinguish false from true echoes.[26] This was the same spin *Portland*'s Executive Officer gave the Kiska Pips on the eve of an invasion a few months into the future, saying that "Our time spent in the Aleutians was good training which we will now put into use."[27] In their remarks, both officers assigned no blame to the climate, but of course everything else flowed from how dreadful the weather was.

During the war, some *Portland* sailors thought that the pips at Kiska were actually troop-carrying submarines to evacuate Japanese troops from the island.[28] We now know, though, that no submarines were used. One *Portland* sailor thought that the blips were Japanese surface ships, and that Sweet Pea's quick radar pickup and voluminous firing gave them a hot welcome that actually delayed the evacuation a day or two.[29] Another veteran wrote that the targets were probably the tops of mountains forty miles away.[30] These ideas are all products of the wishful thinking of men for whom the truth is embarrassing. It was a low point in the career of this great ship and her crew.

The "Kiska Pips" may have been the final element that convinced American commanders that warfare in the Aleutians was impossible. Warfare there was never resumed. The Japanese were gone, and there was no reasonable hope for offensive warfare from that region, either. The weather was simply too terrible for combat. Just going from place to place on a ship in such turbulent conditions was dangerous. Milton Poulos, who served as a messenger for the bridge watches, recalled later that carrying a pot of coffee and some cups topside in the horrible Aleutian weather was "a challenge," but he and other men in similar situations devised a system. Poulos would wait until the ship rolled one way, run up a slippery ladder as far as he could go, and then wait until the next roll before scrambling further, scurrying across wet decks and climbing other ladders, and so on until he reached the bridge. He was a happy man when his "black and blue shins finally got a break" because he was assigned to the radar shack during the Aleutian operation.[31]

On September 12, the task group was smashed by a huge Pacific storm.[32] This gale compared nastily to the one endured by the "Rolling P" in 1937 that led to Captain Dutton's death. True to her old nickname, on this new occasion *Portland* rolled some forty-seven degrees. One of the whaleboats swung so far out on its davit that it broke in two when hit by a huge wave. The crew welded I-beams to the inside of the hangar doors to prevent their being smashed open by the waves. And Sweet Pea was not alone in having a tough time. When neighboring *San Francisco* lifted out of the waves one time, *Portland*'s crew could see her bottom! The turrets on both ships were buried in the ocean when they plowed back into the sea.[33]

*Portland* had been in other storms, and would run yet another one with fatal results in 1945. But this time she suffered no significant damage. When the Aleutians campaign finished, Sweet Pea and the other ships were ordered back to Pearl Harbor.[34] Arriving in Hawaii in late September 1943 she was immediately put back to work, but never again in that ugly Aleutian climate.

## THE GILBERTS

The flexibility of U.S. Navy cruisers was demonstrated throughout the war. Prewar planners anticipated that they would serve from time to time as commerce raiders, defenders of smaller friendly craft, or scouts for the battleships.[35] When the battleships were nearly wiped out at Pearl Harbor, they surprisingly became the main defenders of the carriers. During the war they proved to be excellent in shore bombardment. And, finally, they were both fast enough and powerful enough to be sent on individual missions.

In an entirely different fashion, but again demonstrating her flexibility, when *Portland* arrived at Pearl in September 1943 she was immediately sent to San Francisco to pick up a thousand Seabees and bring them back to Hawaii.[36] This was not the last time she would serve as a passenger ship. Years later, one of the officers thought the entire reason for sending her to California on this occasion was to give the crew, at sea for almost four months, some Stateside liberty.[37] He was speaking facetiously because, to make room for the Seabees, about half of the *Portland* crew had been debarked in Pearl Harbor.[38] Those men had a lot of time off. Waikiki, the bars and brothels on Hotel Street, and dances at the USO and at the YMCA were attractions many of the sailors took advantage of.[39] Some others were sent to special schools in Hawaii for additional training.[40] Bill Reehl was hosted by a large family that lived out of town, a circumstance that may have been infrequent but was certainly pleasant.[41]

Nevertheless, the men still on board felt that they were home again as they passed under the Golden Gate Bridge.[42] The ship was in port long enough for all hands to get two days off the ship.[43] Through the USO, on this visit Joe Arbour also met a civilian family. Throughout the war, these folks invited into their homes about eight hundred men in uniform. Unlike Reehl, whose home visit was a one-time thing, Joe liked his family so much that he stayed in touch after the war.[44]

Sweet Pea returned to Pearl Harbor to deliver the Seabees, who were going to build the airfields once the Marines captured the Gilberts. She picked up her own men and began training herself for the invasion of Tarawa in that island chain.[45] In late October 1943, the Pacific Fleet that *Portland* rejoined, after being away almost exactly a year for repairs and the Aleutian venture, was far different from when she was part of its backbone. In the old days, one or two carriers had to be husbanded, but now about seventeen new flattops of three different types, carrying nine hundred aircraft, swept through the Central Pacific. Back then, one or two battleships and a handful of cruisers provided the big guns, but now a dozen battleships and a dozen cruisers, many of them brand new and all bristling with armament, sped along with the flattops. This formidable armada would escort and support transports carrying more than thirty-five thousand troops to the invasion of the Gilberts.[46] As various units joined the fleet from time to time on the way to the staging area at Efate in the New Hebrides, Sweet Pea's crew was impressed with how the Pacific Fleet had grown.[47] A year earlier, the Americans had been on the strategic defensive, but the time had now come for the U.S. Navy to go over to the attack.

Despite all this vast power, the Tarawa assault in November 1943 was mired in mistakes of preparation, most of which are well known.[48] *Portland* herself had but a few days to get ready. The operations order was revealed to Captain Burhans and his officers only when the ship reached Efate on November 7.[49] Sweet Pea was more familiar than the other ships with Tarawa, since she had been there only thirteen months earlier on her one-ship raid on the Japanese outpost. Early in the morning of November 20, 1943, she began to shell the island, this time in company with what appeared to be countless other warships. Her assignment was scheduled fire in the bombardment of Betio, the island in the atoll where the landings would be.[50] Turret Three's target, for example, was the string of long catwalks that ran out to privies hanging over the water, so Turret Officer Lieutenant Pringer earned the nickname "Pringer the Privy Paster."[51] But Sweet Pea and the other ships fired for only a few hours, and the shooting was ineffective. One important lesson drawn by the high command after the campaign was that naval gunfire should not be designed to saturate the target area, but that "sustained, deliberate, aimed fire" against specific targets was needed to help the Marines take a fortified beach.[52]

The ship was close enough to Betio that Japanese shore batteries returned her fire and shells splashed all around her, although none hit.[53] The ship was, nevertheless, damaged while she was firing. When a destroyer made sonar contact with a submarine near *Portland*'s place in line, the tin can depth-charged her submerged target so close to the cruiser that the concussion loosened some of Sweet Pea's rivets, creating an oil leak that formed a slick behind her. No evidence was ever found that the sub had been sunk, and the firing missions continued. During the day, Sweet Pea fired high-explosive ammunition in her support of the troops ashore, but at night she rearmed with armor-piercing ammunition in case the Japanese fleet should intervene.[54]

It did not, but after a day or two of watching the high-explosive ammunition do little damage to the Japanese fortifications and little good for the troops ashore, someone in *Portland* whose identity is lost to history decided that armor-piercing shells might be better. Sweet Pea fired a few such rounds and got good results, and it was not long before the rest of the fleet began to do the same. The AP ammunition penetrated the Japanese blockhouses and pillboxes, causing great damage and casualties, and the gunners in *Portland* were gratified.[55] This kind of firing, novel at the time, helped the high command learn its lesson about the superiority of deliberate and aimed fire.

The Marines ashore on Tarawa suffered enormously during the three days of fighting. Things got so bad that *Portland*'s sailors circulated a petition around the ship. The men who signed it volunteered to go ashore to help the Marines on the island. Captain Burhans rejected this bad idea, but let the petitioners off lightly by saying he could not spare any of the ship's company.[56]

*Portland*'s crew took great satisfaction from the ship's work at Tarawa. A year earlier she had poked her nose into the atoll, then scurried away because the U.S. Navy could only harass in those days. Now the ocean swarmed with American ships and the sky with American planes and the land with American troops, and the men on Sweet Pea liked that a lot better.[57]

## THE MARSHALLS

After much death and destruction, the Gilberts were finally secured. Sweet Pea's Seabees and others turned these atolls into airbases from which the Central Pacific command gathered information about, and launched attacks against, the Marshall Islands, the next step on the march toward Tokyo. In early December 1943, *Portland* accompanied a carrier task force on a raid to collect intelligence and do some damage to the enemy's defenses in the Marshalls. During this mission, on December 4 the new *Lexington* came under heavy air attack and was torpedoed. Although the damage to the flattop was not extensive, Burhans seemed defensive and even petulant in reporting that the enemy planes never came within range of Sweet Pea, so she fired not a single round in *Lexington*'s defense. Burhans wrote in his own defense that the arc of train for his 5-inch guns was limited, and that with only two AA directors the ship could not track more than two aerial targets at a time. He also complained that while radar for the 40mm mounts had been authorized, the system had not yet reached *Portland.* He quickly anticipated problems even with the 40mm radar whose absence he was then lamenting. He argued that the 40mm tracer rounds would illuminate the ship if Sweet Pea began to rely on them once they were radar-controlled.[58]

That Sweet Pea's skipper fretted about his ship's performance is indicated as well by the inclusion in his Combat Action Report of lengthy subordinate officer statements. One by the Combat Information Center Officer, a mere lieutenant, included eight detailed comments. Another was a two-page report by the sky control officer, a lieutenant commander in charge of anti-aircraft actions.[59] Commanding Officers do not ordinarily use what their subordinates say as evidence to support their own cases. These now seem to have been harbingers of what lay ahead for Burhans.

Meanwhile, though, *Portland* returned to Pearl Harbor for Christmas 1943.[60] In Hawaii, she went into dry dock to have her bottom scraped. There it was discovered that she had yet another rudder problem. This time the bearings had become badly worn and the rudder itself was about to fall off. A couple of the propellers were cracked, too. There was talk that the ship might have to return to the United States yet again, even to the East Coast, for repairs. But the Pearl Harbor shipyard's workers were known throughout the war for their hectic work. They fixed the damage well enough that Sweet Pea was able to participate in the invasion of the Marshalls.[61]

The rudder repairs took so long, however, that *Portland* did not make the main assault on Kwajalein in late January 1944. Instead, she was assigned to help with the assault on Darrit Island in the Majuro Atoll, a secondary goal of the Marshalls campaign. On January 23, 1944, she sailed with Task Groups 51.1 and 51.2 under Rear Admiral Harry W. Hill. *Portland* was the only heavy cruiser and the biggest ship in what was nevertheless a powerful assault force. TG 51.1 comprised seven transports and two cargo ships plus seven destroyers, while TG 51.2 included Sweet Pea, two small carriers, two transports, and a minesweeper.[62] The ships reached Majuro on January 30, and *Portland* conducted about a half-hour of shelling until the troops waded ashore and discovered that there were no Japanese there.[63]

There was one moment of excitement, however. On February 2, as *Portland* and destroyer *Kidd* were patrolling near Majuro, they each picked up a radar contact at eighteen miles. Everyone believed that the Japanese would send their fleet to defend their bases in the Marshalls, and the contact might be the skirmish line of the Combined Fleet. But seaplane tender *Casco* was also expected that day to service some of Sweet Pea's aircraft. As the radarmen plotted the contact, it became clear that it was an American ship. *Portland*'s radarmen identified the zigzag pattern, and yet the stranger showed no identification lights and did not respond to voice-radio queries. Guadalcanal had taught *Portland* that opening fire first on unidentified radar targets can outweigh the disadvantages, and she was ready to shoot. But the Aleutian fiasco had also taught the Captain and crew some restraint. In this case off Majuro, both the cruiser and the destroyer held their fire, and sure enough *Casco* hove into view.[64] A "friendly fire" disaster was averted by *Portland*'s cool appraisal, although there were long and tense minutes before the happy ending.

The cruiser rejoined the main fleet on February 8 at Eniwetok Atoll and participated in the shelling there, prior to the landings on February 19. *Portland*'s primary targets in this operation were on Parry Island, next to the landing beaches and connected to them by the reef.[65] She was close enough to the assault force that her crew listened on the radio as Marines ashore described the enemy they were facing.[66] The Pacific

*Above*, USS *Portland* at sea, 25 January 1933 (National Archives). *Below*, View looking aft from foredeck while at sea in 1944 (U.S. Naval Historical Center photograph).

*Above*, USS *Portland* under way at sea, 23 August 1935 (Naval Historical Center Collection).

*Right*, USS *Portland* in the Cockatoo Drydock, Sydney, New South Wales, Australia, late 1942 (U.S. Naval Historical Center photograph).

*Below*, USS *Portland*, in camouflage, off the Mare Island Navy Yard, California, 30 July 1944 (National Archives).

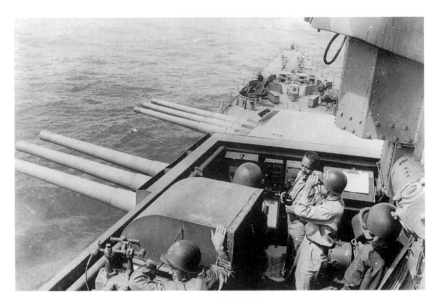

*Above*, Scene on the open bridge during the bombardment of Leyte, October 1944. Officer without helmet is ship's Commanding Officer, Captain Thomas G.W. Settle (U.S. Naval Historical Center photograph). *Below*, USS *Portland* (at right) transfers USS *Yorktown* survivors to USS *Fulton* on 7 June 1942, following the Battle of Midway. *Fulton* transported the men to Pearl Harbor (National Archives).

*Right*, *Life* (November 5, 1945), cover photo of S1c Matthews, 40mm gunner in Fifth Division, USS *Portland* (Courtesy William Partridge).

*Left*, They were young once . . . Willie Partidge in 1945 (Courtesy William Partridge).

*Above*, Horrified *Portland* crew looks on as a dead Marine is brought aboard from Peleliu in September 1944 (Courtesy William Partridge). *Below*, Coal bags were used to speed the transfer of *Yorktown*'s survivors to *Fulton* in June 1942 (National Archives).

*Right*, Shell hit, starboard hangar, Tulagi, November 1942 (From *A History of United States Ships Named* Portland).

*Below*, OS2U "Kingfisher" being hoisted aboard *Portland* in 1944. This is a damaged aircraft from USS *Pennsylvania* that was saved by Sweet Pea (National Archives).

*Above*, General Magikura, Admiral Hara, and the rest of the Japanese party meet *Portland*'s Officer of the Deck as they come aboard to surrender at Truk. *Below*, The signing table on the quarter-deck where the official signing of the surrender terms took place (Both from *A History of United States Ships Named* Portland).

*Above*, The ships officers and men, at Cuckatoo Island in Sydney, December 1942 (From Joe Stables, *We Remember*).

*Left*, USS *Portland* Memorial, Ft. Allen Park, Portland, Maine (Courtesy Joe Stables).

Fleet had grown so large by this time that, like the other cruisers and battleships, Sweet Pea was assigned to a specific fire support area, Number Seven in her case. Her own destroyer, USS *Hoel,* screened her against submarines, while she bombarded targets ashore. Together the two ships comprised Fire Support Group Three, or TU 51.17.3, of which Burhans was the Commander.[67]

The shelling was supposed to be "scheduled for point targets," according to the lessons learned at Tarawa. It quickly degenerated, though, "into a somewhat general area bombardment of the entire island" because of the intensive jungle growth on Parry. The brush was so thick that aerial spotting was impossible. But several times before, *Portland* had demonstrated the ingenuity to solve problems. This time, her gunners tried firing the 40mm anti-aircraft guns into a given area to clear the jungle away and make the targets visible. The medium-sized anti-aircraft batteries, fired sparingly but accurately, trimmed coconut groves that had impeded the sight-lines of the spotters for the 8-inch turrets.[68] About two thousand rounds were used this way, at four rounds per salvo, so the 40mm mounts were kept busy with the chore.[69]

The rest of the crew, however, was mainly bored at Eniwetok, now that Japanese opposition had dwindled to only what enemy troops ashore could throw up. Officers and men alike whiled away the time by reading magazines and detective stories and playing cards. One interesting diversion in the Communications Division was to tune in the radio frequencies of tanks ashore and listen to the conversations of men in ground combat as they mopped up what was left of the defenders.[70]

Nevertheless, during the Eniwetok campaign, two tragedies occurred to *Portland* that must have interested even the most jaundiced among the crew. The more important was that she lost one of her aircraft and its two aviators. On February 21, 1944, an SOC with pilot Ensign Charles Corbett and Radioman Petty Officer Robert H. Carter was lost while conducting an anti-submarine patrol.[71] At Eniwetok, the planes from the battleships and cruisers were pooled for whatever aviation chores were required. This caused *Portland* some distress in routine air operations. Sweet Pea's aviation personnel found that aircraft crews from other ships were sometimes careless about following prescribed procedures. One day, for example, Sweet Pea had to fish out of the ocean a badly damaged plane from battleship *Pennsylvania.* It had gone in because of pilot error. *Portland*'s combat action report made a formal complaint about the matter after the invasion was completed, and officials up the chain of the command supported the analysis.[72]

As a result of the pooling of aircraft, Corbett and Carter were assigned to an area away from Sweet Pea on the day they were lost. Although they had not reported in to their controller since 0834 that day, the cruiser did not learn about their loss until early in the afternoon. Seaplanes and vessels on patrol inside and outside the lagoon conducted an intensive search covering a wide area for several days.[73] Nothing was found in the first week after the disappearance, although there was a ray of hope on February 23. What was thought to be a pontoon was seen floating on the opposite side of the lagoon, but it turned out to be only a discarded mattress.[74] The men were not forgotten as the islands in the atoll were captured, but almost a year later when the atoll was entirely in the hands of U.S. troops *Portland* concluded that they would never return.[75]

The crew believed the SOC was shot down by Marine guns ashore, perhaps even a ricochet.[76] On at least a couple of occasions during the Eniwetok invasion, Sweet Pea herself had ceased firing on Japanese positions when friendly aircraft were seen strafing the area, so the crew knew that an accident because of friendly fire was possible.[77] The Navy's SOC bore some resemblance to the Japanese plane called "Pete," so it might be that Corbett's aircraft had actually been a target of American forces.[78]

Nearly fifty-seven years later, in late 2000, a story circulated among the ship's veterans that Corbett and Carter had been recovered safely, although their survival had not been revealed to *Portland*.[79] The editors printed the story in the association's newsletter, hoping it was based on some recently discovered information. They then researched the matter thoroughly and found that the tale was fiction. The plane and its two men were lost.[80] When added to the dead at Guadalcanal, the pilot and radioman lost at Eniwetok brought the number of *Portland* men killed in action to twenty.[81]

The second sad event was the demise of Captain Arthur Burhans. He had acted strangely before the Eniwetok operation, but the matter became a crisis during this campaign. About 1600 on February 19, *Portland* was inshore of USS *Colorado*. The battleship asked Sweet Pea to move out of her gun-target-line so that she could perform her firing mission. Deeply fatigued, Burhans refused, so the battlewagon fired its huge guns right over the cruiser. The crew was horrified to find that 14-inch guns were firing over her bow while 5-inch guns were firing over her stern. Burhans got the message and moved out, unfouling the firing range.[82]

Apparently there were other odd incidents, although the details were not recorded.[83] One characteristic that is noticeable about Burhans in the ship's records is his verbosity, perhaps a clue to an anxious personality. His report on the Kiska Pips the previous summer was overwrought.[84] His more recent defense of Sweet Pea's not having fired a single shot when *Lexington* was attacked in December was more of the same. Having his junior officers write detailed explanations for the fact that Sweet Pea had not fired, blaming the equipment, and so on do not portray a man of great confidence.[85]

The report on the *Lexington* incident, by the way, was blasted by the cruiser division commander, none other than Rear Admiral Laurence T. DuBose, Burhans's predecessor as CO of *Portland.*[86] Perhaps Burhans was tightly wound and the stress of commanding a great ship in a great war had increased beyond what he could handle. He may also have been a nitpicker. For example, although Burhans came aboard the ship on May 6, 1943, he did not relieve DuBose until another seventeen days had passed.[87] Even though *Portland* was in a shipyard being repaired and renovated, such a long time to relieve was unprecedented in the ship's history and is hard to fathom. One possibility that suggests itself is that he was a nervous nelly about the various inspections of men and materiel he conducted before taking command at long last.

Whatever was true, on February 19 the situation became stark enough under combat conditions at Eniwetok that the ship's senior officers decided that the Captain was ill. The Executive Officer, Commander Wallace Guitar, went to USS *Solace,* the hospital ship anchored nearby in the lagoon, to report his CO's problems.[88] The Senior Medical Officer there was convinced and by 1000 the next day, February 20, 1944, Captain Burhans was placed on the sick list, "diagnosis D.U. (observation)."[89]

*Portland* continued her duties, conducting a firing mission later in the day while Burhans was laid up.[90] Navy routine provides for the next in line to take command, which in this case meant that Commander Guitar became acting skipper.[91] The following day, February 21, 1944, the same day the ship's aircraft was lost, a board of medical examiners headed by the Medical Officer from battleship *Colorado* was convened aboard *Portland.* It met at 0900 by order of Rear Admiral Hill "to examine and report on the physical condition of Captain A.D. Burhans, USN to continue in the duty to which he is now assigned." Yet again, about 1100, with the board still in session, the ship conducted a gunfire mission under Commander Guitar. The board recommended that Captain Burhans report to *Solace,* and he left the ship at 1723 that afternoon, about twelve minutes before the next firing mission began.[92] When he left, the ship's Officer of the Deck thought the former skipper seemed happier than he had been for some time.[93]

Exactly what went wrong with Arthur Burhans cannot be determined with certainty from the existing sources. One of the sailors thought he went crazy.[94] Another repeated a rumor that he had Bright's disease, an old term for chronic kidney ailments.[95] One of the officers repeated a rumor that Burhans suffered from diabetes and that he died within a year or so.[96] The last part of that story is certainly not true, because Burhans lived until 1960. A note in the Naval Academy *Register of Alumni* says that he was retired on November 1, 1944, only eight and a half months after being removed to *Solace,* but there is no record of the reason. It does seem clear that his retirement was for medical reasons, and he was promoted to rear admiral as he left the service.[97]

While the ship awaited a new Commanding Officer, Guitar did everything well. The ship conducted all of her call-for-fire missions during the continuing invasion.[98] Guitar held Captain's Mast, the Navy's nonjudicial punishment hearing, at least once during the eleven days he was in command. On that occasion Guitar decided five cases; he delivered one warning and one sentence of five days on bread and water, and assigned three cases to deck courts-martial.[99] So he was no pushover, even though a temporary Captain.

## CAPTAIN SETTLE

Commander Guitar's temporary command of *Portland* lasted until March 2, 1944. That day, one of the ship's SOCs flew over to the other end of the Eniwetok lagoon to pick up Captain T.G.W. Settle.[100] The new skipper came aboard by aircraft, which meant he was swinging at the end of the crane that hauled the SOC up out of the water. Some in the crew found that ungainly.[101]

Captain Settle, known as "Tex" to his friends and behind his back by all under his command, was already famous in the Navy. He had been a pioneer in "lighter-than-air" aviation, the Navy's blimps. In the early 1930s he set records for speed, distance, and altitude in a balloon. The altitude he reached was an amazing 61,237 feet, higher than most *powered* aircraft have ever been able to climb.[102] In making such flights he had provided data for the research on life-preserving devices like sealed and pressurized cabins.[103] When only a lieutenant, he was named the Inspector of Naval Aircraft and in that position wrote several pieces on the development of airships. He left office only a year before the crash of USS *Akron,* the blimp that brand-new USS *Portland* had tried to rescue in 1933.[104]

Settle was such a giant in the field of airships that he came to *Portland* directly from his post as Commanding Officer of all the Navy's blimps in the Pacific.[105] His fame came home to Sweet Pea one night when he was CO. The crew's movie was a Wallace Beery feature about a name-dropping chief petty officer. In one scene Beery's character bragged about going up with Lieutenant Commander T.G.W. Settle on his record-breaking balloon flight in 1933. Settle joined the crew in "a good laugh."[106]

In the first twenty-four hours he was aboard, Settle showed that he retained many of the characteristics of the prewar Navy. He was there barely two hours when he made an official call on Commander Cruiser Division Four, the type commander for *Portland.* This was Rear Admiral Theodore Chandler, who had been four years ahead of Settle at the Naval Academy. While they were probably acquaintances from prewar service, it is not likely that the call was a matter of one man visiting his buddy.[107] The next day, March 3, 1944, at 0900 morning quarters, Settle read his orders without much fanfare and went to call on Admiral Hill in his command ship.[108] Like the others, this call was a formality at the heart of the old-style naval etiquette.

What no one could have known that March day when this lighter-than-air aviator came aboard the heavy cruiser was that it marked the beginning of a love affair between the new Captain and his crew that would last long after both Settle and *Portland* were gone. The skipper made a terrific first impression on the crew, partly because of his reputation as a balloon aviator.[109] His demeanor was another asset. Although not a big man, Settle walked with an air of superb self-confidence. The sailors thought of him as "all-Navy," a term no one would be able to define to the satisfaction of all, but high praise, nevertheless.[110]

Settle served as CO almost exactly a year and a half, until July 1945, when he was promoted to rear admiral and left the ship.[111] In that time he endeared himself to the crew by his command presence, his many acts of kindness, and most of all his skill in combat.

Settle could display a hot temper, but it usually had a useful effect. One time he was bothered by Executive Officer Al Joyce's penchant for publishing too many wordy memos about this or that. He called Joyce into his cabin to speak about the matter and told the XO point-blank that too much paperwork was sweeping the ship. Joyce replied, "Aye, aye, Captain," and Settle turned away, thinking the conversation was over. Then Joyce continued, "I'll get a memo out on it right away." The skipper looked back and grimaced, "Goddamit, man, what the hell do you think I'm talking about?"[112] End of longwinded memos.

Settle's action reports were much more concise than those of Arthur Burhans. Describing the April 1944 bombardment of Satawan Island in the Carolines, Settle wrote tersely, "No opposition was encountered. It is believed that expected results were obtained."[113] In fact, his longest report of all may have been one to criticize the reporting system itself. He pointed out in some detail that ships' commanders had to file redundant reports in different formats because of the demands of various higher-ranking levels of the task organization. His argument was that the time spent on filling out and submitting these reports took his officers away from their primary duties of supervising and training the men in their departments. Settle's complaint was couched in reasonable terms. It was not, he said, "a proposal to eliminate reports, but rather one to further simplify them to a point where a minimum of extraneous and duplicatory material is required."[114]

Although his tone was civil, the Captain's feisty side shows through here, also in sharp contrast to the whining that often characterized Burhan's remarks. On the same occasion, he complained pointedly that other ships' commanders misused the voice radio circuits. That report won the resounding approval of the admiral in command of the amphibious force, who was also angered by the poor radio discipline of too many of his Captains.[115]

Settle's personal touches made the officers and men love him. A few days after the ship was attacked by a midget submarine, the still-nervous lookouts reported a periscope and torpedo tracks. After some scary moments, it turned out to be a paravane that had somehow gone adrift. The Captain withered the officer in charge with, "That was no periscope your lookouts reported." In doing so, he omitted the fact that the officer had relayed the report by nervously shouting it himself. But Settle immediately gave the officer a big smile that relieved the younger man.[116] Another time a few officers who hoped to become naval aviators were scheduled to go to a nearby carrier for flight physicals. But the XO, Joyce's successor, was angry that they wanted to transfer from *Portland,* so he gave them some excuse that prevented them from taking any of the ship's boats. Later, Settle asked one of the officers how the physical went, and was told they had not gone because no boat was available. "Hell," the Captain said, "Take the gig," his own personal boat. They did, had their physicals, and loved the man ever after.[117] Yet another time, *Portland* was refueling at sea when the bridge phone talker discovered that the man on the bridge of the oiler at the other end of the line was a friend from his hometown. The two young sailors were having a gabfest when Sweet Pea's Officer of the Deck told the man to keep the line clear, since it was the Captain's personal circuit. When Settle found out about it, he simply said, "Enjoy your visit with your friend, sailor." Years later, the man was still raving about what a good guy Settle was.[118] In fact, "Tex" loomed so large in the minds of most of his men that some believed his name, T.G.W. Settle, was "Thomas George Washington Settle."[119] It was not; he was Thomas Greenhow Williams Settle.[120] The combat skill the crew most remembered Settle for came later: how he helped prevent *Portland* from ever being hit by a kamikaze.

As the new skipper settled in, *Portland* was assigned to Task Group 52.8 as it went on some wide-ranging air strikes in support of the Southwest Pacific theater of Douglas MacArthur. In April 1944, the general decided to leapfrog a huge length of New Guinea by attacking Hollandia, almost six hundred miles farther west than his most advanced units. It was one of the general's greatest strategic ideas in a career of such brilliance. Because the invasion area was beyond the range of most of his land-based air, though, he asked for carrier aviation to support the assault.[121]

As a result, *Portland* was again in a force that included *Enterprise,* with whom she had spent so much time around Guadalcanal in 1942.[122]

As the cruiser joined the group, "Big E" rendered honors to port. Such formalities can be routine, but Sweet Pea's crew thought there was a special touch as the old carrier recognized the arrival of one of the old ships from those days when the Allies were hard-pressed. *Portland*'s men were thrilled when their ship rendered its own return salute.[123] On the way to New Guinea, this carrier's planes attacked Yap in the Carolines, and men topside and below noticed how oppressively hot the weather in that region was.[124] After the landings at Hollandia, *Portland* and some other cruisers and destroyers were detached to bombard the Japanese in the Nomoi Islands and to assist in the raids on Truk, the Japanese island fortress in the Carolines.[125] Sweet Pea would come back to Truk in 1945.

While *Portland* was operating off Hollandia the rudder problems that had bedeviled her from the beginning of the war, and which *Enterprise* would remember from the Battle of Santa Cruz, acted up again. On May 5, 1944, Navy inspectors visited Sweet Pea.[126] They discovered that the repairs accomplished at Pearl Harbor in January had been mere patch-ups. As a result, a high-speed turn was a frightening proposition, as water poured in around loose rivets, and the ship made noises "like a freight crossing a steel trestle."[127] Not surprisingly, then, in early May *Portland* was ordered to return to Mare Island for repairs and overhaul, to the sadness of not one soul on board.[128] They were headed Stateside again!

10

# Mid-1944

On her way to California in May 1944, *Portland* again carried fighting men, this time a group being transferred back to the United States, adding to the number of strangers who were always uncomfortable riding in what they might have recognized as the "Rolling P."[1] During that voyage Stateside, the ship's company was repeatedly warned about the dangers that awaited them at Mare Island, such as the evils in bars and brothels ashore, the temptation to stay away over leave, the need to maintain security about the ship's past and future combat activities, and other matters that today seem less consequential than they were then. It is possible that the officers had learned something when *Portland* last visited there a year earlier. Or perhaps the command had become more fussy. Or maybe it only now appears different from earlier visits to Mare Island because in 1944 a ship's newspaper existed and it chronicled the command's concerns.[2]

The brass worried about little things, to be sure. Sailors were advised not to waste all their money in Pearl Harbor, a midway stopping point, since "our second stop is the important ONE." They were also told they should lay in an extra supply of "small stores"—underwear, socks, handkerchiefs—in preparation for the visit to California or to home on leave. More importantly, they were cautioned not to talk to anyone about where *Portland* had been, what was being done to her in the yard, or where she was going next. Such information, they were sternly told, would likely find its way to the enemy. And in a front-page editorial that must have been written by Captain Settle or his XO, the temptation of going AWOL and the penalties that would result were laid out in excellent fire-and-brimstone style.[3]

The main purpose for the yard visit was to repair once and for all the steering problem. But while she was there the cruiser enjoyed major work on all her systems. All the main battery and AA guns were re-barreled, the firerooms were re-bricked, most of her machinery was overhauled, and minor damages topside were all repaired. The yard installed a new fire-control radar system for the 40mm guns, the same update that Arthur Burhans had been waiting for with mixed feelings.[4] And *Portland* finally got the SG, a radar that was intended only for surface search.[5] Yet again, while the work was being accomplished, the ship became uninhabitable for its company. The officers moved into the Mare Island bachelor officers' quarters, and the enlisted were housed in a nearby barracks.[6]

The crew enjoyed the liberty again, of course, this time on the schedule called "port-and-starboard," when half the ship's company was free to leave while the other half remained on duty.[7] Since the ship was in dry dock and all her machinery removed or shut down, she was in a status called "cold iron," meaning she could go nowhere and fight against no one. Some of the crew wondered, therefore, why so many men had to be kept on duty. The on-duty sections stood sentry watches but little else. The situation did lead to one comical moment. One night some saboteurs got into a machine shop not very close to the ship and blew it up. The Officer of the Deck called away general quarters, to the bewilderment of the crew. They had no battle stations, and since none of the equipment was in working condition they could not have manned any stations they may have been assigned to in the past.[8]

It is sad to report that sabotage was not limited to some strangers. Unhappily for *Portland,* her reputation as a fighting ship—and a fighting *man*'s ship—was sullied at Mare Island by the misbehavior of a few members of her crew. These sailors hoped to extend the ship's stay in California by damaging some of the electrical cables in the after AA director. The damage they did was slight, they were caught, and the ship left the yard exactly on time. The perpetrators, though, were court-martialed and Sweet Pea had to leave a few behind to serve as witnesses when she got under way on August 7, 1944.[9]

While the crime cannot be condoned, it is at least understandable considering that most of these men had been away for the best part of a year. But such culprits were few. For some, the trip to California was a marvelous chance to catch up with loved ones who lived in the Bay Area. A year earlier, when he had first reported to *Portland* at Mare Island, Merle Choate had tried to marry his Oklahoma girlfriend, Jean Worsham. He thought the ship would be there long enough for the wedding, so he phoned Jean and asked her to come to California. She arrived in San Francisco on the very day the ship left for what turned out to be the Aleutians campaign, and they did not see each other.[10] They finally did get married when *Portland* was in San Francisco briefly in October 1943 to pick up the battalion of Seabees.[11]

But the Choates had only two days together before Merle shipped out again for the operations in the Gilberts, Marshalls, and at Hollandia. At long last, in the late spring and early summer of 1944, the couple had some extended time together. One thoroughly unexpected but exciting event occurred in a San Francisco bar where they were sipping a couple of beers. Mrs. Choate earned her spurs that day when a U.S. Marine who was unhappy that the bartender had shut him off began smashing the place. As these things can do, his anger turned into a general melée. Not involved, the Choates pressed themselves against a wall and tried to make their way out. But Merle was attacked by a different Marine, who entered the fight for some uncertain reason and quickly got the sailor-husband in a choke hold. Choate was about to pass out when suddenly the Marine went limp and let him go. Jean had smashed the man on the head with the three-inch heel of her shoe. As her victim lay on the floor bleeding, Merle stared worriedly, thinking he might be dead. The leatherneck began to groan, though, and at that the Choates slipped out and got away unhurt.[12]

After all the yard work, the ship again conducted underway training exercises. The value of such preparation was clear to the officers. One of them admitted that after being away from the bridge for so long, he had actually forgotten the procedure that shifted steering from the pilothouse to the secondary steering station.[13] The ship had labored with steering difficulties since the beginning of the war and had gone to Mare Island this time primarily to have them corrected. And now the bridge officers had to relearn how to operate the steering apparatus. Some of the sailors' skills had lapsed, too, and now there were new men who had to be taught for the first time why things were done as they were. One youngster who was assigned to tap the anchor chain as it was hauled up out of the water was asked what he was listening for. He admitted that he had no idea.[14]

Still, *Portland* got past all this rustiness and inexperience and sailed for Pearl Harbor on August 23. Again she doubled as a passenger ship, carrying another load of about six hundred Seabees. When she got to Hawaii, she dropped these men off, picked up about three hundred soldiers and thirty war correspondents for further transfer, and headed off for the combat zones.[15] This was the trip made by John Brennan, the Australian reporter who had reminded the *Portland* men that some Australians away on combat duty were not happy about the ship's visit to Sydney the year before. One of the other newsmen on the voyage, incidentally, was Joe Rosenthal, who six months later would become famous for his picture of the flag-raising at Iwo Jima.[16] The crew seemed to enjoy having the journalists on board. *Life* magazine artist Paul Sample submitted a few of his drawings about life aboard ship to *Port Beam,* the ship's newspaper. One picture shows two bare-chested sailors, one man in dungaree pants sitting on a bollard, the other in short pants standing next to him but slouching so he can rest his forearm on the sitting man's shoulder. Quite lifelike, the drawing brings these men out of the past, casting them probably exactly the way they looked in 1944.[17]

The newspaper *Port Beam* had an impressive career. It may have been initiated by Captain Settle who, while giving credit to the "organizers of this publication" as if they were other than he, nevertheless wrote in the first issue that the paper could "prove useful in disseminating items of general naval interest as well as news of the activities of individuals and groups in the ship's company. It should serve to familiarize officers and men with the personalities and activities of other divisions of the ship, and thereby help to more completely weld the crew into a single 'team.'"[18]

These would certainly be the goals of a Commanding Officer, and upon reading the text of the newspaper's various issues one can see that the skipper's intentions became the foremost reason for the publication of the newspaper. Radio Officer Vince McNamara, listed as "advisor" to the all-enlisted masthead staff, wrote in his diary for April 20, 1944, that "Today, we rather officially got the ship's newsletter underway."[19] This shows that the paper did not start spontaneously from the grass roots, since no junior officer would have done such a thing without the

Captain's approval. Moreover, there is that expression "rather officially," which most probably was employed precisely. If so, Settle would be the "official" who created the newspaper.

Surviving copies of *Port Beam* ran from the spring of 1944 during the Hollandia operation to about the end of that year as the ship returned to the war for the campaigns in the Philippines.[20] The first issue, printed on April 28, was called *The Pilot,* but it offered a prize to any member of the crew who proposed a better name by the time the next issue went to press. A week later, the May 5 edition was called *Port Beam,* the suggestion of W.C. Barrett, a machinist's mate petty officer from B Division. Barrett won $10 for the idea and the name stuck for the rest of the run.[21]

The editor for most of the life of the paper was Radioman First Class J.G. Stofer, although Bob McDannold took over the job later on.[22] The staff comprised radiomen mostly. They had access to the news that came into the ship and was sometimes relayed in the pages of *Port Beam,* they could all type, and Lieutenant McNamara was their division officer. The paper usually ran about eight pages, and one copy was printed for every fourth man in the crew, so all hands were asked to read it and pass it on.[23] Although Captain Settle originally said that the paper would give to loved ones "within censorship limitations, a clearer idea of a 'man-of-war's-man's' life in the war areas," after *Portland* left Mare Island in the summer of 1944, the crew was warned that the "paper is to be read aboard ship and may not be sent through the mail."[24]

The skipper's interest in *Port Beam* is further shown by the fact that every issue had a lengthy article about some navy regulation or other instruction of command interest. For example, the first issue ran a front-page story about the new rules that covered rotation back to the United States for personnel who had been overseas for more than eighteen months.[25] Later first-page stories covered the offense of wearing unauthorized ribbons, how much leave and liberty the ship would be able to allow during the upcoming Mare Island yard period, the rules on giving interviews to the media, and the patriotic necessity of buying savings bonds and not cashing them in prematurely.[26] These items would be interesting to the sailors who were the paper's reading "public," but disseminating them would be essential for the Commanding Officer.

The paper also published stories of pure human interest to the crew. "The Lucky Bag" was a regular feature of what is sometimes called "three-dot" journalism; it usually included quick notes about personalities.[27] There was once a little piece about Joe Pagel, "the most bemedaled crewman aboard," who as a seaman 2/c won the Navy Cross and the Purple Heart at Guadalcanal, but who was "still a good storekeeper," as if the two characterizations were mutually exclusive.[28] "The Lucky Bag" often made wry comments on happenings about the ship. One time the column pointed out that as soon as the pay list was posted many men would immediately run to the pay office to complain. Once there, they always found out that the storekeepers had it right. "Really, storekeepers do not get a cut," the columnist wagged.[29]

The newspaper also thought its readers wanted to know who was in sick bay. One week two men identified as Carpenter Day and Dick Dransfield, a fire-control technician, were laid up by minor injuries and D.F. Allen of Fifth Division was there recovering from an appendectomy.[30] Reporters wrote about the crew's washroom, said to be so crowded at night that only those willing to crawl in on their hands and knees could gain entry. There was apparently a lot of "rough-housing" during shower time because the editors proposed a new campaign medal for those who used "the scrub shack between 1600 and 2000," and offered a design for the ribbon. It would have "a white toweling background set off by red and blue stripes. . . . The red is for razor rash, and the blue is for the 'black and _____' which you are as you emerge from your nightly shower."[31]

A ribald sense of humor was present in the story about "Skinny Pearson," who fell off the lookout platform onto the bridge, no doubt after falling asleep. Pearson got up, dusted himself off, and calmly walked off in a way even "Ripley's Believe or Not" would have doubted, *Port Beam* reported.[32] When Seaman Steel from Fourth Division fell off the catapult tower, the newspaper unsuccessfully scoured the ship for reports on what happened, probably intending to ridicule him, too.[33] Bill Reehl was featured in one issue when he began to wear an earring and was heard to boast that his mother would think him a "regular pirate" by the time he returned home.[34] But Reehl was not the only one who wore an earring, *Port Beam* told its readers. Chuck Martin had his ear pierced by one of the boatswain's mates and inserted a ring from which he hung a cross not likely to be thought a pirate's insignia.[35] These and other stories were probably best kept on board ship. Imagine what might have happened if the paper had gone home and the appropriate wife read the report that "R.C.C." began his letters with "Dearest Mildred," when the editors thought his wife's name was "Evelyn."[36] The newspaper poked fun at one yeoman, the navy word for typist and file clerk. He was W.W. Inkman, a pun the reporter did not seem to notice when he pointed out that Inkman had recently gained thirty pounds while on leave.[37] In one issue, a cartoonist caught the *Port Beam*'s own printer, crew-cutted Joe Arbour, as he whimpered, "Please be good," to a machine with an out-tray and an in-mouth that chewed paper. The caption called the machine "Minnie Multilith," no doubt 1944's top-of-the-line copier but one that routinely misbehaved when Arbour needed its help.[38]

*Port Beam* reported on the activities of the ship's chapter of the Servicemen's Christian League, which may have descended from Chaplain Linzey's work in 1942. The League aimed to help Sweet Pea's Protestants "maintain the faith they were born into." The paper covered a series of talks by members of the crew at the Sunday evening Vesper services. Doctor Joers covered "Christ at the helm," remarks said to be "inspiring." W.H. Martel, a corpsman, was scheduled to speak on "The General Teachings of the Bible."[39]

The glimpses of the crew in these pages are fascinating, and their accuracy is attested to by the fact that when John Hall left the ship in the late summer of 1944, he asked that all subsequent issues of *Port Beam* be forwarded to him so he could keep up with his former shipmates.[40] One can wish only that there were more. Akens sold the same cigarette lighter three different times, Levy wore toeless sandals, Kostic had underwear that some prankster tinted pink with Mercurochrome, Remly was devoted to fishing, and Healy loved the Boston Red Sox.[41] Seeping through these notes in their lamentable brevity is a vibrant crew of young Americans, most only boys when they enlisted and obviously clinging to that boyishness, but already more adult than any of them could have imagined they would ever become.

As *Port Beam* reached the pinnacle of its success in the late summer of 1944, Sweet Pea was sailing back to war. Leaving Hawaii with the three hundred soldiers and thirty newsmen, she headed south, crossed the equator, and again staged a shellback ceremony. This time the crossing occurred on the international date line, which made the initiation even more rigorous than usual, since at the end the initiates would be Golden Shellbacks.[42] One pollywog named "Blackie" Oliver tried to hide, but was discovered and given even worse treatment as a result. After they shaved his head, the shellbacks made him crawl into a long canvas chute with draw-strings at each end. The inside was coated with graphite grease, making the whole experience simply awful. Then the shellbacks "paddled the hell" out of the unfortunate man and fire-hosed him when he tried to get out. The worst came at the end, when the shellbacks mixed some Pet milk with toothpaste and corn starch, put the concoction into a condom, and ordered Oliver to bite the end open and drink it all.[43] The overt sexuality of so much of this ritual showed only that the men lived in a world that deprived them of normal outlets for their libido. No one seemed threatened, and even the victims enjoyed the experience, *once it was over!*

The civilian correspondents were included in this initiation into the mysteries of King Neptune's domain, too, and they took it good-naturedly.[44] The journalists enjoyed being indoctrinated into all the peculiarities of shipboard life. At the end a couple of them wrote a piece for *Yank* magazine expressing their delight at learning what a gedunk was and where the fresh water was turned off when the evaporators ran low.[45] They were so tickled to be included in the shellback ceremony that they created the "Society of the Double Cross." They laughingly made the ship's officers "provisional" members so long as they would buy drinks for all the correspondents at the next opportunity.[46] When they left *Portland* in the Solomons, the newsmen referred tongue-in-cheek to the shellback ceremony by telling the crew how they appreciated the sailors' "dexterity with the paddle and razor."[47]

## PELELIU

Sweet Pea was headed for Peleliu in the Palau Islands when she left the Solomons in September 1944. The landing at Peleliu should have been cancelled. After Admiral Halsey's carrier planes struck the southern Philippines, he reported that there was no need to start the liberation of the Philippines in those islands, since the Japanese seemed to have withdrawn their defenses from them. Consequently, the invasion was moved up a month, and the location of that landing changed to Leyte, an island in the central part of the archipelago. Peleliu had originally been thought necessary as an airbase for support of the more southerly assault on Mindanao. Now that it had been cancelled, Peleliu was irrelevant. Nor could the island be used by the enemy as a base to attack the Americans as they invaded the Philippines, because its airfield could have been easily neutralized.[48] But for no good reason, Admiral Nimitz ordered that the island be taken anyway.

*Portland* had been there before. On March 29, the fast carrier task force she was escorting attacked several of the islands in the Palau chain.[49] But no one on board could have been prepared for what happened in the invasion. *Portland*'s section of the assault fleet was gathered and organized in Tulagi, the island in the Solomons where Sweet Pea had been hastily and temporarily repaired nearly two years earlier.[50] In 1942, all the waters nearby and the palm tree to which she was moored were busy with Japanese air and surface forces. By mid-1944, though, Tulagi was far back in the rear echelon, with facilities that allowed American invasion units to load up. The work of preparation done, *Portland* got underway with her task force for Peleliu on September 6, 1944.[51]

In the Gilberts and Marshalls campaigns, Sweet Pea had been in the Fifth Fleet under Admiral Spruance. Now, however, she was in the Third Fleet, commanded by Admiral Halsey. There was only one set of ships, but the commander and his staff changed, and with them the nomenclature of the units. The system was invented for three reasons. First, when Halsey completed his mission in the South Pacific in 1943 and that theater was cleared of the enemy, he and his staff reported back to Admiral Nimitz in Pearl Harbor. Nimitz did not want to have to pick Halsey over Spruance for command of the great fleet that had been built up, or vice versa. Second, alternating command every four months or so would give one of the staffs time to prepare for the next operation while the other was carrying out the current mission. Third, the nomenclature might confuse the Japanese in their analysis of radio traffic. So, when Halsey was in command of the fleet, it was called the "Third," and when Spruance commanded, it was called the "Fifth."

As she got underway to leave Tulagi, *Portland* fell in as a member of Task Unit 32.5.1, which comprised two other task units: TU 32.5.2, *Maryland, Pennsylvania, Indianapolis,* and *Honolulu,* plus four destroyers; and TU 32.5.3, *Idaho, Mississippi, Louisville, Portland,* and five more destroyers.[52] The old battleships here were slower than any of the thirteen ships that had brawled with the Japanese on November 13, 1942. But each one of these task units was remarkably more powerful than Task Force 67, which had won the Cruiser Action that night.

Sweet Pea took her place in the naval gunfire line at Peleliu before dawn on September 12, and began firing at 0700.[53] One sailor said it was like the Fourth of July, with some ships firing heavy explosives and others spewing rockets.[54] But little of the pyrotechnics did the landing force much good when the Marines began to crawl ashore on the 15th. For the first time, the Japanese decided to spend themselves dearly. Instead of fighting above ground, as they had done most of the time earlier in the war, the defenders this time built themselves subterranean fortifications, using the phosphate mines that dimpled the entire terrain on the surface, and digging underground tunnels to link them together.[55]

The Japanese engineers did an excellent job in this construction. *Portland*'s director officer noticed through his binoculars that a large enemy gun came out through a heavy steel door in the side of a ridge, fired a round at the Marines on the beach, and then disappeared inside again. To try to silence this weapon, Sweet Pea fired five salvos of her 8-inch batteries against the emplacement. But between those salvos the Japanese gun came out of its cave to bombard the beachhead. *Portland*'s gunners had to give up. The officer said in disgust, "You can put all the steel in Pittsburgh into that thing, and still not get it."[56]

Another of the cave guns was hit by an armor-piercing projectile and smoked slightly for several hours. But the following morning that very gun was again in action and required further attention. Such well-hidden and fortified weapons were silent only when the ship's guns were firing at them, and they would come out again to do their damage as soon as *Portland*'s attention turned elsewhere.[57]

Sweet Pea was positioned about a mile offshore, close enough to allow her to again use her anti-aircraft guns unconventionally. But this time, the 40s were fired at the enemy to support the Marines as they went in, not just to clear the jungle to improve sight lines for spotters on the bigger guns.[58] Her position was so close that the crew could see what was happening on the beach and inland. Vince McNamara watched a group of Marines move off the beach into the jungle but come running back out under machine-gun fire. Several of the men he watched went down, and many of them never moved again.[59]

Within a couple of days, dead bodies began floating by the ship.[60] Chuck Martin, one of the ship's divers, helped to fish out of the water some of those dead American boys. He thought they had probably not even reached the beach before being killed when their landing craft was sunk.[61] Some boat coxswains with wounded Marines aboard stopped alongside *Portland* instead of going to the hospital ship much farther out. One of Sweet Pea's own Marines, Pat Miles, had been frustrated until then by his assignment to a cruiser when he wanted to be in the amphibious infantry in the Fleet Marine Force (FMF). But he admitted that he changed his mind when an LCM, a medium-sized landing craft, came from Peleliu out to the cruiser "loaded with wounded and dead Marines." Miles was sobered by the experience, thinking, "It's one thing to want to be there, but then you think about yourself being all chopped up or dead, and it's another deal."[62]

Another leatherneck who once served in *Portland*'s crew had not escaped infantry duty, as Miles did. Audell "Johnny" Johns left the ship at Mare Island in 1944 and was wounded at Saipan on June 30 when Sweet Pea herself was still in the yard. Johns was proud of his service both on the ship and on the beach, but Miles was right in thinking that his chances of escaping death or injury were probably better on the cruiser, as Johnny's transfer had proven.[63]

Former coxswain Willie Partridge has photographs of Marine casualties who were brought aboard from Peleliu. In one, a man already dead was in a body bag on a stretcher being carried by four sailors. Another shows a litter hanging by four lines from a crane as it is lifted out of a landing craft. Most telling are the faces of the *Portland* sailors. In the first picture, some men were on the main deck where the dead man was being carried, others were one level up, and a few more farther up than that. They were all horror-stricken. A youthful officer crossed his arms in apparent unconcern, but his face was tightened in agony. Some of the sailors were stunned while a few looked hurt as they stared at the young Marine, healthy and fit like them only minutes ago, but now mutilated and dead.

The casualty was buried at sea that night.[64] Some of the men in the crew were regularly assigned to this duty. Whenever burial detail was called away, for example, Merle Choate would report to the quarterdeck in the specified uniform, most often working dungarees but sometimes dress whites or blues. He wondered to himself why he was assigned that duty, but when others asked he would always chuckle confidently, "I figure I'm the ideal sailor," meaning that the authorities who picked him thought he was good-looking enough for the solemn chore. During a burial at sea, three men on a side would hold a board on which lay the remains in a body bag weighted with a projectile, all under the national flag. The chaplain would conduct a service, and on signal Choate and the others would lift the inboard end and slide the corpse from underneath the flag into the sea.[65]

Servicemen in the Vietnam War wanted their bodies brought home if they were killed. Many men were killed or wounded in Vietnam trying to retrieve already dead buddies, so important to all was the notion of being taken home.[66] When the *Portland*'s sailors were asked whether they worried that, if killed in action, they might be consigned to the deep instead of taken home, they seemed not to understand the point of the question. As Ron Hicks said, "It was sad but it was the right thing to do. Not even if I had been killed would I have thought my body should go home."[67]

Wounded men who were delivered from Peleliu to Sweet Pea received impressive solace. During previous battles, the ship's medical department had gained considerable experience in treating strangers. At Peleliu, the tradition continued. Once, when a landing craft brought some wounded alongside, *Portland*'s Senior Medical Officer told the coxswain that his sick bay was overloaded. But the doctor gathered up some pain-killing drugs, jumped into the LCM, and treated the injured men for miles on the bouncy journey to the hospital ship.[68]

A different ship's doctor ran afoul of Captain Settle a few months later in a similar situation. The doctor was on the main deck, triaging the wounded brought aboard from one of the landings in the Philippines, when Settle noticed. The skipper yelled down:

> "What are you doing down there, Doctor? Do you realize you've deserted your post?"
>
> "Be that as it may, sir, but these guys need my help."
>
> The Captain was seriously irritated and hollered down again to the doctor, "You took an oath to serve the Navy by following orders."
>
> The doctor went about his work, cooly replying, "With all due respect, Captain, I took an oath when I became a doctor to render help where and when I could, and that's what I'm doing."

Settle seemed to understand that he was wrong, grunted and walked away.[69]

Sweet Pea herself had a couple of near misses during the Peleliu campaign. After several days of nearly incessant firing, she withdrew from the line to replenish her ammunition. During the night of September 19, while she was tied up alongside an ammunition ship, a small Japanese aircraft flew over without warning and attacked her. The two bombs the snooper dropped missed, but only by about one hundred feet, frightening everyone on board.[70] During the loading operation all the hatches to the magazines had been left wide open, so a hit would have turned the ship into a pyre. There would have been nothing to prevent massive flooding, either, had the ship's hull been punctured.[71]

*Portland* immediately cast off and sailed away from the ammunition ship. Overnight, Settle and his officers created a new loading plan. When work resumed the next morning, every single person on board—cooks, typists, radarmen, pharmacist's mates, *everyone*—was put to work so that the time of exposure would be minimized. All labored so hard and so quickly that the replenishment took little time and the ship was soon safely away.[72]

Back on station a few nights later, the ship found itself surrounded by geysers, as if enemy shore batteries were firing at her. But no flashes could be seen. It was finally determined that the rounds were from USS *Pennsylvania*'s 14-inch guns. The battlewagon was bombarding Japanese positions on the other side of the island, and some of her shells had gone over the target and the entire island to endanger *Portland* and other American vessels near her.[73]

Despite his earlier complaints at Eniwetok, Captain Settle found that not much had been reformed about the poor discipline on radio circuits. Now he was much more pointed in his criticism, saying that the radio circuits were tied up by "Administrative traffic, . . . verbose drafting and procedures; unnecessary testing, repeats and call-ups." He seconded the suggestions of his radio officer, F.S. Knight, that a shorter and less frequently used voice format for reporting what ammunition the ship had on hand should be adopted. Knight loathed the practice of calling, then saying "Message for you, over," and only then giving the message, and Settle concurred that it should be eliminated. The Captain himself recommended that the ships send routine things by the older visual methods like semaphore or flashing light, and save the modern radios for tactical matters.[74]

Settle did favor some of the newer gadgets provided the ships for this

invasion. He singled out for praise the charts that could be placed under
the Dead Reckoning Tracer in the Combat Information Center. He also
liked the target grid maps, and the simulations of radar scope
presentations that enabled the crew to check what land features they were
picking up on their scopes. On her own, innovative *Portland* began at
Peleliu to equip her aircraft with cameras. The pictures were invaluable
to the ship's Gunnery Officers in planning future missions.[75]

On September 29, 1944, the Marines finally did secure this nasty
little island that was not needed for American victory. When they did,
*Portland* and her task force withdrew to Manus in the Admiralties, there
to prepare for the coming invasion of Leyte.[76]

11

# LIFE ON BOARD

The long days and nights of the Pacific War only rarely included the excitement of battle and the horror of death and injury. Most of the time was spent in everyday events, not unlike what the men would have been doing at home. *Portland* was its own living community, and almost everything that might happen in a town of about twelve hundred people happened on board this heavy cruiser. There were no women, of course, but that this many people slept all their nights on the ship, ate all their meals on the ship, worked all their days on the ship, cleaned all their clothes and spaces on the ship, and entertained themselves on the ship made Sweet Pea a hometown for them all.

The ship had machinery that not only moved them through the water but also heated their living spaces in the cold or ventilated them when it was hot, and lighted them all the time. In this ocean-world, the ship converted salt water into fresh for drinking and cooking. Sweet Pea stored all the food the crew would need for long weeks at sea or got more from replenishment ships she would meet from time to time. Her cooks baked all the bread and pastries, cooked all the meat and vegetables, and boiled large amounts of water every day to make the ubiquitous coffee.

## THE MEN

The men themselves, of course, worked the machines that did all these things. They came from everywhere in the United States. Merle Choate was from Oklahoma, Edwin Allred from Tennessee, Charles Morton from Massachusetts, Henry Hight from Arizona, and Willie Partridge from Georgia. John Geriak was from Connecticut, Bill Reehl from Pennsylvania, Tom Goff from Iowa, Ron Hicks from Oregon. They enlisted for a variety of reasons. When Herb Gibson joined in early 1940, the Great Depression lingered and the $4 a week paid to a young sailor recruit seemed like a good deal to him. On December 7, 1941, the raid on Pearl Harbor angered sixteen-year-old Reehl, but it was three weeks before he could talk his parents into lying about his age so he could join up. Even later, Ted and John Mahala in Salem, New Jersey, had to get a Navy chaplain to intervene so the twin brothers could serve together in the same ship.[1]

Like Reehl, other *Portland* sailors were too young to enlist legally, but they lied to the recruiters, none of whom seem to have had a rigorous attitude about such legalities. Reehl got through only because no one at the recruiting station asked him for a birth certificate.[2] Allred was too young when he was sworn in in Tennessee, as were Ted and John Mahala when their grandfather signed the requisite papers at their enlistment, and Fernando Valdes when he got his mother to sign by threatening to run away if she didn't.[3] Marine Corps recruiters could look the other way, too. Pat Miles tried to join the U.S. Navy but failed the physical when the doctors found a minor heart murmur. Later, doctors working for the Marines found the same murmur but got a second opinion from a civilian doctor who returned a glowing physical report, and Miles found himself in the Corps. He ended up on a ship anyway, USS *Portland*.[4]

Given the national crisis, this sloppy inspection of the prospective recruits is understandable. Joe Arbour was too small to enlist legally, but he ended up as one of Sweet Pea's photographers. He weighed but 106 pounds, and even when discharged he was still officially twelve ounces too scant for his height.[5] The system, such as it was, differed a great deal from a few years earlier when so many men preferred to be in the much smaller Navy rather than face the jobless days of the Great Depression. One example of how hard it was to get into the prewar Navy was Ray Koepp, who served in *Portland* from about 1937 to about 1940. Koepp was turned away by the Navy recruiter at first because he had a scar on his cheek, a little overbite in his teeth, and a few ingrown toenails. But he wanted to enlist so much he had all of the deficiencies corrected over the next six months. Even then, though, he was put on a waiting list before being finally allowed to enlist near Christmas in 1935.[6]

The Navy calls basic training "boot camp" because of the leggings recruits wear throughout the program. Most *Portland* men went to boot camp at either Great Lakes outside of Chicago, or San Diego.[7] But basic training was conducted at more esoteric sites, too. Charles Morton went to a newly created boot camp at Sampson, New York; Ron Hicks to another one in Farragut, Idaho; and John Fynan to a third in Newport, Rhode Island.[8] Wherever they went, in boot camp the recruits were supposed to learn fundamental things about the Navy: how to recognize ranks and rates, how the disciplinary system and some of the equipment worked, physical fitness, and so on. Before the war, boot camp was rigorous and about three months long.[9] But for those who joined right after Pearl Harbor, when the manpower needs were too desperate to allow any serious training, boot camp lasted only three weeks, just about enough time to get uniforms fitted and too trivial to be of much value.[10] About mid-1942, the Navy realized that it had been shortsighted, and those who joined then and beyond were trained much more intensively in boot camp. Most importantly, they learned how to fight fires.[11] The Navy had realized that damage control helped American bluejackets and their officers when *Yorktown* was hit at Midway and saved *Portland* at Guadalcanal, among others. Throughout the war, this skill kept afloat innumerable other ships.[12]

Right after boot camp, a few men got advanced training in the jobs they would fill when they finally reached *Portland.* For example, Arthur Bentley went to electrician's mate school in San Diego, W.C. Barrett went to machinist's mate school at Great Lakes, Henry Hight to radioman school at San Diego, and Eldon Peterson to typing school also in San Diego.[13] Ron Hicks was originally sent to machinist's mate school, too, but since he didn't know trigonometry he failed to qualify and had to report to *Portland* as an unskilled sailor.[14]

Most of the enlisted men during the war were like Hicks and arrived on board without special skills. Such men were almost invariably assigned to a deck force division, of which there were six. First, Second, and Third Divisions comprised the officers, petty officers, and seamen who were assigned to the main battery, the 8-inch guns in Turrets One, Two, and Three, respectively. Fourth Division had the 5-inch dual-purpose mounts, Fifth Division the intermediate anti-aircraft guns, at first 3-inch, then 1.1-inch quads, and finally 40mm guns as the ship upgraded, and Sixth Division the smaller 20mm AA batteries.[15]

The work of these divisions was the central reason for the ship's existence. *Portland*'s guncrews worked feverishly every day to improve the skills of firing her guns. Men in all the deck divisions cleaned, maintained, and repaired the weapons, and practiced loading them, aiming them, and/or firing them almost daily.[16]

The men in the deck divisions had plenty of other work, too. For his first few months aboard, for example, Joe Arbour was the range finder for Turret One when the ship was at general quarters in battle or drills, but he served his division as a compartment cleaner otherwise.[17] *Portland* was a steel ship that was always in a body of water, so the sailors spent plenty of time chasing rust. The men chipped and painted, cleaned and polished. They also did more skillful jobs like streaming anti-mine paravanes, operating the boats, or putting out sleds for aircraft recovery, as well as the technological things around the guns themselves.[18] The training in even the mundane jobs was very good. One man who was in a deck division for only a few months could still recite more than fifty years later what he had been taught: "'Chip it, scrape it, wire-brush it, red-lead it, then paint it.' And when painting, 'worm and parcel with the lay, then turn and serve the other way.'"[19]

When they painted high places, such as the stacks and the sides of the upper decks, the sailors would rig a chair from a site higher than the spot to be worked on. When the ship rolled one way, the sailor would swing in and be able to paint, but when it rolled the other way he would fall away and have to wait for the next roll. In a ship once thought of as the "Rolling P," these swings were often huge in distance and time.[20] There was always work: the maintenance of the anchors and the boats, the rigging of brows, access ladders, and canopies when in port in rear areas, and on and on, were all jobs done by the deck divisions.[21]

These jobs could be dangerous, too, whether in or out of combat. One time when the ship was under air attack, Fernando Valdes kept firing and firing for a long time while a Japanese bomber flew right at his anti-aircraft gun mount. He was never sure whether his gun or some other finally hit the plane, but as the enemy drew very close a round wrecked one of its wings and flipped it over and into the water. Cheering with the rest of the sailors nearby, Valdes then noticed that the crew's sightsetter was gone. Looking over the side to the deck below, he saw the other man hanging on a hook that had punctured his jaw. The sightsetter had been so sure that the kamikaze was going to hit that he had jumped. He was rescued by three other sailors who lifted him off the hook "like a huge human fish—the catch of the day," Valdes thought.[22]

The work was perilous in peacetime, too. Before the war there was the November 4, 1940, accident that killed Boatswain's Mate Hall and injured Seaman Brents while *Portland*'s crew was practicing minesweeping outside of Pearl Harbor.[23] George Dolezal's 1942 injury, when the lines on the winch parted and swept across the deck, nearly amputating one of his legs, took place during the war but not in combat.[24]

These treacherous tasks could sometimes teach the young men valuable lessons for life. Valdes recalled one time when Boatswain's Mate 2/c Dieterle took him up the mainmast to clean the lights at the end of the yardarm. Valdes had to crawl out to the farthest end of the yardarm while the famous "Rolling P" made him swing very far away from the vertical. Adding to his anxiety was the fact that the "sailors walking on the deck below looked about a half inch tall." The only reassurance he had the entire time was that Dieterle held the long line attached to the back of Valdes's safety belt. That job got done "real fast," Valdes recalled, but he had learned an important thing about service aboard *Portland:* the men had confidence in each other. "I trusted Dieterle to hold on to his end of the rope. Trust is what brought us all together . . . and that's what made *Portland* great."[25]

Every once in a while a man would report to the ship and be placed immediately somewhere other than a deck division. Most of the other divisions were called by letters. For example, there was B Division, which worked in the boiler rooms; C Division for all the communications personnel; E Division for the electricians; R Division for machinery repair; and so on. Jack Lassen came straight from boot camp and upon arrival found himself lined up on the quarterdeck with all the other "boots," as all sailors insultingly called rookies. A petty officer mustered these men and then asked if anyone could type. Lassen said he could and was sent immediately to C Division as a radioman striker.

As a striker, Lassen was assigned all the warm-body jobs that existed everywhere on the ship. He swept and swabbed, carried messages, went for coffee, and of course typed message traffic. But his progress in radio work was taken seriously, too. Lassen was taught Morse Code and how to encrypt and decrypt messages, and then given time to study and practice these skills. All radio traffic came to *Portland* by continuous-wave transmissions in radio-telegraphy using Morse. Fifty years later, Lassen remembered the ship's call sign: NACB, or "dah-dit, di-dah, dah-di-dah-dit, dah-di-di-dit." Although the Navy almost never uses Morse anymore, Lassen can still "read" the code whenever he hears it on a ham radio station. When the young striker got good enough to copy at eighteen words per minute, he was put on the watch bill, where he actually sent and received ship's messages. He ultimately made Second Class Petty Officer as a radioman, so as imprecise as the selection system was, it certainly worked in his case.[26]

Some of the men assigned at first to one of the deck divisions transferred out when opportunities became available elsewhere. For example, Al Lucas was placed in Third Division when he arrived, but several months later worked his way into the R Division shipfitter shop. Boatswain's Mate 1/c Stratton in Third Division was so angry to lose Lucas that he wrecked the younger man's bunk space when he learned of the transfer.[27] Sometimes, though, a move out of a deck division would be mutually desired. Tom Goff, for example, was a redhead with very fair complexion. When he worked around the guns, he sunburned so badly that he lost a lot of working time in sick bay. As a result, he was given an inside job, cleaning the chiefs' quarters. But one day a chief petty officer in "S," the Supply Division, recruited him because Goff, too, could type. He mastered the complex Navy system of supply so quickly that he was promoted to storekeeper first class petty officer, a jump of four pay grades, in only one year. This was a great achievement because that system involved all replacement equipment, all foodstuffs, all fuel, and all ammunition.[28]

Transferring from one division to another sometimes created problems for the sailor. Each division had a quota of men who had to be assigned to help with the preparation and serving of food, the mess cooks. Bob McDannold came aboard and was assigned to Fifth Division, which promptly sent him on temporary duty to the galley as a mess cook for a few weeks. Then he was transferred to First Division, which immediately sent him mess cooking. Finally, he passed the Radioman 3/c test and was assigned to C Division in the radio gang. He went mess cooking for a third time.[29]

Many men learned sophisticated skills right on the ship. Chief Petty Officer Art Bentley had scores of sailors under him in the electrician gang who learned on the job all there was to know about *Portland*'s complex direct current electrical system.[30] Willie Partridge was an experienced welder in civilian life. He had been shipbuilding in the yard at Charleston, South Carolina, when he decided to follow his father's and brother's footsteps into the service. The Navy wanted to use his already highly developed skills, and he was offered a petty officer's rate as a shipfitter if he would come in as a welder. He declined because he wanted to be a gunner, and the Navy sent him to *Portland*. When he reported to the ship, Sweet Pea bowed to his desire, too, and placed him in Fifth Division. He now shared responsibility for the 40mm guns and became a sighter for one of the batteries.[31]

It was called "making a rate" when a seaman became a petty officer in a specialty. For Lassen and Goff, it was a matter of learning certain skills and passing certain tests. For men in the deck divisions, it was likewise, although their skills were often more manual. To make gunner's mate, one had to study technical books and learn the fundamentals of *all* the Navy's guns, not just the type the man's division was assigned to. Then the sailor had to pass a test that proved he actually had learned such things. But for all there was a quota. In the wartime Navy, a man could not be promoted unless his ship had an opening in that particular job. He might be lucky and find such a need very quickly, as Goff did in his rise to storekeeper first class within a single year. On the other hand, Bill Reehl passed the test for gunner's mate third class in March 1944 but had to wait several months until an opening occurred before he could be promoted.[32]

The Navy expected men to be resourceful and bright enough to learn their duties even as the ship was taking them to battle. Those who were good at their jobs ordinarily were rewarded quickly. Though slow to make third class, Reehl was promoted four times while he was aboard *Portland*. To achieve each one of the new grades, he had to find time to learn from manuals and pass the tests about the guns he served and others he might not ever see.[33] John Fynan recalls the same tough schoolwork to make electrician's mate third class, and he gives credit to his boss, Warrant Electrician Eldon Guhl, for instilling in him "a study ethic that has lasted all my adult life."[34]

Work in the other divisions varied but was just as arduous. Machinists, water tenders, shipfitters, and electricians maintained, operated, and repaired the engines, the boilers, the evaporators, the electrical and other systems. Radarmen maintained their equipment and practiced tracking and evaluating electronic targets. The ship became a finely tuned machine as the war progressed. And of course there were always the back-breaking work parties to take aboard fuel, ammunition, food, and other stores. Some former sailors recall the working parties as much as anything else about their careers aboard Sweet Pea. Fernando Valdes was certain that he was assigned to every single working party that was ever called away during his three years on the ship.[35]

Life aboard the heavy cruiser was not all work, though. There were many events, like the talent show planned for the day of the Pearl Harbor raid and the dancing exhibition put on by the Samoans in 1943. For example, the "*Portland* Band" was organized in late 1943 by Chaplain Whitman and Lieutenant Thomas. The group suffered in the early going for lack of good instruments. But when the ship was in Mare Island in the spring of 1944, the chaplain was given permission by Captain Settle to buy what the band needed. Thereafter, practice was held "night after night" in one of the mess halls for some fifteen musicians, including:

Guitar: Romero
Sax: Rief, Cook, Wilson, Lewis, Brannigan, McBuremo
Trumpet: Smith, McClellan, Mond, Heinolds
Trombone: Hedberg, Nesborn
Drums: Utz
Piano: McKillip.

In time the band became "pretty good," according to the sailor who reviewed it in the ship's newspaper. The crew certainly liked the performances.[36] Smaller, more specialized musical groups also grew up around the ship, to the enjoyment of all.[37]

How men reported to *Portland* was almost as varied as their origins. Some crewmen were Regular Navy sailors who had joined before the war for fixed terms of service. These sailors usually came to the ship alone or in very small groups, and found her in Long Beach or Pearl Harbor.[38] Others who joined the ship once the war had started were often in drafts of a hundred or more men when they arrived. Ron Hicks was in one large group that reported at Mare Island in March 1943 when *Portland* was being repaired and modernized after the torpedoing at Guadalcanal. This was the occasion when the petty officer in charge split the men in half, arbitrarily sending Hicks's group to *Portland* and the other to *Indianapolis*.[39] Chuck Martin was sent from boot camp to Mare Island, where he was waiting in a barracks one day for something to happen. A petty officer came in, took a look at a muster list, called out about a hundred men whose last names all began with the letter M, and took them all to Sweet Pea.[40] Two other long-time *Portland* sailors, J.C. Banks and Ray Peugh, reported to the ship on December 13, 1941, in Pearl Harbor. They were survivors of battleship *California,* which had been torpedoed alongside Ford Island. Because the Navy needed their skills, and this nearby cruiser was ready for sea, away they went in *Portland*.[41]

Joe Arbour had an adventure getting to the ship. He was ordered to *Portland* after fire-control school, but an ailment held him up in the hospital at Treasure Island, so he missed the ship's movement to the Aleutians campaign. When he was well, the Navy put him on a train with several other pubits—poor unfortunate bastards in transit—who shared the nightmare ahead. By the time they got to Bremerton, Washington, *Portland* had departed, so for a while they were given temporary duty around the base. They were finally loaded on a Liberty ship that fed them only twice a day as it sailed slowly through the uncomfortable North Pacific to Adak via stops in Sitka and Dutch Harbor. Since there was no place at Adak to house them, the men were sent to ammunition ship *Shasta* for temporary lodging. At long last, to their great relief, *Portland* came into port and picked them up.[42]

The men who had been in the ship's company in 1933 when *Portland* was commissioned were held in especially high regard. They were called plankowners because symbolically they owned a theoretical share of the wooden main deck. During the war, the plankowners were exalted as if they shared the ship's original soul. A count was kept of them each year when the ship's birthday was celebrated. There were still forty-two such men on board in 1939 when the ship was six years old. Most by then were fairly high-ranking petty officers, but there was one seaman 1/c, "Bunky" Schneider, the manager of the ship's gedunk stand.[43] The final plankowner was not piped over the side until October 3, 1944. He was Chief Water Tender Otis Rutland, who had served in *Portland* for eleven and a half years.[44] During that time, he put in a long tour as the ship's Chief Master-at-Arms, roughly the chief of police, who never, *ever,* was seen without his .45 pistol in its belt holster.[45] He also served an important collateral duty as "Queen of the Court" during the shellback initiations.[46] Chief Rutland was even rumored to have smuggled a cute blonde aboard one time, a story more likely due to his status than to any truth in the report.[47]

These plankowners were also revered in the postwar years. The *Newsletter* as late as 1994 pointed out that H.B. Benge, who had joined the reunion association, was a plankowner in the Marine detachment. He served a year or so in *Portland* and then went to the Naval Academy, after which he returned to the Corps and rose to the rank of colonel before retiring.[48]

The crew included many far less "salty" men than these plankowners, to be sure. Ron Hicks and his colleagues from the Far West were so little traveled that they thought the cruiser was named for Portland, Oregon. Hicks himself learned the truth only in 1945, when the ship was feted in its Maine namesake. Some "boots" believed that the ship they slept on the first night at Mare Island was *Portland,* even though it scarcely resembled the photos they had seen of the great ship. They laughed at themselves the next day when they realized their temporary home was an old ferry, *Calistoga,* which had been commandeered by the Navy for the crew while the *Portland*'s innards were being ripped apart.[49]

## SLEEPING AND EATING

In some ways, *Portland* looked as if a bunch of sea wanderers had captured it. Most of the berthing spaces were far below decks, and were cramped and hot rooms with several tiers of three bunks, each surrounded by and crammed between narrow and sometimes heavily traveled passageways.[50] As a result, in the combat zones (that is, practically the entire Pacific Ocean) many of the men chose to sleep not in their bunks but all around the topside decks. They worried they might not be able to get to their battle stations when the bugle sounded and the watertight doors along the route were slamming shut as they ran through them.[51] Willie Partridge took pride in being able to sleep in his bunk, wake up with a start, and still get through the doors and up the ladders before being sealed off. But his attitude was unusual.[52] Most of the sailors found ways to sleep near their general quarters stations, some right on the deck.[53] Joe Arbour folded a blanket four times to give him a cushion as he slept on the steel deck.[54] Bill Reehl thought ahead when visiting Pago

Pago and bought a Polynesian sleeping mat made out of palm leaves to use as a mattress on the hard surface.[55] Others were able to buy cots from sailors on the troop transports, stow them all day in some hiding place topside, then drag them out at bedtime.[56] Edwin Allred never returned the hammock he was issued during the few days when he first reported aboard before he was assigned to a berth in a sleeping compartment. For the rest of the war, he rigged that hammock at night near his battle station in one of the gun mounts.[57]

Sweet Pea's men ate pretty well. Before the war the crew was served family style. One mess cook would work two tables, each of which seated ten people and a petty officer who acted as mess captain. The mess cook would set up the tables before each meal and apportion such standard items as fruit and bread. He would then go to the galley to get his allotment of the main food rations, then come back and serve the table, starting with the senior man. The "boot" at the table would get what was left over. Of course, that was one good reason to work hard to make a rate.[58]

By 1942, when the crew size beefed up to the wartime complement, meal service became entirely cafeteria style. Sailors would line up with a regular, steel, sectioned tray and a ceramic mug, with their flatware in their shirt pockets, and be served from behind a counter by mess cooks. No plates or other crockery graced the crew's mess: the mess cooks would put the various items into this or that section of the tray. Portions were rigorously limited by the chief commissary steward, for most of the war a man named "Pete" Soulis. He was regarded with respect by most of the crew, although the same sailors often found him tight-fisted with the rations. One day he told his mess cooks to give the men all they wanted, to their delight. At the same time, though, he held down one finger where the crew could not see it, in a surreptitious signal to his men that he meant that they should serve only one portion, regardless of what he was saying.[59] A story went round the ship that Soulis told some mess cooks who were peeling potatoes when an abandon-ship drill was called away to "Put lifejackets on the spuds, the men can swim."[60]

Soulis was a colorful character, to be sure. The crew thought that when the meal was good, Pete would be on hand, eagerly looking for compliments. When it was less so, he was nowhere to be found. He was notably generous to the work crews that brought foodstuffs aboard and stored them in the various refrigerators and closets. If they did a good job, they knew he would treat them to ice cream and cake, so of course they worked hard and efficiently. Once in a while a work crew was tempted to steal some food. A case of beets was missing one time and the Supply Officer penalized the division that had been the work crew by making the sailors eat beets off a piece of canvas. The officer made it clear that he could not understand why the men would take beets and not something more worthwhile.[61]

The food was substantial, and many men, such as gunnery phone talker John Geriak who had been on the ship since before Pearl Harbor, gave it a simple review: "The food to me was very good. We always ate good."[62] There was always fresh bread and ice cream, made right on the ship. When Sweet Pea left port, her lockers were always filled with fresh meat and vegetables, so the crew ate very well for however long it took for the fresh supplies to run out.[63] From the very beginning of her career in 1933, Sweet Pea was intensely concerned to stock enough food. By the end of the war, this logistical problem had become a science worthy of mention in a combat action report. When the ship was in combat for long periods, the crew had to be fed on station. In 1945, Captain Settle reported how *Portland* did it. All available topside spaces were stocked with selected items so that rations were readily available around the clock to serve to men who were unable to leave their battle stations to get to the mess decks. Menus were planned so that hot food could be served on station, even after dark. Sandwiches of "hot minced ham, turkey, beef" were welcome treats at unusual times, Settle reported. And he raved about the cooperation from all departments, especially the repair parties who served these ad hoc meals to the entire crew over a period of about two hours.[64]

For three big holidays, the ship laid a spectacular meal on the tables. Thanksgiving and Christmas menus would give each man a choice of roast turkey with all the trimmings, or baked ham also fully loaded. The third holiday was the ship's birthday, a feast that marked the anniversary of Sweet Pea's commissioning on February 23, 1933. It featured the same offerings as the other two holidays, turkey or ham with fabulous side dishes and desserts, coffee, cigars and cigarettes. The menu for December 25, 1943, varied almost not at all from those on the other holidays:

GREEN OLIVES   SWEET PICLES [*sic*]
CREAMED TURKEY SOUP AU CROUTONS   SALTINES

ROAST YOUNG TOM TURKEY
CRANBERRY SAUCE
OYSTER DRESSING   GIBLET GRAVY
VIRGINIA BAKED HAM
PINEAPPLE SAUCE
CANDIED SWEET POTATOES   MASHED POTATOES
CREAMED PEAS   SCALLOPED CORN
FRUIT SALAD
MINCE PIE   PUMPKIN PIE
FRUIT CAKE
HOT PARKER HOUSE ROLLS
BREAD   BUTTER   COFFEE
CHRISTMAS CANDY   CIGARS   CIGARETTES   MIXED NUTS[65]

A few of the men, to be sure, were critical of Sweet Pea's food. Dewey Stimson said the crew was fed horsemeat, and he disliked the Australian butter, which spread like glue, he said.[66] Milton Poulos hated the "lime jello" that was given to the crew every day for weeks on end one time when food supplies ran low. The weather was so hot and humid that the stuff usually ran to liquid before the men could eat it.[67] Such disdain is not surprising since the sailors were mostly youngsters, nearly all of whom had never been far from home cooking before.

In fact, the eating *was* sometimes less than spectacular. When the ship was at sea for extended periods of time, it had to depend on underway replenishment for food, fuel, and ammunition. If a food resupply ship did not appear for a few weeks, the fresh food would run out and the crew would eat only whatever canned and packaged supplies had been stored. Powdered milk and eggs were routine at these times.[68] One such time of belt tightening was before, during, and after the Battle of the Coral Sea, and another was for several months after the invasion of Leyte, as we shall see.

## COMBAT

The men stood watches, of course. Even when not *expecting* combat, the ship was nevertheless *ready* for it. On those occasions she steamed in what was called Condition Three, which divided the crew into three sections. One section was always on watch, while the other two were doing ship's work, or resting, studying, or doing all the other things across the human spectrum.[69] Bridge watches were manned by men from the deck divisions: helmsmen, phone talkers, lookouts, and so on. Engineroom and fireroom watches found men from those divisions ready to respond instantly to orders from the bridge. In Condition Three, a third of the guns were manned and ready, so many deck-division men were stationed there. There were other watches that weren't so obvious. Merle Choate, for example, stood smoke watch. His chore was to patrol topside near the stacks and, using his sound-powered phones, tell the fireroom when the smoke became too visible. The idea was to make sure that enemy forces over the horizon did not discover the ship early because of a smoke trail it might be creating.

Choate may have saved his ship on this watch one night when *Portland* was in a formation of cruisers steaming single file. As the dark hours wandered past midnight, he noticed that the vessel behind Sweet Pea seemed to be closing the gap between the ships. Finally, she drew to only fifty yards or so and he became concerned. Although his phone circuit went only to the fireroom, he informed the talker down there. That man did not have a line to the bridge, either. But he could tell by the tone of Choate's voice that this was a serious matter, so he relayed the message to the talker in the engineroom, who *was* connected to the bridge. Three phone talkers and a radio call later, the other ship made a hard turn to starboard and slowed down to reach the correct interval.[70] No one ever said anything to Choate about it, but the officers who should have been more alert on both bridges were probably deeply relieved.

*Portland*'s Marine detachment usually was composed of two officers, about three non-coms, and thirty-five or so men. They served as Captain's orderlies and ship's buglers, guarded the brig, and performed other security and ceremonial duties. They also manned one of the topside 5-inch guns.[71] As brig guards, the Marines were loathed by the sailors in the crew.[72]

*Portland* had her share of troublesome men, and her brig was frequently used. It had two small cells, with a place in between for the Marine guard. There was just enough room in the cell for the culprit to lie down. If a man were disobedient or late returning to the ship or got into a fight with someone superior in rate, he usually faced confinement. A Captain's Mast or a deck court-martial had the power to lock him up for three to five days on bread and water, called "piss and punk" by the irreverent crew.[73] Sailors were usually treated harshly by the Marines who guarded them. But when Marine Private First Class Pat Miles earned brig time for swinging at a sergeant, the guards were his buddies, and they took care of him by smuggling food into his cell.[74]

One thing that united the men on the *Portland* was the loss of shipmates. Some of the old-timers can remember every one of them. The torpedo killed eighteen at Guadalcanal, the two aviators disappeared at Eniwetok, and then a man went overboard in 1945.[75]

The man who went overboard was Seaman 2/c Virgil Stonestreet, who had transferred from the deck force to V Division. In the predawn darkness on May 6, 1945, he was preparing to crank the engine on an SOC that was going to be launched from the port catapult for dawn patrol. The man in the cockpit, S1c Alfred Saenz, saw Stonestreet at work, then turned his eyes into the cockpit for his own preflight job, and heard a loud clatter. Looking out, he saw that Stonestreet was gone. Several other men near the catapult heard the clatter, too, from the crank as it fell to the catapult. One man said he heard a loud splash and looking over the side saw the splash receding down the side of the ship. The men immediately threw a life ring and a dye marker over the side, and the ship and one of the destroyers turned at once to search the area. The plane Stonestreet had been working on was quickly launched and joined in. Although the searchers found the life ring and the dye marker, no sign of Stonestreet was ever seen despite the fact that the weather was clear, the sea smooth in a very light wind, and most of the hunt occurred in full daylight. After several hours of looking, Sweet Pea gave up, leaving another of her men in the deep.[76]

On April 2, 1945, about three weeks before the Stonestreet accident, four other men, unnamed in the action report, were slightly wounded in action. And ten days after that, on April 12, 1945, Gerald Pacheco and William Shoup, both seamen 2/c, were wounded by shell fragments in an air defense action off the coast of Okinawa. The injuries were not life threatening and both men were retained to convalesce on board.[77]

Like rescued men who were treated in Sweet Pea's sick bay, her own crew received very good medical care. During combat, injured could be taken to one of three aid stations: sick bay, the wardroom, and an after site on the fantail. The one on the fantail was wiped out by the torpedo hit at Guadalcanal, killing one of the doctors and three of the enlisted corpsmen. Pharmacist's Mate Walter Martin's battle station was to rove the ship topside, where he felt exposed. He had an excellent view of the Battle of Surigao Straits, described later, but was never comfortable while the shells flew over in both directions, from U.S. battleships to the north and Japanese battleships to the south.[78]

USS *Portland* was primarily a fighting vessel, but in many ways it was like a small town. In her, men worked, played, rested, and fought the enemy. As she steamed toward the Philippines in October 1944, one such fight, the biggest naval battle in all history, was about to engulf Sweet Pea.

12

# LEYTE GULF

When *Portland* left Peleliu in late September 1944, she was detached from the fast carrier task force and assigned to the bombardment force of General MacArthur's navy, the Seventh Fleet, at its base in the Admiralties.[1] Her new mission was to support the seaborne infantry as it made its way ashore at Leyte, the island in the central Philippines where MacArthur would finally make good on his pledge to return.

Both Admiral Nimitz's Central Pacific theater and General MacArthur's Southwest Pacific campaign had been highly successful. The creation of these two Allied forces that had been driving against the Japanese Empire from different directions since early 1943 was a political compromise. The Navy had made very clear in 1942 that it would never tolerate MacArthur as the overall commander in the Pacific, because the ocean would be the main environment. But he was too big a national hero to be placed under the lesser-known Nimitz. So the United States split the war in the Pacific into two theaters. MacArthur moved from Australia along the northern New Guinea coast and the other nearby islands, while Nimitz took the route across the Central Pacific described earlier in these pages: Gilberts, Marshalls, Marianas. The twin prongs kept the Japanese off balance and unable to guess where the Americans might strike in either theater. By the summer of 1944, the two American commanders disagreed on what should come next, but MacArthur's promise to liberate the Philippines won out. "I shall return" became the American strategy, because both theaters would combine in taking Leyte.

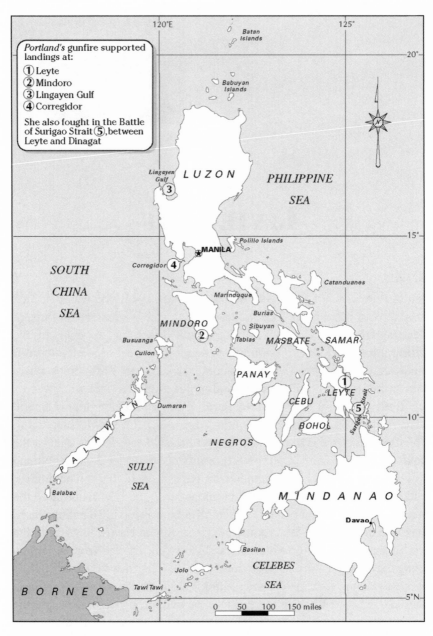

Map 4. Philippine Campaigns, October 1944–March 1945

Sweet Pea arrived at Leyte on October 18, 1944, two days ahead of the scheduled landings.[2] Her crew thought she was the first large American ship into Leyte Gulf. She lobbed rounds at the beach for those two days, trying to draw fire so the enemy defensive positions would reveal themselves.[3] When the troops did go ashore on October 20, it seemed to the men on the cruiser that the Japanese did not offer much resistance.[4] That judgment may have been shaped by the fact that they had been to the bloodbath at Peleliu only a month earlier.

At Leyte, as at Peleliu, the ship switched from one firing area to another, depending on where targets were discovered. Again, Captain Settle was unhappy with this ad hoc system, saying that it led mainly to inaccuracy in bombardment. He proposed that all ships be assigned to a single firing position from the days before the landings through the end of the campaign, in order to allow them to maximize their familiarity with the terrain and consequently with the enemy in front of them.[5] It is hard to imagine why Settle's proposal had not been adopted long before.

Only a few days after arriving on the scene, though, *Portland* and all the other gunfire support ships had to give up the bombardment mission and go fight the enemy in a sea battle. The details of the Imperial Navy's plan, *Sho Ichi Go,* were complex but can be summarized simply. By ruse and daring, the Japanese intended to get their gunships into Leyte Gulf from two different directions in order to destroy the thin-skinned transports and supply ships that were supporting the invasion. The southern pincer of this attack would come through Surigao Strait, in two separate groups, and *Portland* and the other warships were alerted to head them off.[6]

Early on the morning of October 23, Seventh Fleet had learned of the first Japanese force of two battleships, a heavy cruiser, and their escorts coming into the strait.[7] The enemy's flotilla was a formidable force that was nearly identical to the one *Portland* had faced on Friday the 13th in 1942. There was, however, a big difference on the American side. At Guadalcanal two years before, Task Force 67 had no battleships to go up against the Japanese and only two heavy cruisers. But now, across the mouth of Surigao Strait, American Admiral Jesse Oldendorf lined up six Seventh Fleet battleships and five heavy cruisers, while along the sides of the strait he placed dozens of PT boats and destroyers, all of which could launch torpedo attacks.[8]

Oldendorf's battlewagons and cruisers were old, prewar ships that in 1944 were intended only for shore bombardment. The battleships could not hope to keep up with the fast carriers and their modern escorts, nor to cope with the newer Japanese battlewagons in a sea battle. Five of them are worth naming: *California, Maryland, Pennsylvania, Tennessee,* and *West Virginia.* All five had been sunk or badly damaged at Pearl Harbor.[9] About two and a half miles ahead of them, Oldendorf created two lines of heavy cruisers, including *Portland,* to extend his battle line.[10] By aligning his force this way, the admiral had created an automatic "T-capping" in which the slow speed of his battleships did not matter at all. The Americans were arrayed across the strait, while the Japanese were in column, steering directly toward their doom. In the predawn darkness of October 24, the smaller Japanese force would be annihilated.

*Portland*'s crew knew the enemy was coming, and most were near their battle stations awaiting the call. Lieutenant Vince McNamara, for example, slept on a cot next to the searchlight platform, where it was cool and breezy.[11] Sweet Pea was plodding slowly along with the other cruisers in the left wing, astern of *Louisville* and ahead of *Minneapolis,* and about two and a half miles in front of the battleship line. Her Executive Officer, Commander Allen R. Joyce, was the same man whom Settle had criticized for his flood of paper. Whatever else he was, though, Joyce was a fighter; he had won a Bronze Star at Guadalcanal when he was Sweet Pea's Navigator. The XO did not want to be caught unprepared at Surigao, as he thought the ship had been two years before. About 0200, then, Joyce recommended to Captain Settle that *Portland* go to general quarters, although the Japanese could not yet be seen on the radar.[12] Settle agreed, and at 0210 the crew rushed to battle stations.[13]

Then all waited for more than an hour and a half. Finally, the excellent scouting report that had alerted the Americans to the Japanese intentions was matched by the excellent American radar. At 0300 *Portland* picked up the approaching Japanese twenty-six miles out, and at 0352, when the enemy came within range, Oldendorf opened fire.[14] Sweet Pea targeted Japanese cruiser *Mogami,* which was second in line behind battleship *Yamashiro.*[15] Enemy shells whistled by *Portland* as the Japanese fired back.[16] More than fifty years later, Charles Morton could still replay the way Sweet Pea rocked from the impact as huge Japanese shells hit the water nearby.[17] Since there would be no anti-aircraft action,

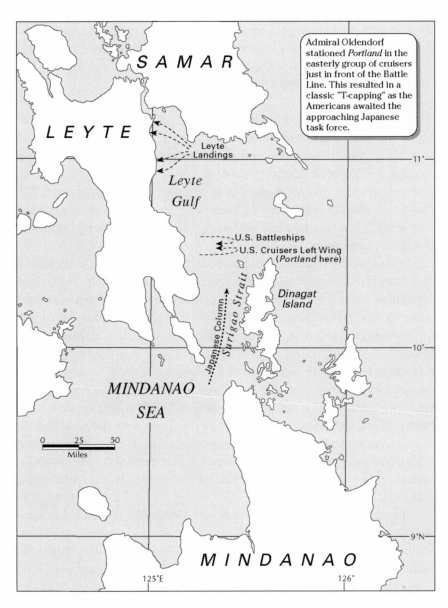

Admiral Oldendorf stationed *Portland* in the easterly group of cruisers just in front of the Battle Line. This resulted in a classic "T-capping" as the Americans awaited the approaching Japanese task force.

SAMAR

LEYTE

Leyte Landings

Leyte Gulf

U.S. Battleships

U.S. Cruisers Left Wing (*Portland* here)

Dinagat Island

Japanese Column

Surigao Strait

MINDANAO SEA

0    25    50
Miles

11°

10°

9°N

125°E                                126°

MINDANAO

Map 5. Battle of Surigao Strait, Oct. 24, 1944, 0300 hours

the AA crews had again been told to get down on the deck. Some of them, though, again took positions where they could see the action.[18] Not Merle Choate on smoke watch topside; he prudently made sure to keep the stacks between himself and the Japanese guns.[19]

No more one-sided a naval battle has ever been fought. Only four minutes into it, *Portland* checked fire to switch targets since *Mogami* was being pelted by many other ships and was already "burning brightly." The second target, destroyer *Shigure,* turned away in those four minutes and sped to the south in an attempt to flee the holocaust. The range was already almost ten miles, so *Portland* looked for something else at 0402, but only her original target, *Mogami,* was available and she blasted it some more.[20]

In fact, all the Japanese ships engaged were sunk, save the destroyer that managed to escape. Oldendorf sent the cruisers to pursue the second part of the enemy force, which had approached but then turned around when its admiral had discerned the deadly trap ahead. Marine Pat Miles, on *Portland*'s bridge at the time, said later that they found mainly "flotsam and jetsam and dead bodies."[21] Sweet Pea joined the other cruisers in firing at one fleeing enemy vessel, and by 0540 it was burning and unable to move. The cruiser offered to pick up Japanese survivors, who characteristically declined the rescue.[22] Some of the men were happy to let the enemy sailors drown because they knew that only twenty-four hours earlier other Japanese units had attacked hospital ship USS *Comfort,* an atrocity in their minds.[23] Just about then, the pursuing cruisers were called back to the battle line and the Battle of Surigao Strait was over.[24]

It had been a savage couple of hours. One Japanese battleship sank at 0411, the other at 0421, the heavy cruiser at 0535, and destroyers at various times in the same period.[25] If ships have souls, the American battleships that had been assaulted on a day of supposed peace at Pearl Harbor must have rejoiced. In fact, the Battle of Surigao Strait was so easy that the greatest danger all faced during the entire time came when the task force ran out of room on its route of march. Oldendorf ordered a 180-degree turn in order to maintain the broadside firing. But *California* did not turn at all, and *Minneapolis* made only a ninety-degree turn, so the entire formation nearly piled up. Captain Settle won the crew's admiration when his emergency shiphandling avoided a collision during this chaos.[26] The failure of the U.S. fleet to act upon Settle's earlier complaints about the TBS had caused this near disaster. Things were so hectic on that overly used radio circuit that *California* and *Minneapolis* failed to hear the turn signals, thus putting the entire formation in peril.[27]

The Battle of Surigao Strait, only a portion of the enormous Battle of Leyte Gulf, was a decisive victory for the U.S. Navy. In it, USS *Portland* took its unique place in history. By playing a role in the slaughter, *Portland* became the only heavy cruiser ever to fight enemy battleships in nighttime engagements *twice*. It does not matter that here at Surigao Strait she was on the side of overwhelming power, while at Guadalcanal the Japanese had had the preponderance of strength. Both times Sweet Pea was on the winning side, and both times her fighting contributed to the victory.

Meanwhile, the northern pincer of the Japanese effort to sneak in on the invasion had enjoyed more success. About dawn, *Portland* and the rest of the Pacific Fleet received an unencrypted message from Nimitz's headquarters in Pearl Harbor that to the north of Leyte Gulf a group of escort carriers and destroyers was under attack by a large flotilla of Japanese battleships and cruisers in another part of this huge battle.[28] These heavies had slipped by and were now threatening the precious transports and supply ships off the landing beaches. *Portland*'s crew was shocked when the ship received orders to speed to the rescue, because in their weariness the men thought that one huge surface action a day was enough. Worse was that their magazines were nearly out of armor-piercing ammunition. Sweet Pea had arrived off Leyte with her magazines two-thirds loaded with the high-explosive ammunition most useful for shore-bombardment. The firing overnight in Surigao Strait had consumed 327 rounds of her armor-piercing shells and she now had only enough AP for about six salvos from her main battery.[29] Happily for all concerned, the gritty little flattops and their tiny escorts up north drove off the much stronger Japanese force, so *Portland*'s group was able to resume its task of bombardment.[30]

The invasion went on without further disruption, except for the many air attacks. J.T. Paul, the "Einstein of the 40mm gang," kept count: *Portland* went to general quarters eighty-seven times from her arrival at Leyte to her departure on November 3.[31] Still, by early December the invasion had gone so well that the United States had major bases ashore on Leyte. The island was so secure that some of *Portland*'s officers spent a little social time in officers' clubs there.[32] The ship continued to fire support missions for troops still fighting farther inland, and went back to the Palau Islands one time for replenishment. During that visit, Admiral Oldendorf presented Captain Settle with the Navy Cross for the ship's outstanding performance at Surigao Strait.[33]

The Battle of Leyte Gulf effectively ended the Imperial Japanese Navy. But Japan now had another horrible weapon that *Portland* and all the other ships in the Pacific Fleet would have to face.

## KAMIKAZES

During the last year of the war, the U.S. Navy in the western Pacific was beset by what amounted to a prototype of the guided missile when the enemy began employing the suicide attacks that became known as *kamikaze*. The Japanese word means "divine wind," and it was first used to describe the typhoon that destroyed Kublai Khan's invasion fleet in the thirteenth century, thus saving Japan from conquest. Some Japanese leaders in 1944 hoped that suicide attacks on the American fleet would save their nation yet again from foreign conquest.

The very first such mission struck and sank an escort carrier off the coast of Samar during the Battle of Leyte Gulf on October 25, 1944.[34] *Portland* suffered her own first attack about a month later, when she returned to the Philippines after a few days at Peleliu, away from the war zone. As she sailed into Leyte Gulf on November 29, 1944, the crew was advised of the new Japanese tactic.[35] Barely had the warning been given when a kamikaze attacked the ship. As Lieutenant McNamara wrote in his diary, "They weren't fooling!"[36] It was a fixed-wheels aircraft, with a bomb slung below its belly as it approached *Portland* from the port side forward. The crew was terrified: although the tracers from the AA batteries in that area of the ship were obviously hitting the plane, the pilot kept boring in.[37] Gunners aimed for the engine and the cockpit, because such shots had been successful against orthodox aerial attacks. But they were not against this determined suicide attacker. Finally, a few rounds from Coxswain Willie Partridge's 40mm hit the kamikaze's starboard wing. Having lost its aeronautical stability, the plane flipped over and slammed down into the water so close aboard that everyone near the bridge on the port side was splashed. The ship's bugler leaned over from his station and laughingly handed Partridge an El Roy cigar for his good shooting. Partridge kept that trophy for more than sixty years. From then on, Sweet Pea's gunners aimed for the wings of the suicide planes.[38]

Now that the Japanese had turned to suicide attacks, the air action around Leyte became frantic. *Portland* went to general quarters for air defense five times that day alone.[39] The sailors remember that not all the suicide attackers were courageous patriots eager to die for country and emperor. Several in Sweet Pea's crew recall one supposed kamikaze who belly flopped in the middle of the U.S. fleet and allowed himself to be captured, because he wanted to live.[40] Nevertheless, most of the enemy pilots were legitimate suiciders who tested the fortitude of Sweet Pea's sailors. Bill Reehl was more terrified of the kamikazes than of anything else he faced during the war. "Just the idea that they would deliberately fly their planes into ships was demoralizing," he reported.[41] Partridge admitted that he was scared during every moment of combat, but never so much as when under suicide attack.[42] Marine Pat Miles, assigned to a battle station on one of the 5-inch AA guns, chimed in, saying that as a loader he would sometimes be holding a 5-inch/25 shell in his hand just as a suicide plane bored in toward his position. He reckoned that he had no chance if the kamikaze should hit near him because the "little bomb in my hand" would certainly explode and disintegrate him as it did. As Miles put it, "man, you talk about terror. I was terrified."[43]

Miles had good reason to be so fearful, and when the attacks intensified several weeks later during the American invasion of Luzon at Lingayen Gulf, things were even worse. On January 6, 1945, *Portland* faced the most ferocious kamikaze attack the fleet had so far experienced. Instead of the remark "Steaming as before," which customarily opened each watch's log entry, the ship's log on that day read, "Under air attack as before."[44] The fleet had to fend for itself, for there were almost no friendly fighters to help out.[45] Captain Settle wrote officially and with uncharacteristic petulance about the paucity of planes flying combat air patrol, complaining that America's "enormous national numerical and qualitative superiority in aircraft" should not leave her naval units "so vulnerable to enemy air attacks."[46]

Another factor that contributed to how awful these attacks were was the fact that the American radar could not pick up the Japanese aircraft as they attacked from over land. The radar was blocked by the land masses, and operators were almost never able to pick up the enemy until they got out over the water. By then, though, there were only minutes or even seconds before the attacker hit.[47]

In 1945, Japan's only defense against the U.S. Navy was the suicide tactic, and on January 9 the kamikazes had a field day. Before the bombardment task unit could get on station for gunfire support, the ship right alongside *Portland* in the next column and the one right next to her in the same column were both hit by kamikazes.[48] The attack on the abeam ship, *Louisville,* killed Commander Cruiser Division Four, Rear Admiral Theodore E. Chandler, one of the few flag-rank U.S. officers to die in action.[49] When Chandler was killed, command of the cruiser division passed temporarily to Captain Settle of *Portland.*[50]

The ship in the same column with Sweet Pea was *Columbia,* which, because she had more AA guns, had just moved from behind *Portland* to right ahead of her. But as soon as *Columbia* took her new station a kamikaze dove. He passed *Columbia,* and seemed headed for *Portland,* where some men on the bridge froze in horror. Sweet Pea's gunners, though, kept up a steady and voluminous fire, when suddenly, as if to avoid what was coming from *Portland*'s fewer guns, the suicide pilot rolled over and hit *Columbia* on her after gun deck. Yet again, *Portland* was not hit, but again her men found themselves helping to rescue sailors from another ship.[51]

It was at Lingayen that *Portland*'s sailors began to think that "Tex" Settle was truly special. To a man, they were sure that his resourceful and radical shiphandling techniques kept Sweet Pea from being hit by the suicide bombers. When a kamikaze dove to attack, Settle would give wild steering and engine orders to turn the cruiser and change her speed in order to throw off the aim of the suicide pilot. He often gave abrupt commands like "right full rudder," "shift your rudder," and so on, allowing the ship only enough time to come to some radically new heading before giving a new order. He did the same with the ship's speeds, issuing analogous engine-order-telegraph commands like "all ahead full," "all stop," "all ahead flank," in rapid succession, probably not always giving the ship time enough to change speed before he gave something new.[52] Sometimes he would take the wheel *himself* and put the ship into radical turns even at full speed.[53]

He had done this kind of maneuvering during the first attack in November, when Lieutenant McNamara wrote in his diary, "The

Captain really threw the ship around and did some beautiful maneuvering."[54] And he continued to do so thereafter. Dewey Stimson, a sailor in First Division, gave full credit to the "cool and excellent ship handler taking care of the *Portland.* "[55] Willie Partridge was willing to give thanks to "the good Lord," but quickly added that the ship had "a wonderful skipper," and praised Settle's radical ship-handling.[56]

Many in the crew believed that Settle's experience in aviation had taught him the maneuvering that enabled him to avoid suicide planes.[57] He would drive his heavy cruiser like a PT boat or a fighter plane when under kamikaze attack. The captain's "flying" his cruiser had its desired effect, because despite the frequency of the attacks USS *Portland* was never hit by a kamikaze. Large numbers of the U.S. vessels were hit in the Lingayen operation. One of *Portland*'s sailors kept a diary in which he noted that in the first five days of the operation, kamikazes hit every man-of-war in Sweet Pea's group except *Portland,* cruiser *Minneapolis,* and battleship *West Virginia.* He listed the ships damaged by suicide attack during those days: escort carriers *Omanney Bay* and *Manila Bay*; cruisers *Louisville* (twice), *Columbia* (twice), HMAS *Australia,* HMAS *Shropshire*; battleships *California, New Mexico, Mississippi*; and several escorting destroyers.[58] A different diarist noted that in one twenty-four-hour period on January 17, twenty-four ships were struck.[59]

Some of *Portland*'s success in escaping this onslaught was due to the fact that most of the suicide pilots who got through to the main body of the U.S. fleet aimed for aircraft carriers.[60] The list above, however, shows that not all did. The skillful shooting of *Portland*'s experienced AA gunners had a lot to do with it, too. Besides aiming for a kamikaze's wings, another tactic they devised was to shine their searchlights into the face of the pilot, seeking to blind him as he dove on Sweet Pea.[61] In his endorsement of *Portland*'s combat action report, the admiral in battleship *California,* which had been hit, applauded the searchlight idea.[62] But the men in the crew gave most of the credit to Tex Settle's maneuvering.

There probably are some who will think that Sweet Pea was only remarkably lucky. Such doubters should read the accounts of the kamikaze attacks on USS *Louisville* and HMAS *Australia* in Morison's naval history of World War II.[63] Only then should they consider making an argument against *Portland*'s skill in avoiding the suicide planes. In fact, her never being hit by a kamikaze in this terrible phase of the war is another reason why she may have been the greatest of all the U.S. Navy's cruisers.

Settle carried out his wild maneuvers when other ships usually remained in formation. One time he darted *Portland* all over the harbor while all other ships remained at anchor.[64] Such unorthodox behavior caused an admiral to dress him down on at least one occasion.[65] A sailor-diarist wrote that Settle replied that as long as he was in command, he was responsible for the safety of his ship and its men and he would therefore do as he saw fit.[66] We cannot know if this rejoinder actually happened or if the story were only apocryphal, but the crew surely believed it.

Maneuvering radically was something ships had long done when under air attack. In this history alone, several carriers have done so: *Lexington, Yorktown,* and *Enterprise.* But oddly, it was frowned on when the kamikazes entered the war. Settle may have thought he was stating only the obvious when he explained why his ship was not hit by suicide attack at Lingayen although thirty-five other ships were, including the two nearest. He explained *Portland*'s escape: "Maneuvering the ship by radical use of speed and rudder." He admitted that one had to take care not to foul gun-target-lines by smoke, or by forcing directors to turn into their stops, or by causing ammunition passers to lose their footing.[67] He must have been astounded when ComCruDiv Thirteen disputed his assertion, saying that maneuvering should be employed under kamikaze attack "only to bring the maximum number of guns to bear, or turn tail at night."[68]

Sweet Pea's sailors reported that Japanese pilots avoided *Portland* because it was not so easy a target as the ships that stayed in tight formation.[69] Another time a pilot, not a kamikaze but a regular bomber, dropped his ordnance on the very spot in the sea that *Portland* had just vacated because of Settle's swift course change as the plane approached.[70]

While the bridge watch loved to see the Captain at work on such occasions, men in the engineering spaces were not always so thrilled. Orders coming from the bridge were not only difficult to follow, but physically demanding to obey. Men would often have to run from one place to another to throw switches or spin heavy wheels to open or shut valves. The heat of the engine and boiler rooms made such activity arduous. Settle's wild orders also put great pressure on *Portland*'s aging machinery. Merle Choate remembered that the sailors in his below-decks division sometimes took refuge in humor, saying, "He doesn't aim the guns, he aims the ship!" But they found it scary to see all the pressure gauges running in the red and to watch so many of the boiler safety valves pop.[71]

On at least one occasion, Settle's maneuvering nearly cost innocent lives. Quartermaster "Buddy" Fountain was on the helm one day during an air attack when the skipper gave him "right full rudder" as the ship was at maximum speed. The Captain and the Navigator were immediately distracted by the ship's gunfire mission and left the bridge to go aft a short distance to observe the shooting. But *Portland* continued to turn and its circle was about to take it right into an LCI, a landing craft full of troops. Fountain yelled for someone to give him a helm order, but no one with that power could hear him. So, on his own initiative the quartermaster shifted his rudder to "left full." A moment later, Settle came running into the pilot house and saw that the ship was closing on the LCI. Because Fountain's unauthorized left rudder had not yet stopped the swing of the ship, *Portland* was still drifting right toward the landing craft. Settle ordered left full rudder. Instead of replying, "Left full rudder, aye, sir," to acknowledge that he had received the order, Fountain immediately replied, "My rudder *is* full left, sir," to confess that he had already done so. Settle looked at him and broke out into a big smile, recognizing that the helmsman had saved the day. He told Fountain that what he did was "the right thing," praise that Buddy never forgot.[72]

The Okinawa campaign from April through June 1945 was the peak of the kamikaze war against the fleet. Navy commanders thought that the Army general in command of the forces ashore moved his troops rather too deliberately, thus costing many ships and sailors who were supporting him, but the general stuck to his strategy.[73] So Okinawa evolved into a ninety-four-day operation from the opening of shore bombardment to the end of hostilities. During it, the kamikazes sank thirty-six American ships, damaged another 368, killed nearly five thousand sailors, and wounded nearly five thousand more.[74] *Portland* was on station for all but eighteen of those days.[75] Crews throughout the fleet became piano-wire tight, and Sweet Pea's was no exception.[76] One time gunner Partridge took a bead on a plane banking near the ship. He was prevented from shooting down what he should have recognized as an American fighter only because, as he put it, "Old Frank Hayes on the corner of the bridge closed the safety, and helped me off from firin'."[77] It was not unusual for friendly aircraft to be fired upon during the kamikaze raids. At Lingayen a few months earlier, a large number of F4U Corsairs had drawn American anti-aircraft fire as they courageously followed the kamikazes all the way to the wavetops to try to defend the very ships that began to shoot at all planes nearby, including them.[78]

The pressure felt by the crew because of these suicide attacks was palpable. Most officers began joining the enlisted men in sleeping near their battle stations.[79] Up until this time, *Portland* had maintained an alert status that kept her prepared for enemy action while nevertheless accomplishing essential ship's work, such as cleaning, repairing, and cooking. To accomplish these two assignments, she divided the crew into four sections, numbered I, II, III, and IV. On any given day, two of them were duty sections to do the normal things, one from midnight to noon, the other from noon to midnight. The other two were security sections, standing watch at their battle stations on the same twelve-hour rotation.[80]

Such a system did not work at Okinawa, though, because *all* hands were at general quarters nearly all the time. As a result, Captain Settle created Condition One Easy. Condition One meant that battle stations were fully manned and ready throughout the ship. In One Easy, however, while all hands had to be at their stations, only one man at each site had to be awake and alert, manning the phones. The others could relax or sleep or even get essential work done, but since they were at their stations they would be ready to fight in a moment. Many of the men thought One Easy was anything but easy. Paul Hupf, for example, pointed out that since most of the battle stations were cramped, no one was really able to get any rest.[81]

The crew knew how serious all of this was, though. One night the phone talker at one station fell asleep during One Easy, and a veteran petty officer put him on report. At Captain's Mast, Settle assigned the case to a court-martial. The trial itself was interrupted again and again by the incessant air attacks, and by the time the man was finally brought before the bar the petty officer who had witnessed the offense had been transferred. Not wishing to let a man who had fallen asleep on watch get off without penalty, the court nevertheless found the man guilty. Settle overruled the verdict, however, citing the lack of evidence.[82] But no doubt the message was heard throughout the ship: the one man awake during One Easy must *stay* awake!

## OTHER PHILIPPINE CAMPAIGNS

This story has drifted ahead of itself, but it should finish what happened in the Philippines. On November 1, 1944, a week after the Battle of Leyte Gulf, *Portland* went to Ulithi, the fleet's forward base. Because she had been in combat only since October 17, it did not seem significant that she was in port less than a day and no stores came aboard. No one knew it at the time, but it was going to be twenty weeks before Sweet Pea had another chance for a major replenishment. On November 2, she fell in with a carrier task group that sailed back in a big hurry to the Philippines to make strikes on Luzon. She was able to restock her magazines again at Kossol Roads the first few days of December, but then she returned to Leyte to help the ground troops still fighting there.[83] By this time the Americans had begun to build harbor facilities on Leyte, and *Portland*'s crew had the experience of dealing with "bum boats" that visited the ship from Tacloban. The sailors were quick to note that the Filipino girls were not only pretty, but happy to see the Americans who had liberated them from the Japanese.[84]

Despite what joy the crew gained from this flirting, much more serious was the fact that the ship did not have time to get fresh vittles. On December 12, without having replenished, *Portland* left with a few other cruisers and destroyers to escort a landing force that was sent to capture the island of Mindoro. Happily, the landing was unopposed, so the fleet's gunfire was not needed by the troops ashore. On the other hand, the ships came under what were now routine kamikaze attacks. *Portland* was credited that day with shooting down another attacking suicide plane.[85] Cruiser *Nashville* was damaged enough by a kamikaze that she had to be sent back to Leyte. The Imperial Navy even sent a destroyer to intervene, but an American tin can made short work of the challenge.[86] When Sweet Pea ended the Mindoro operation, she was approaching desperation. She reached the Palau Islands on December 23, but by then there was even less food on board, and there was none to be had at Peleliu, either.[87] In 1944, Christmas dinner, usually the huge and festive meal described earlier, was some aged pork that had been taken aboard the ship more than four months earlier when *Portland* topped off leaving Mare Island.[88] Crew morale slumped, and the ship's fighting efficiency dipped, too, although plenty of war remained to be fought.

# 13

# 1945

The Navy's success in keeping its combat fleets supplied was one of the great engineering and logistical feats of all time. As the war progressed westward toward Japan, the distance from the major base at Pearl Harbor became too great for the warships themselves to return for replenishment. Consequently, two systems were developed.

The first part of the Navy's logistics system was the underway replenishment, or unrep. Even during the fighting in far-off places, large ships called AOs, AFs, and AEs—oilers, refrigerator vessels, and ammunition ships, respectively—would bring their much-needed cargoes to the warships on the fighting line. While the supply ship and the warship steamed along side-by-side, transfers of all these things, plus replacement personnel, were accomplished in a way that amazed even the sailors who saw it all the time.[1] The unrep ships also carried the greatest of all morale-boosters: the mail.[2]

Mail delivery at sea was never regular during the war. A warship would get mail only when it was in port or when a supply ship would deliver it. On a terrific day, the ship could get thirty or forty bags of mail.[3] But for long days and weeks in between such bonanzas, sailors might receive no word of any sort from home. As a result of these irregular schedules, men who had regular correspondents would often get many letters at a single mail call, although not always in the same order in which they had been written. So letters from wives, girlfriends, and others sometimes referred to events the sailor did not yet know had happened.[4]

Most men heard frequently from their families. Merle Choate's mother wrote him nearly every day, a frequency he could not keep up with. After all, he reported, "'I love you,' 'I miss you' can be said only so many times." Somehow, though, Mrs. Choate managed to say those identical things in a way that made Merle keep her letters for a long time and re-read them with great pleasure several months after receiving them.[5] For many other men, there was also the girl back home, and the mail between two lovebirds must have been pretty intense. We have seen how, during the war, Choate married a girl with whom he had stayed in touch through writing. Likewise, Bill Reehl and his high school girlfriend wrote such love letters that they decided to become officially engaged on his 1944 leave. They had started high school together, but then Reehl enlisted when illegally young. The girl continued in school and had just graduated after Bill's second year in the Navy. Long before the war was over, she found someone else, and Reehl moved on to a long-term happy marriage himself.[6] Despite the odd outcome in this case, the ability of the mail to promote romance was unquestionable.

There were some laughable moments about the mail. For example, Joe Stables found a letter on his bunk one night when he came down off watch. He was so excited to get it that, in the darkened compartment where all others were asleep, he took out the flashlight he carried on watch to read it right away. The flashlight had a red filter to preserve everyone's night vision. The four pages in the letter were empty, without a single word written on them! He complained to his shipmates all morning until he looked at it again in the daylight. Sure enough, his sister had written in red ink. The event was a joke in the Stables family for years thereafter.[7]

The crew could sometimes suffer because of the poor mail system. In 1945, when Bill Reehl's mother died back home in Pennsylvania, his father tried to get the Salvation Army or the Red Cross to notify the Navy so Bill could find out quickly. That idea worked better than the U.S. Mail because a chaplain was able to give Reehl the bad news in an office in Okinawa long before his father's letter ever reached him.[8] There was, of course, no provision for emergency leave under these circumstances. No sailor would find out about the crisis until it was long over, and transportation to get him the many thousands of miles to his hometown would be almost as slow as the mail service.

Still, the crew loved getting mail. It would often include food, since all the folks back home knew that however good Navy chow was, it could not replace what Mom did. Merle Choate's mother and sister frequently sent him oatmeal cookies, which he always shared with his good friends to demonstrate what a good guy he was and to keep open the possibility of their sharing with him some other day. One time his mother tried to smuggle him a small bottle of recreational whiskey, packing it in with the cookies. She would have been horrified to discover that the bottle broke somewhere in transit and the booze soaked into the cookies. But she might have enjoyed the fact that those were the most popular cookies her boy ever received, as his buddies fought over them to get a little hit.[9]

Nothing could have been more disappointing than *Portland*'s December 28, 1944, mail call. Not only had the ship not received any mail for a long time, but there had not been enough time to take on even fresh food for weeks, so the men were already in a state of deep irritation when the mail arrived. The Fates apparently sought to add to the neglect the men in *Portland* already felt. The Christmas packages that arrived that day were mostly "wet, torn or crushed and had to be thrown away."[10]

Although servicemen overseas did not have to pay for postage on their letters home, outgoing mail from the ship was censored. Officers were assigned to read the letters sent by the men in their divisions, and to read each other's outgoing mail, too. The latter inspection was *pro forma,* since officers were generally trusted not to tell anyone where they were or what they were doing. But every American serviceman everywhere was disgruntled that his most intimate expressions could be read and sometimes deleted by his "boss."[11] *Portland* was no exception, and the sailors had reason to object. One officer wrote in his diary that one of the sailors whose letter he had censored that day was "Quite sure of himself" for proposing to his girlfriend and at the same time asking for her ring size.[12] The sailor never learned of this mocking. Because of this lack of privacy, the men often tried not to reveal much of what was really on their minds.[13] They knew, though, that if they ever did write something that was supposed to be secure, they would be punished. One time in the Aleutians, Choate wrote about needing machetes to cut the fog, and he was taken to Captain's Mast, where he could have been demoted or fined for his offense. The Captain gave him a "severe warning," and Choate learned his lesson. But he was not a happy man for having his mail read.[14]

The second part of the Navy's wartime supply system in the Pacific was the development of forward bases. The farther west the war went, the more time-consuming and difficult it was for even the unrep ships to return to Pearl Harbor. As a result, the Navy built bases closer to the action. After Kwajalein and Eniwetok in the Marshalls were taken, a major forward base was established at Majuro, where *Portland* had been a gunfire support ship during the unopposed landing in February 1944.[15] Ships could pull into the lagoon there, anchor, and receive all kinds of replenishment: ammunition, incidentals, food, fuel, new personnel, and mail.

## ULITHI

In late December 1944, after the Leyte and Mindoro campaigns and before the invasion at Lingayen Gulf, *Portland* visited Ulithi, where she picked up the ruined Christmas packages. Ulithi was the Navy's final, and greatest, forward base. Located in the Caroline Islands, about 310 miles southwest of Guam in the Marianas, it was a coral atoll of more than thirty islands, with a reef nearly all the way around that created a lagoon fifteen miles long and five miles wide. Ulithi had been taken on September 24, 1944, and since the Japanese did not think it worth defending, there was no opposition. American engineers turned the atoll into a major base so quickly that Admiral Nimitz called it "the Navy's secret weapon." He refused to allow reporters to comment on Ulithi, for fear the enemy might attack it.[16]

In addition to the logistics support Ulithi supplied for the ships, it also had a recreation site, the island of Mog Mog at the northernmost point on the atoll. Sailors were allowed to take liberty at Mog Mog. The natives had been removed, so there were no women there. But excellent facilities had been built by the Seabees on which men played baseball and other sports. *Portland* had a terrific baseball team about the time she pulled into Ulithi. There was a league of sorts among the various divisions aboard the ship, and the champion was the Fox Division nine. Eleven athletes, including star pitcher Zylon Sanders, a Radarman 3/c with a great fastball that struck out more than ten opponents per game, were in the team picture. These guys developed their 13–0 record by beating several teams from Sweet Pea and from other ships, as well.[17]

The Navy hoped the men would avail themselves of the games and other recreational opportunities. But of course, there was also beer.

Drinking was the main reason most sailors went to Mog Mog. Per day, each enlisted man on liberty at Ulithi was allowed two cans of beer, room temperature but free of charge.[18] A lusty black market grew up, as it did in every GI recreation area where the beer was rationed. Nondrinkers could get almost anything they wanted for their allotment of brew.[19]

Some of the men found Mog Mog tiresome. Merle Choate, for example, thought that the two to three hours of liberty invariably led to a fist fight. Like most others, he seemed not even to notice the other facilities and thought that the only attraction over there were tents under which men drank. So he stayed away.[20] But there were subtle pressures to go over to Mog Mog, even for those who chose not to drink. Once in a while a nondrinking sailor in the liberty section would opt to stay aboard, and it would cost him. Homer Peace, for example, declined to go ashore one day and found himself assigned to mess cooking so that a mess cook could take his place in the liberty party.[21] It is unlikely he made that mistake again.

The officers had facilities on Mog Mog, too. There was an officers' club where they could *buy* drinks without limit, including all kinds of whiskey in addition to beer.[22] The building was right next to what had been the native cemetery, with its huge, mossy, and well-aged gravestones of all sizes and shapes that reminded one man of England's Stonehenge.[23] The area around the club was prohibited to enlisted men who, in huge numbers, were confined to another end of the same island.[24]

The ages-old story of sailors and drinking would find plenty of evidence in the history of USS *Portland.* Bill Reehl said years later that the crew did little drinking aboard the ship, but almost in the same breath he described how the ship's bakers made "raisin jack" and reported that sometimes liquor was smuggled aboard when the ship was in the States.[25] Indeed, he may have known about the radarmen who brought aboard twenty-eight fifths of illegal scotch, hidden in boxes with cathode ray tubes. A boatswain's mate named "Rabbit" Robinson was famous for making "some potent stuff in the forward Bos'n locker that would knock your socks off with just a small amount." For his trouble, Robinson went up and down the promotion ladder more times than anyone could count.[26] The men in the engineroom, where there was plenty of steam and electricity to create stills, made something called "Engineroom Joe," which was decidedly *not* coffee, but heavy on the alcohol.[27]

Chief petty officers had been around the Navy a long time, so they knew the rules and their way around them. At New Caledonia one day, four cases of Clorox bleach were delivered to the ship and hustled off to the CPO quarters by a bunch of chiefs, who ordinarily did no such heavy lifting or laundry. The other enlisted men got the joke and noticed that the chiefs were in "good spirits" for several weeks.[28] Nor were officers above sneaking a drink on board the ship. *Port Beam*'s Editor-in-Chief McDannold let an officer use a corner of the newspaper's little office to ferment some berry juice. The caper came to no good end when a surprise Captain's Inspection was called away on the ship's public address system, leaving MacDannold with the still-fermenting juice and little time to dispose of it. He tried to remove the stuff but dropped the bottle of contraband going down a ladder next to the hangar bay. Now the entire area smelled like a distillery. In the little time he had before the inspection party arrived, McDannold poured carbon tetrachloride all around. He thought that since the chemical removes smells by removing the air, it was his one chance to avoid big trouble. It worked, although MacDannold nearly asphyxiated when the carbon tet snuffed out the air he was breathing. As the inspection party left the newsroom, one officer said to another, "That hangar could be used for 'sick' call if we ever get real crowded in sick bay—it really smelled sanitary."[29]

Of course, there was a lot of drinking ashore, where it was at least mostly legal, but it often led to trouble, too. Coxswain F.G. Zedler remembered one night in the Philippines when a large number of tipsy officers boarded his boat, overloading it. His protests that some would have to get off were overruled by the passengers, so he shoved off with only three to four inches of freeboard, a lot of drunken brass, and not nearly enough life jackets. Fortunately, he made it to the ship with no trouble.[30] One night in Pearl Harbor a huge brawl broke out among hundreds of enlisted men waiting for too few motor launches to take them to too many ships at too many anchorages out in the harbor somewhere. Most of the men were drunk, and in the heat and the line, pushing and shoving turned into a fight that grew to sheer mayhem. There were no fatalities, but countless minor injuries were suffered.[31]

## BACK TO WAR

On December 28 in Ulithi, *Portland* finally took on fresh stores, so her food shortage was relieved. She received little rest, though: as soon as she refueled, she got underway and headed back to the war in the Philippines.[32] She stopped at Tacloban, Leyte, but only briefly, and on January 2, 1945, Sweet Pea went to sea with the rest of the fleet for the invasion of Luzon at Lingayen Gulf.[33] That was when the kamikazes were out in great number as the ships approached the Gulf to support the landings.

In addition to the AA fire *Portland* threw up with the various task forces she served in, her main mission continued to be gunfire support of troops ashore. Even after the new battleships with their 14- and 16-inch guns arrived in the fleet to replace their sisters sunk at Pearl Harbor, *Portland*'s 8-inch main battery still threw a heavy shot at the enemy. And she was good at the gunfire mission. One Marine radioman ashore at Tarawa openly expressed his relief one day when the ship's call sign told him that he was working with *Portland*.[34] One of the reasons her fire was so accurate was that her SOC aircraft did a great job in spotting. Other ships were heard to tell their own pilots to get lower, saying that *Portland*'s pilots did so.[35] One time, a soldier ashore at Lingayen Gulf complained by radio to a spotter plane from another ship that the pilot was flying too high and should go lower. The aviator demurred, saying the enemy fire was too great. The soldier on the ground sniffed that *Portland*'s pilots had flown that low yesterday. In fact, that day the senior aviator, who was stationed on one of the battleships, had ordered the planes not to descend below six thousand feet. But when *Portland*'s pilots told Captain Settle they could not spot from that high because they could not see the targets, Settle told them to do what they had been doing before.[36] All these policies contributed to Sweet Pea's greatness as a shore-fire ship.

In February 1945, *Portland* was taken out of the force supporting the Lingayen invasion and was sent to help recapture Corregidor.[37] Known as "The Rock," this little island was famous for its resistance in 1942. Sweet Pea was supposed to participate in an air and naval bombardment for a few days until February 16, the day of a combined amphibious and airborne assault.[38] The biggest ships in the task force at Corregidor were three cruisers: *Portland, Minneapolis,* and HMAS *Shropshire.* Sweet Pea conducted scheduled fire missions, using optical fire-control systems and having the rounds spotted by her own SOCs. Not much shooting was needed, actually, since she fired only twenty-seven main battery rounds.[39]

An unusual feature of the Corregidor assault was the use of paratroopers. The sky filled with parachutes as the men and their equipment came swinging down.[40] Different colors indicated what the chute was carrying, making the sky a rainbow for a few minutes. The men aboard *Portland* could see what a difficult place Corregidor was for an air drop, with sheer cliffs on one side and enemy troops on the other. But the landing itself went without too much trouble, and Sweet Pea's gunfire was not even requested after the preinvasion bombardment.[41]

She made herself useful even so. Her aircraft flew around the landing site to direct U.S. destroyers in rescue missions for paratroopers who missed their mark and splashed into the water. A few parachutes failed to open, aviation radioman Atilano Valencia reported sadly. He added hopefully that he could not tell whether they were carrying men or material. As a matter of fact, no men were lost in the jump.[42]

Japan's defense of Corregidor was crushed over the next several days. The last of the enemy blew themselves up in their ammunition dump in the tunnels the Americans had built before the war.[43] By then *Portland* had already returned to Lingayen.

## OKINAWA

The phenomenal economic and military power the United States brought to bear worldwide in World War II was shown in February 1945. While its forces and those of its allies were pushing the last remnants of German resistance out of Italy and puncturing the Siegfried line in western Germany, Americans were also mounting a major invasion of Iwo Jima in the Bonin Islands, about 660 miles south of Tokyo, and pursuing the Japanese occupation forces all over the Philippine Islands.

The naval units in the Philippines operation were in the Seventh Fleet, still commanded by Thomas Kinkaid. *Portland* remained in this organization until early March, when it rejoined the Fifth Fleet. Spruance's Fifth Fleet staff had been busy planning the next operation while Halsey's Third Fleet had commanded the ships during the Philippine invasions. Barely had her work around Luzon and other northern parts of the archipelago ended when the next campaign began. In late March 1945, she sailed in company with a major carrier task force into the waters off the Ryukyu Islands to begin the Okinawa campaign.[44] It was the twelfth amphibious assault Sweet Pea had supported, a list that shows how central to the American cross-Pacific offensive she had been: Guadalcanal, Kiska, Tarawa, Majuro, Eniwetok, Hollandia, Peleliu, Leyte, Mindoro, Lingayen, Corregidor, and now Okinawa.[45] Because she had been assigned to combat in the Philippines in February 1945, Sweet Pea missed Iwo Jima. That and the Marianas operation in July 1944 were the only major campaigns in the entire Pacific War that did not include USS *Portland*.

Okinawa was unlike most of the other places attacked by the U.S. during the Pacific War. It was a huge island, not an atoll, although a coral reef did encircle it. Okinawa extended about sixty miles from north to south and was between two and eighteen miles from east to west. Before the assault, almost half a million people lived there.[46] Because the government in Tokyo regarded the place as Japanese territory, American intelligence estimated that about seventy-five thousand enemy troops were assigned to its defense.[47] The fighting there would prove to be a major land campaign, marked by defenses that included stone fortresses as well as the caves and underground bastions Americans were becoming accustomed to. It would take nearly three months for a joint landing force of soldiers and Marines to defeat the enemy at Okinawa. The fighting set new standards for savagery; besides the thousands of combatants killed and wounded, about as many civilians became casualties and hundreds of thousands more were left sick, injured, and/or homeless before it was over.[48]

*Portland*'s first firing mission at Okinawa began a few hours after midnight on March 21, ten days before the assault craft swam ashore. By early morning she was in peril. About 0830, six Japanese bombers came over the ships. They must have been especially interested in Sweet Pea, for her gunners had to down three of them. Only minutes after that attack, a torpedo porpoised off *Portland*'s port bow, attracting the attention of the bridge watch to that track and another one, both of which narrowly missed both Sweet Pea and the nearby *Pensacola*. They had been fired by a Japanese midget submarine. On Sweet Pea's bridge, Lieutenant R.V. O'Brien traced the wakes back to their origin about four hundred yards away, and sighted first the periscope and then the conning tower of a midget submarine which itself was surfacing, perhaps unintentionally. Captain Settle tried to ram the sub by some characteristically radical shiphandling, only to miss by perhaps twenty feet. *Portland*'s 20mm and 40mm AA guns pumped more than four hundred rounds at the surprising target.[49] But the sub was too close for them to depress sufficiently and they missed. The enemy submerged, to suffer a long depth-charge attack by several American destroyers, but the Japanese escaped.[50]

These were the final torpedoes fired at *Portland,* bringing the total to *eleven!* Treaty cruisers were supposed to be vulnerable to torpedo attack, and in fact one torpedo had nearly killed this ship. But she was still fighting after all these attacks. Was Sweet Pea lucky? Of course she was. But the skill and determination of her officers and men in fending off these attacks were the most important ingredients in her combat record.

The men on board were not only excellent warriors. For example, at Okinawa, as curious young Americans will frequently do whenever they find themselves in previously unknown places, Lieutenant Vincent McNamara took some time from the savagery all around him to sightsee. Before the fighting ripped Okinawa apart, he found the terrain beautiful as he looked through his binoculars. He told his diary about the pretty countryside with its little farms and the shacks the people dwelled in. He was impressed by the terraced hillsides and the small burial places he called "cribs" that "dotted" the hills and could be seen from his vantage point offshore.[51]

On a few occasions *Portland* went to rest and refuel at Kerama Retto, a cluster of small islands with a great central area the fleet used as a forward base. It lay about fifteen miles west of Okinawa.[52] McNamara's diary learned that although "very few" people lived there because the islands were so mountainous, he could see a few small gardens on the terraced hills and an occasional tiny hut with a straw roof.[53]

One time, the young officer also noted that not even animals were safe from modern warfare's terror. As *Portland* fired on a beach target at Okinawa, a horse ran out of a barn and down to the beach, then back up the road. McNamara watched as a 5-inch shell hit and disintegrated the unlucky animal. One of the phone talkers reported in not officially approved language, "My God, Captain, we killed a horse."[54]

These bucolic moments afforded only temporary relief from the demands of warfare, though. Okinawa was the longest and bloodiest island invasion the United States undertook during the war. American commanders must have anticipated that the going would be hard, because before the ground forces landed *Portland* created a landing force in case the troops ashore might need help.[55] They did not, so Sweet Pea's riflemen stayed afloat. But there were nevertheless scary moments for others in the crew. On a spotting mission over Okinawa pilot Jim Young found himself in the middle of American aircraft making a dive-bombing attack. He failed to realize that the carrier planes were dropping their bombs from *above* him and that he was in their target lines until the bombs began exploding under his SOC. He dashed away to safety.[56] Another day a destroyer ran aground off Okinawa. As its crew off-loaded ammunition to lighten the ship so she could crawl off the sand bar, Japanese artillery blasted the tin can, and it had to be abandoned.[57] A few days later another destroyer grounded on the same sand bar. This time, Navy commanders ordered *Portland* and several other heavies to surround her while she lightened ship. Sweet Pea's crew was happy to see that the shore-based artillery wanted no part of the Navy's big guns. The stricken ship was easily refloated and she sailed away without having received a single enemy round.[58]

The fighting ashore at Okinawa converted the place into something far different from what Vince McNamara recorded during the first few days offshore. Chuck Morton thought that the island was almost entirely ablaze. He saw American troops bulldozing dead Japanese into holes in the ground, then dousing the corpses with gasoline and lighting them off. The smell carried across the few miles of ocean to where Sweet Pea patrolled.[59] While the Marines and soldiers ashore and the destroyers on picket duty suffered the most from Japanese tenacity and suicide attacks, *Portland* also endured great pressure. Because of the frequency of the kamikaze attacks, the crew was at general quarters the whole time the ship was on station off Okinawa. Since deck officers were at their guns all night, officers from other divisions stood bridge watches, even those who normally were on different stations, like radio officers, for example.[60] Sweet Pea was a good neighbor for other units, too. Reminiscent of when she became a gas station for the PT boats when she lay crippled at Tulagi in 1942, off Okinawa in 1945 she became a floating gedunk stand for some of the fighting men ashore. A Marine officer visited the ship one day and asked if he could buy soap and candy for his men. Sticking to regulations, a storekeeper petty officer replied that he could not sell to a person who was not in the ship's company. Some of *Portland*'s officers thought that was "BS," so they lined up to buy the Marine everything he wanted. They even gave the visitor some jars of baby food that Al Beaudoin's mother had sent when she thought he was becoming too thin. Years later, Vince McNamara met the visitor, who said his troops thought the baby food was as good as prime rib![61]

On April 7, Admiral Spruance received word that the giant Japanese battleship *Yamato* was underway from Japan with several escorts and headed for Okinawa. To fight the enemy task force, he threw together a surface action unit, Task Group 54.7, which included *Portland* along with several of the new American battleships. It might have been an interesting shootout, not to mention Sweet Pea's third fight against a battleship. But aircraft from the fast carriers in Task Force 58 sank the behemoth later that same day, so the American gunships resumed their other duties.[62]

Okinawa has been generally thought of as the height of the kamikaze war. On the afternoon of April 12 alone, eighty-two attacking planes were shot down. Still, suicide pilots hit a battleship, nine destroyers, and one destroyer escort.[63] Again it was not just luck that kept *Portland* from being hit by these determined suicide pilots. Captain Settle made a strenuous effort to ensure that the gun and director crews were highly trained in aircraft recognition. It paid off on April 6 when several kamikazes dropped out of the clouds to catch the task force by surprise. Sweet Pea's guncrews were so quick in identifying the planes as enemy that she immediately fired at the four planes headed for her and splashed them all. Captain Settle thought that the speedy recognition and "heavy and effective" AA fire was the reason the ship had not been hit.[64]

Many of the other ships in formation wrestled much longer with identifying the aircraft and as a result suffered hits when the attackers crashed into them. Settle argued that another reason for the slow response of the American ships was the poor discipline of American aviators. He was proud that only once in the entire campaign did Sweet Pea fire at a friendly aircraft, but he nevertheless criticized the pilots for their poor "operational discipline . . . in the vicinity of our surface naval forces."[65] This time the Captain stopped short of suggesting that others emulate his radical maneuvering. No doubt he did not wish to incur the wrath of a superior again, as he did when he wrote about his shiphandling after Lingayen Gulf.

For the first time, the enemy at Okinawa used "window," shreds of tinfoil scattered by planes during an air attack. It had the effect of wiping out the American radar for fifteen minutes, and it remained a problem for up to an hour after being deployed.[66] The Japanese also sent out suicide boats to attack the larger American ships. Although *Portland* was never targeted by one of these, she still had to be alert to the danger from this quarter. One close call happened when *Portland* picked up her mail from destroyer *Zellars* one day. Just as the transfer was complete and all lines were cast off, a kamikaze aircraft came out of nowhere to smash into *Zellars* just below the tin can's bridge. The plane's engine flew through the thin-skinned destroyer and splashed into the water only a few yards from *Portland*'s side.[67]

To minimize the fatigue all the crews were suffering, the fleet adopted a policy of taking each ship off the line every fourth night, so the men could get some sleep at Kerama Retto.[68] Except for that respite of a few hours every several days, though, *Portland* was on station off Okinawa for nearly a month. She departed on April 20 for Ulithi, where replenishment of food, fuel, and ammunition awaited her, plus the usual beer and ballgames on Mog Mog. But she was right back on station off Okinawa on May 8, where she stayed for yet another month.[69]

On June 17 she left again, this time for the Philippines, where she remained anchored for over seven weeks. Sweet Pea needed this time away from the war. Her crew was worn out, like the men on all the ships of the fleet off Okinawa. Part of *Portland*'s difficulty was that there had been great turnover in personnel in recent months, so many of the key positions were now filled with inexperienced men, causing the tension to mount. But perhaps more importantly the ship itself was being "plagued by a series of material deficiencies." As Captain Settle put it, *Portland* had been "operating in the war theater continuously since early October," and the one short period at Ulithi in December for replenishment did not include any time for maintenance and repair.[70]

At Leyte Gulf, then, some sophisticated repairs were made to *Portland*'s engines and other machinery during June and July 1945. For example, the cruising turbine was overhauled.[71] On July 24, moreover, Settle was relieved as CO by Captain Lyman A. Thackery.[72] Thackery came from Allied Headquarters in Europe and Settle, freshly promoted to rear admiral, was sent to Washington to await future assignment.[73]

The ship herself got underway for Okinawa on August 3, by which time the island was secure.[74] Even so, Sweet Pea conducted anti-aircraft drills against aircraft-towed sleeves to keep the gunners' skills honed in case the kamikazes should reappear.[75] No one knew it, of course, but *Portland* had fired her last angry shot, because she arrived in Buckner Bay, Okinawa, on August 6, the very day the United States dropped the A-bomb on Hiroshima.

# 14

# WAR'S END

The Pacific War came to a surprisingly abrupt end. Like nearly everyone else in the world, the crew of *Portland* had been kept in the dark about all aspects of the atomic bomb. Some of the men heard rumors that their sister ship *Indianapolis* was on a secret mission when she left the shipyard in the States in July 1945. She had been there for repairs after a kamikaze attack, but no one aboard Sweet Pea knew that on her return she had carried parts of the nuclear weapon to the airbase at Tinian.[1] "Indy" then went to her death only a few days later.

*Portland* herself had just anchored in Buckner Bay in finally peaceful Okinawa when the crew heard about the atomic attack on Hiroshima.[2] Merle Choate was taking a nap and resisted being awakened, jokingly groaning to the men who were shaking him, "I'm not going to get out of this bunk for anything less than the end of the war." They laughed and shouted back, "THIS IS *IT!*"[3] Like American service personnel everywhere, *Portland*'s sailors were thrilled at the news of Hiroshima and, three days later, Nagasaki, because they were confident that Japan's surrender would follow and they would go home.[4] At the time some were hoping for even more atomic devastation of the hated Japanese.[5] With the news on August 14 that Japan had surrendered, the fleet put on a "VJ-Day" fireworks display that may have frightened some Okinawans into thinking the war had resumed.[6]

Some fighting persisted for a few days after Hiroshima. Battleship *Pennsylvania*, which had been severely damaged at Pearl Harbor on the *first* day of the war, was also severely damaged on the *next to last* day. At anchor not far from Sweet Pea, she was torpedoed in an air attack.[7] But for the most part the ships in the U.S. Navy kept low profiles after the A-bombing of Japan. No one ever wants to be the last man killed in a war.

A good part of the victorious Pacific Fleet went to Tokyo Bay over the next two weeks to participate in the ceremonies marking the surrender of the Japanese government and to begin the occupation. But *Portland* was assigned her own important mission. Japanese forces in the far reaches of the Pacific and on the Asian mainland had to surrender, too. As early as August 22, outlying Imperial Army and Navy headquarters began formally laying down their arms. The earliest surrender was at Mili Atoll in the Marshalls, and it was followed by separate ceremonies in Korea, the Ryukyus, the Bonins, and at Truk, all on September 2 to coincide with the events aboard USS *Missouri* in Tokyo Bay. It was at Truk that Sweet Pea was the star.[8]

Because of her outstanding record, *Portland* was selected as the site of the surrender of the headquarters of Japan's forces in the Pacific.[9] An atoll in the Caroline chain, Truk had been occupied by Spain in the sixteenth century and then captured by the Germans after Spain's defeat by the Americans in 1898. In 1919, the Japanese took over the Carolines under a League of Nations mandate. Because Truk has a magnificent harbor, Japan built the island up as her great forward base, analogous to America's Pearl Harbor. At Truk, the Japanese constructed several airfields, fortified many defensive positions, and created extensive ship repair facilities. As a result, it became the great mid-ocean air and naval base for the Imperial Army and Navy.[10]

Truk was widely regarded among Americans as the strongest of all the Japanese positions in the Pacific. During the war Admiral Nimitz wanted very much to fly his flag there. He ultimately decided against an invasion, partly because it would be too costly and partly because better bases for further assaults against Japan could be found in the Mariana Islands of Saipan, Tinian, and Guam.[11] As American forces pushed across the ocean to assault the Japanese Empire, the invasion of the Marshalls in February 1944 included an attack on Truk by a fast carrier task force. It was a three-day blitz that left the fortress effectively neutralized.[12] On several other occasions, American carriers pounded the island, just to keep it that way. *Portland* was with them in April 1944, when she was called on to shell some of Truk's defenses.[13] Because these raids made Truk no threat to Allied forces that were moving further west toward Japan, the bastion was bypassed. Still, the word "Truk" always conjured up apprehension in the minds of Americans who fought in the Pacific.[14]

In September 1945, vaunted Truk was the location of the enemy's headquarters that would have to surrender all of Japan's Pacific holdings. The ceremony would take place on *Portland*'s deck. The ship left Okinawa on August 25 and arrived three days later in Apra, Guam. There, late in the afternoon of August 31, Vice Admiral George Murray, the overall U.S. commander in the Marianas, came aboard with his staff.[15] Almost in a trade for the high-ranking officers, twenty-one of Sweet Pea's enlisted men left the ship that day, headed home for discharge.[16] Merle Choate thought he was going to be one of them, and was disappointed when he learned he was not on the list. Later on, though, he was glad that he had gone to Truk.[17]

On September 1, Sweet Pea was escorted by destroyers *Ralph Talbot* and *Stack* and destroyer escort *Osmus* as she sped to Truk with Admiral Murray embarked.[18] Task Unit 94.3.2 steamed at twenty-two knots so as to enter the harbor at exactly 0800, the time the Japanese had been told to receive it.[19] No one trusted the enemy, however. On the way to Guam to pick up Admiral Murray, *Portland* conducted firing drills with live ammunition, fully two weeks after the Japanese government had announced the surrender.[20] On the way to Truk, the group zigzagged around several base courses, taking no chances about possibly recalcitrant enemy submarine skippers.[21] On the morning of September 2, as the task unit approached the fortress island, *Portland*'s crew was arrayed in dress whites, but all were at their battle stations, just in case.[22] *Portland* launched one of her SOCs to patrol for submarines. As he carried out his mission, pilot Jim Young worried that some of the huge number of Japanese in the garrison at Truk might not have heard about the surrender, and he kept an eye out for anti-aircraft gunfire. The flight was uneventful, though, as Japanese behavior throughout the event was unimpeachable.[23]

The ships simply stopped, without anchoring, about a mile and a half south-south-west of South Pass at Truk. It was as if they were emphasizing that staying there was not part of the plan. At 1029, a seven-man Japanese delegation came aboard *Portland*.[24] Likewise, seven American officers awaited them.[25] The Japanese were taken to the wardroom, where they were instructed on what their duties would be, and at 1110 they were escorted back to the quarterdeck. Eleven minutes later, they began to sign the surrender documents. When they finished, Admiral Murrary signed for the United States and the Allied Powers. While the officials worked on the surrender documents, one man from Sweet Pea's Fifth Division nonchalantly walked over to the surrender table and stole one of the glass paperweights for a souvenir.[26] Admiral Murray then turned to the "crowd," which comprised only the surrender parties and the crew of the cruiser, and made this announcement: "All Japanese held islands under the command of Lieutenant General Shunzaburo Magikura of the Imperial Japanese Army and Vice Admiral Chichi Hara of the Imperial Japanese Navy having been surrendered to me, acting in the name of the Commander in Chief United States Pacific Fleet on this date, 2 September 1945, are hereby and henceforth proclaimed to be under United States control."[27]

Murray made no effort to give a summarizing MacArthuresque speech and the ceremonies concluded forthwith.

Although *Portland*'s men had been apprehensive entering the harbor at Truk, their intimidation ended when they saw the Japanese officers. Some smirked that the man in charge was quite short while his aide was enormous.[28] Merle Choate said the younger man was "the biggest goddam Jap I ever saw!"[29] Ron Hicks had to finagle his way up front in order to see. He thought that the Japanese admiral seemed happy that the war was over while the general was miserable.[30] Edwin Allred noticed that the admiral wore a badly wrinkled uniform, and Willie Partridge harrumphed that the general's dress uniform was rather tattered. They both wondered about the living conditions endured by the enlisted men on Truk and what they would have looked like if this is what the Commanding Officers were wearing to such an important ceremony.[31] In fact, the Truk garrison had been cut off from surface or air supply and reduced to near starvation after U.S. forces bypassed it.[32] It might not have been that formidable a bastion by 1945, after all.

Having completed their depressing duty, the Japanese officers left *Portland,* got into their little boat, and headed for shore.[33] An American seaplane that had been standing by took the documents and flew away somewhere official. And that was that.[34] *Portland* spent a half-hour right after lunch refueling *Osmus,* which then departed on another mission. The rest of the task unit got underway at 1405 to take Admiral Murray back to Guam. Sweet Pea arrived there about twenty-four hours later on September 3, 1945.[35] So far as the sailors knew, no occupation force landed on Truk. Nor did the crew know how the stranded Japanese garrison at Truk ever got home to Japan.[36]

Every man on board was given a set of official Navy photographs that recorded the event, and today most of them cherish those pictures and their own role in the surrender.[37] A few of the sailors have added to their souvenirs of the event. Years later, the Federated States of Micronesia issued a postage stamp with a picture of Sweet Pea on the day of the surrender in the lagoon at what is now called "Chuuk." Some of *Portland*'s veterans have the stamp.[38] The flag flown by the ship that day in Truk was originally given to the City of Portland, Maine, during the ship's visit back home several weeks after the surrender.[39] But city officials apparently did not know what to do with what the crew thought was a hallowed banner, and merely stored it in "the archives." In 1994, following a petition by the *Portland* veterans' association, the city gave the flag to a delegation of the former sailors so it could be displayed in the Nimitz Museum in Fredericksburg, Texas, "on a long term loan."[40]

On April 4, 1997, The History Channel broadcast a program on the wreckage of the Japanese ships sunk by the raids in the lagoon at Truk, which has become a haven for marine life of all sorts. Divers come from all over the world to study the spectacle. The show included footage of the surrender ceremony on board USS *Portland*.[41]

## Magic Carpet

Having returned Murray to his headquarters at Guam, *Portland* thought she was forgotten by naval authorities as she lay anchored in Apra harbor. After a few days without orders of any sort, the Communications Officers began to check back files to see if something had been missed, but they could find nothing. Captain Thackery, also impatient, finally sent Lieutenant Graeme Robertson over to the Command Headquarters. He was met there by the Chief of Staff for the Marianas Command, Captain Oliver Naquin. Luckily, Naquin had a warm interest in Sweet Pea and did not just dismiss the young officer out of hand. Only days earlier as a member of the surrender party, he had ridden *Portland* to and from the surrender in Truk. But he had an even closer tie than that: Naquin had been an Engineering Officer aboard Sweet Pea in the first year of the war, including the 1942 battle at Guadalcanal and the difficult days tied to the palm tree at Tulagi.[42] He now chuckled at the worrisome depiction of the ship's plight he was hearing, because he knew that *Portland* had somehow failed to get her orders. He gave Robertson his headquarters' copy of the message the cruiser had missed: "USS PORTLAND, HEREBY DETACHED, PROCEED VIA POINTS XRAY AND ZULU TO PEARL TO JOIN TF 11 FOR FURTHER TRANSFER TO CINCLANT [Commander-in-Chief, Atlantic Fleet] FOR NAVY DAY OPERATIONS."[43]

Imagine what Robertson must have felt when reading those words. Sweet Pea was going home to celebrate the end of the war!

On September 12 in Guam, the ship picked up about eight hundred servicemen who qualified for rotation back to the States and took them to Pearl Harbor. Since peacetime sailing rules now applied, she was allowed to make only sixteen knots on the way, so the voyage took longer than it had during the war, when she often sped at twenty knots or more in transit. But this time she proudly flew a "Homeward Bound" pennant, 960 feet long, one foot wide.[44]

In Hawaii, she dropped off the passengers and was the subject of a flattering newspaper story, under the headline "VETERAN PORT-LAND SHEDS HER WAR PAINT." A photo showed six of her sailors in a line, holystoning the main deck. It had been painted the less visible blue-grey during the war, but could now be returned to the shiny white that peacetime expectations required.[45]

At Pearl, Sweet Pea continued her service in Operation Magic Carpet, which provided "rides home" from the far reaches of the Pacific war zone for many veterans with long service time. This time she took aboard six hundred new passengers bound for the East Coast. She got underway with old companion *Enterprise* and three other carriers, four light cruisers, and a large number of destroyers headed for the Panama Canal.[46] All of these ships were being rushed to the Atlantic coast to participate in the Navy Day festivities at the end of October. It was a fitting way to end the war for the veteran men and vessels that had won the war in the Pacific.

Morale on the ship was very high, of course. George Loock, an officer in the engineering department, thought, "10,000 miles from Guam to New York! With the war over it was truly a pleasure cruise."[47] Captain Thackery tried to keep the youthful enthusiasm somewhat disciplined, nevertheless. On October 2, while still in the Pacific, the skipper held Captain's Mast and administered minor punishment to a quartermaster petty officer who was inattentive on watch and to an electrician's mate petty officer who performed poorly during a steering shift drill.[48] Those men had unilaterally ended their period of enlistment early, but Thackery would have none of it.

The task group arrived at Panama on October 8. It took about eight hours to transit the canal, and then the crews were allowed four days of liberty in Colon.[49] It was a wild time for many. But Chuck Morton thought the Panamanian locals were like those everywhere the fleet pulled in: "just trying to take the sailors' money."[50] Not everyone went ashore. Marine Pat Miles was not allowed to go. En route from Guam, he had not taken his salt pills at sea and as a result lost some work time when admitted to sick bay with heat exhaustion. To worsen his penalty, his five days of brig time did not begin until the day the ship reached the Canal.[51] For Malcolm Marks, this opportunity for liberty in Panama was a waste of time. He was frightened by the doctor's lecture about venereal diseases, so he stayed aboard even when his section had liberty.[52]

Bill Reehl thought the free time was intended to let the men blow off steam before arriving in the U.S. ports they would visit. They had, after all, been at sea in effect for over a year since they left Mare Island in August 1944, with only brief stops in such places as Tacloban, Mog Mog, and Buckner Bay.[53] If Reehl was right, the underlying fear of misbehavior was valid because every night the ship was in Panama many of the sailors returned late from liberty.[54] Those who did were given stiff punishments at Captain's Mast. One man, for example, four hours late in returning, was given twenty days confinement on bread and water with a full food ration every third day. That was the harshest penalty, but others punished that day were demoted, fined, or confined.[55]

## THE VICTORY LAP

No one complained about liberty in New York City. The ship and her task group left Panama on October 12 and arrived in the big city five days later. On the way, the crew was told that *Portland* had won the Navy Commendation Medal for her heroism at Guadalcanal, but what lay ahead was even more exciting than that expected news.[56] The very entry into the harbor was wonderful for these men who had witnessed little but warfare over the past four years. Merle Choate had never seen the Statue of Liberty before, and steaming past it was thrilling for him. So were the boats' whistles blowing, the USO barge with a small orchestra playing "Sentimental Journey," and the five or six young women dressed only in bathing suits despite the cold air that chilled all the sailors, veterans of warmer climes.[57] As *Portland* approached her berth at the Brooklyn Navy Yard, George Loock's father followed her from his office building, using the binoculars he had kept on his desk all throughout the war to watch ships coming and going.[58] Alongside the pier were huge signs, many of them proclaiming "Welcome Home" and "Well Done."[59]

For some of the sailors who had accumulated enough discharge points, New York was the end of their *Portland* careers. On October 17, only two hours after the ship tied up in Brooklyn, about two hundred men from her crew were sent to separation centers near their homes.[60] Choate, for example, saw little else but Miss Liberty, because he left the ship that very day, caught a train, and two days later was in the separation center in Norman, Oklahoma.[61] He missed what nearly everyone thought was the best liberty in *Portland*'s entire history. For many, it was like a trip to an amusement park, which the raucous greeting in the harbor only began. Ron Hicks, for example, went to Rockefeller Center, the Museum of Natural History, and Carnegie Hall, where he saw the Woody Herman band in concert.[62]

But every man had his own unique experience. For its November 5, 1945, issue, *Life* magazine wrote a major story about Sweet Pea's visit to the big city. The cover picture showed one of the 40mm sighters, Seaman 1/c Matthews. On his uniform were proudly displayed a gunnery badge, a "gun pointer first class" badge, and several ribbons and battle stars for campaigns in the Pacific. Another picture showed *Portland* sailors in Jack Dempsey's bar.[63] Being in New York was so wild that the ship's Marines worked out a special liberty deal, duty sections be damned! When a man would get off watch on the quarterdeck, he simply went ashore, whether he was in the liberty section or not. The Marines could get away with this because only their buddies, the sentries at the gangway, were paying attention to which men left the ship and which returned and when. A Marine would come back only for his next watch and at its end promptly shove off again.[64] Some sailors, not beneficiaries of this "open gangway" liberty enjoyed by the leathernecks, simply failed to come back to the ship on time. Just citing two days that were typical, a half dozen were missing from quarters on Sunday, October 21, and thirteen were late on Tuesday, October 23.[65]

As the final stop on this triumphal tour, in company with several other ships, *Portland* went to Portland, Maine, where the city she was named after treated her royally.[66] October 27 was Navy Day, and the ship's trip was timed so she would be in Portland on that date.[67] A young officer, Lieutenant (jg) Jack Hunt had been sent ahead to help with the arrangements. He was surprised and pleased that the city officials actually sought his advice on dinner parties, dances, banquets, parades, and so on, because they wanted to get it right for "their" ship.[68]

What no one could predict was the weather, which was awful as Sweet Pea pulled into Casco Bay on the morning of October 25, 1945. The rain pelted down so wildly that the ship did not go to dress quarters for entering port, as planned. A tug that brought official guests out to meet the ship was tossed around so badly that some of the passengers got seasick.[69] When the little vessel reached the cruiser, the stormy water hurled it into the cruiser's gangway. The collision ripped the ladder from its stanchions, imperiling the sailors who were stationed there in great ceremony. The ship thereupon moved to smoother waters more inland, but the rain continued to fall heavily.[70]

Oddly enough, none of the sailors have ever spoken or written about the ugly weather that greeted them on arrival. They had such a great time in Portland that the awful entry into the port was quickly and permanently put out of their memories as a minor glitch. The ship's log, though, recorded the official welcome home. At 1000, even while the ship was still underway trying to find its more comfortable berth alongside the Navy Supply Pier in Portland, Maine's Governor Horace E. Hildreth, Mayor James Barlow, and other officials of the state and the city came aboard. The mayor presented Captain Thackery with the key to the city.[71]

While they did not seem perturbed by the foul weather, the sailors certainly noticed this greeting and the pride in the ship that it represented. The personal greetings sailors received from individual people in the city were also terrific. One man wrote in his diary, "We had the works—a parade—speeches and lots of fun. It sure was great."[72] Chuck Morton said, "We had a gas in Portland. It was great liberty."[73] Bill Reehl recalled that "the city of Portland opened their [sic] arms in a tremendous welcoming ceremony. . . ."[74] Ron Hicks reported that the "people there really liked the ship and the crew, and they had pictures of the surrender at every display area."[75]

The city loved this ship, and the ship returned the affection. On October 26, Captain Thackery presented the flag flown by Sweet Pea on the day of the Truk surrender to H.C. Bibby, one of the city's officials. It should be noted, however, that ceremonies had to share the daily routine with other events. For example, later on October 26, a Miss Pauline Warne severely sprained her wrist when she was accidentally pushed against the side of the gangway. She was given first aid by Chief Pharmacist's Mate Jackson, who accompanied her to the Maine General Hospital, where X-rays were negative.[76] Meanwhile, Captain Thackery continued to try to hold the line on discipline, administering punishment at Captain's Mast on twenty-two sailors who had returned late to the ship from liberty in New York City.[77]

*Portland* was home, but she was soon to be called one more time into the service of her country, with dreadful results.

# 15

# THE FINAL MISSION

After the visit to Portland, the end-of-war celebrations wound down, but Sweet Pea was yet again pressed into serious work. Several million GIs in the European Theater of Operations (ETO) had to be brought home. A heavy cruiser like *Portland* with her own crew reduced by discharges had a lot of space for these soldiers. Not surprisingly, *Portland* and several other veterans of the Pacific War were sent across the Atlantic for the first time, to collect America's boys and bring them home.

On October 31, 1945, *Portland* went to the Boston Navy Yard, where she was outfitted for the European Magic Carpet.[1] The Marine detachment and the aviation division both debarked, since they were thought unnecessary for the ocean-liner duty that lay ahead, and they were never to return.[2] A number of sailors whose enlistments were nearly complete were also transferred ashore, ninety the first day in Boston and thirty-one the day after that, including a dozen Marines.[3] Incidentally, while all these men were departing the ship to leave the Navy, smaller numbers were coming aboard to join the ship's company. About twenty new men reported on October 23, about fifteen on October 24, an officer and eleven men on October 25, eighteen on October 28, about a dozen on November 3, and about two dozen on November 7.[4]

The soldiers who would soon be passengers were, however, the biggest concern once the ship got to Boston. The plan was to lodge many of them in crew compartments where bunks were now empty because of all the discharged men and others who were sent on leave.[5] To make even

208

more passenger space, both the starboard and port hangars were refitted, since the SOC aircraft had flown away. Bunks were installed there, six high, so that each hangar could serve as lodging for about two hundred troops.[6]

Some men from the crew were reckoned temporarily unnecessary and were put ashore. Some of them took trains to New York, where they were berthed in USS *Olympia,* Admiral Dewey's flagship during the Battle of Manila Bay in 1898. There they enjoyed "open gangway" liberty, and got to know New York City pretty well as a result. Fernando Valdes recalls that, after the fighting *Portland,* the old *Olympia* seemed "quaint, almost cartoonish, like 'The Little Engine That Could.'" As he lay in the dark and the ship moved and creaked in the current and tides, he thought he could "almost feel the ghosts of sailors past moving silently about their daily routine, murmuring as they went."[7]

Those in the crew who were still aboard *Portland* were not happy about the reduction in their number. While the ship's work had settled into a peacetime routine, pretty light compared to the Condition One Easy that had been almost permanent for months at the end of the war, the chores to be done by each man on these Magic Carpet cruises would be increased a great deal because of the smaller crew.[8] Nevertheless, the first Magic Carpet voyage in November, to Le Havre and back to New York, was uneventful. The ship flew across the Atlantic at twenty-four knots. Remembering that she was once known as "Rolling P," it is not surprising that the going became pretty rough. One sailor suffered first- and second-degree burns to his face and neck when a coffee pot was thrown onto him "by a sudden list of the ship."[9]

That the trip itself was generally so unexceptional came as a pleasant surprise to the Navigators. The ship had never been to Europe before and no one on board had any experience in getting across the stormy North Atlantic. Loran, a modern electronic triangulation system, was available and Sweet Pea had the necessary equipment. But Loran had not been used in the western Pacific because the places where outlying stations might have been located were in the hands of the enemy during the war. Consequently, the quartermasters who had been trained in Loran sometime back had never operated it in serious conditions. Still, as one would expect from *Portland* sailors, when Captain Thackery asked them about getting to Europe, they said they could do the job. They dusted off the Loran gear and got to work. Then they discovered that unlike the

Pacific, where a noontime sun line could almost always be acquired by
sextant, the midday sky in the fall and early winter was always overcast
or worse in the Atlantic. So they had to trust to their dead reckoning and
they tried to believe in the Loran, but in fact they worried their way across.
At the end of the trip, personnel on the navigation bridge burst into smiles
when the quartermasters discovered that they had "hit England almost
right on the mark."[10] It was a relief for some others in the crew, too, who
perhaps tongue-in-cheek spread rumors that those same quartermasters
were somehow drinking the "juice" out of the gyrocompass.[11]

Sweet Pea stopped for about twelve hours in Plymouth, England, on
November 21, 1945, then reached Le Havre on the Channel coast of
France the following day. At 2120 she began embarking passengers, and
completed the loading at 0240. In a little over five hours in the nighttime
darkness, *Portland* took aboard twenty-eight army officers and 1,214
enlisted solders, and she left Le Havre five and a half hours later, at 0804
on Friday, November 23.[12] Everyone wanted to get those veterans home
as soon as possible, and Sweet Pea pulled into Pier 51 on Manhattan's
west side in mid-afternoon on the 29th.[13]

    In sum, then, the first Magic Carpet trip across the Atlantic went
well. But even *preparing* for the second voyage in December had some

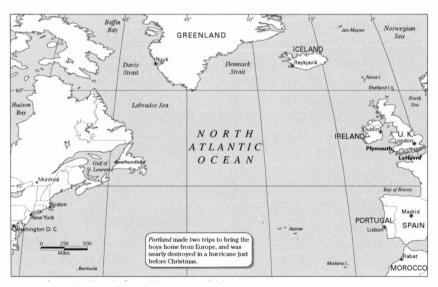

Map 6. Operation "Magic Carpet" Nov.-Dec. 1945

unsettling moments. First of all, the skeletonizing of the crew continued, as the national demobilization program got into high gear. On December 1, about one hundred men were sent to various sites that were now officially called Personnel Separation Centers. Some were located at expectable places, such as Bainbridge, Maryland; Boston, Massachusetts; Bremerton, Washington; Charleston, South Carolina; Great Lakes, Illinois; Jacksonville, Florida; Memphis, Tennessee; Minneapolis, Minnesota; New Orleans, Louisiana; Norfolk, Virginia; St. Louis, Missouri; or Toledo, Ohio. But few would have predicted that others would be located at Camp Wallace, Texas, Lido Beach, New York, Norman, Oklahoma, Sampson, New York, or Shoemaker, California![14]

Just two days before *Portland*'s departure, Captain Thackery was relieved on December 4, 1945, by Captain Lowe H. Bibby.[15] A change in the command of a ship always brings difficulties, no matter how qualified the new skipper may be. Worse, some sailors who thought they were going to be home for Christmas for the first time since the war began were actually recalled from leave to make the trip.[16]

*Portland* left New York bound for Le Havre on December 6. She carried passengers *to* Europe this time, a total of 235.[17] One among them was thrilled to be going over. He was an Army major who had somehow finagled a ride in Sweet Pea to visit his girlfriend in France. On the way, however, he came down with acute appendicitis, and yet again *Portland*'s doctors performed an emergency appendectomy while the ship was underway in rough waters. Although the soldier was supposed to be bedridden for a week or so after the operation, he simply got up and walked off the ship when she reached Le Havre. He later sent a thank-you note, but said nothing about whether the Army had penalized him for not reporting as ordered to the Army hospital upon debarkation.[18]

Sweet Pea did not stop in Plymouth this time but went directly to France, arriving on the 13th. Again she began taking aboard westbound personnel almost the minute her passengers were debarked, and again it was overnight, from 2150 to 0050. This time the manifest listed forty army officers, seven naval officers, 997 soldiers, and one civilian technician, a total of 1,045.[19] Most of the passengers had been serving overseas for a long time, veterans of the First Army, Third Army, 82d Airborne, and various other units.[20] They had been gathered outside Le Havre in camps named for cigarette brands. When they saw the huge ships they were sailing in—a carrier, a battleship, and a heavy cruiser—

it seemed that the Navy truly had provided a Magic Carpet that would take them home.[21]

Staff Sergeant Claude Warble of Hummelstown, Pennsylvania, for example, had been in the European Theater since September 1942. Originally assigned to the motor pool of the 104th Cavalry Regiment, Warble endured the V-1 and V-2 blitz of London in 1944 and served in the rear echelon during the liberation of western Europe. Before going overseas, he had married a girl he met while in the Army but then shipped out after they had been together only a few months. He had not seen her in more than three years by the time he left Camp Chesterfield for the *Portland,* and could hardly wait to be with her again. To Warble, who was being repatriated as a member of the 84th Signal Battalion, Sweet Pea looked like a homeward-bound luxury liner.[22]

For the crew, on the other hand, it was a chore taking on all these troops who were totally unfamiliar with shipboard routine. That there were so many soldiers and so few sailors in the markedly smaller crew surely added to the burden.[23] And yet, Sergeant Warble remembers that the sailors were friendly and helpful to the soldiers who were squeezed in here and there.[24]

*Portland* left port hastily again, only seven hours after the last soldier came aboard, at 0750 on December 14.[25] This time she went to sea in a task force that included carrier *Enterprise* and battleship *Washington.*[26]

For the soldiers who had been overseas for so long, that the ship was serving white bread was a miracle. Sergeant Warble remembered that it seemed like angel food cake. He was also pleased that the cooks were happy to give the troops whatever they wanted to eat. When one soldier asked for another slice of bread, the *Portland*'s cook asked if he wanted some meat on it. The soldier laughed, saying, "No thanks; I don't want to ruin the taste of the bread!"[27]

Not all the bonhomie was due to simple kindness. Within hours after the embarkation of the troops, there were major card and craps games going on all over the ship. The soldiers had lots of money, some from having run black-market operations in France just before boarding. Those funds wildly inflated the ship's economy. Sailors Don Martin and Al Clark ran a craps game. To get started they had to pay a shipmate $35 for a 25¢ pair of dice! In about five hours, just serving as the house, the two *Portland* men cleared $600, an enormous sum for men whose monthly pay was about $50.[28] Another member of the crew, Robert

Braswell, *sold* his *bunk* to a passenger, for $500! The soldier had a duffle bag filled with money, locked and otherwise secured in several ways, and was carrying a loaded German Luger in his belt. Because he couldn't leave the bag, he hired Braswell to bring him food at the rate of $20 a meal. Braswell also provided him with a scrub bucket that the rich soldier used as a latrine. Braswell would empty it in the crew's head from time to time, always for a fee. On his way off the ship in New York, the passenger pressed several hundred dollars into Braswell's hands. The next day, the sailor wired home $4,000, much more money than he had earned in four years in the Navy. He bought a car with *part* of what he had earned working as the wealthy soldier's personal servant.[29]

*Portland*'s compass had been damaged on the way to Europe.[30] No one was concerned about that casualty as she left Le Havre, though, since all she had to do was stay in formation with the two larger ships. At 1110 on December 16, then, she fell in astern of USS *Washington,* which Sweet Pea's deck log reported was "said to be" on a westerly heading at the time.[31] Although the sea had been glassy calm as the ship pulled out of port on the morning of December 14, it began to rain two days later. No one worried about that, either.[32]

## THE *PORTLAND* HURRICANE

What was first only a rainstorm became a deluge during the next day, December 17, 1945, and by that evening the weather had blown up into a full-fledged hurricane. It grew to include winds in excess of ninety knots and seas sometimes growing as high as ninety feet from trough to cap, although the swells were short.[33] All the ships bobbed around like so many corks. The embarked soldiers thought it ominous when Captain Bibby ordered some empty fuel tanks to be filled with salt water as ballast. Although none of them were mariners, the soldiers could all see that the skipper was trying to make the ship more seaworthy. And when the crew began taking tons of ammunition from ready boxes high in the ship's superstructure and throwing all those rounds over the side in order to give Sweet Pea a lower center of gravity, everyone knew the ship was preparing for serious trouble.[34]

Captain Bibby faced two problems, each conflicting the other, perhaps neither of which could be solved even separately. On the one hand, he needed to keep radar contact with the battleship, because without a gyrocompass he had no idea where Sweet Pea was truly headed. But he needed to find a course by magnetic compass that *Portland* could ride safely, which might not be the one the much larger *Washington* would choose. Although his engines were making turns for ten knots, the cruiser was actually moving through the tempest at only five to seven knots. And the helmsman could not stay within twenty-five degrees of the ordered magnetic course, no matter what it was.[35]

The quartermasters who were keeping the log on the bridge during these watches wrote in great detail, as if making a record of a momentous occasion. Indeed it was: "2000 In radar contact with Washington; seas very heavy and mountainous; short swell; height of waves increasing (estimated average height 80–90 feet). Anemometer out of commission, wind logged 70–75 knots by estimate; wind velocity increasing rapidly. Rolling very heavily with water splashing high on starboard superstructure; forward and aft."[36]

The sea began to pour into the ship through every opening. Water ran about six inches deep down some of the internal passageways. When it backed up as the ship pitched, rolled, and yawed, some internal offices and shops were flooded by a wave as high as seven feet, not out in the weather, but *inside*.[37] Shipfitter 1/c John J. Horace was one of the men who had joined *Portland* only since her return from the Pacific. He was making his first cruise in Sweet Pea, and it was an experience he talked about for the rest of his days. He took up a station alongside one internal passageway while a couple of cooks manned the other side. The sailors would reach out to grab soldiers being washed along in the tide, again *inside* the ship.[38] The crew in two of the firerooms sloshed around trying to keep their heads above water that sometimes grew to twelve feet depending on the ship's roll, and not always successfully.[39]

A huge safe broke loose in the radio shack and by pitching to and fro endangered all personnel in the room. It took conspicuous bravery to leave the compartment, go out into the dangerous weather to get below, and find a line strong enough to hold the free-wheeling safe. Those who did so had already experienced the conditions, so they showed special courage in fighting again through the ferocious winds and enormous seas to get back to the radio room and lasso the offending safe to secure it.[40] Lieutenant Barney Kliks and the men who did the work took about an hour to reach the shack. They went one careful step at a time, "whenever the ship hit the center of its roll," and had to rest every now and then.

When they finally reached the radio room, they collapsed in fatigue, but were quickly roused by an all-hands announcement that anyone with first-aid experience "get to the sick bay on the double."[41] Many of those men went back out into the maelstrom and then below to try to help out there.

For hours the task force was hammered by ocean and buffeted by wind, causing considerable damage to all the ships. The flight deck of *Enterprise* was so seriously damaged that she entered New York harbor looking as if the Japanese had got her again. *Washington*'s enginerooms flooded so badly that she temporarily lost all power. She floated adrift until rescued by craft sent out from the French coast.[42] In *Portland* things were not that desperate, but water in the casing of Number Two main engine's turbine caused so much vibration that the engine had to be shut down.[43]

Captain Bibby told a reporter after the event that it was the worst storm he had ever seen in his twenty-eight years at sea.[44] *Portland* was a generally unstable ship to begin with, and when faced by the worst storm in more than a quarter century it rolled so much that conditions on board can only be guessed. In a ship at sea, a storm never lets up. A person cannot just go somewhere else and be away from it. For long minutes, hours, days, the ship never stops rolling, never stops yawing, never stops pitching. Bad seems to get worse as her bow slaps into the water with increasingly louder shocks. Items that were not stowed properly, and even some that *were,* come flying from every direction. As the shell of the ship is bent by unimaginable forces, it makes enormous cracking sounds. Everyone hears them and everyone is sure that in the next instant the ship will be ripped apart and watery death will roar through the tears in her hull. Soldiers who had never been in anything like these conditions were terrified, as were even sailors who thought themselves pretty salty. Merely holding on was as much as a man could do. Many of the passengers were berthed in the aircraft hangars, and although the hangar doors had been welded shut to give them some security, nothing in a tempest like this could make anyone feel safe.[45]

J.J. Horace said years later that he never heard *Portland* referred to as "Sweet Pea."[46] One can easily understand why: December 1945 was the greatest—the *worst?*—moment in the history of the "Rolling P." All hands in Central Damage Control watched the inclinometer, a pendulum that was calibrated to mark the size of the roll. It was widely believed that the ship would capsize if it rolled to forty-five degrees.[47] Memories about how far she actually did roll in that storm varied. One man said "almost 45 degrees," another said "48 degrees," and a third "52 degrees"![48] The ship's log was much less dramatic than any of those recollections, but still recorded "about 40°."[49]

The damage with the greatest consequences would come at about 2150 when a powerful wave stove in one of the hangar doors. Inside the room, 189 soldiers were fearfully holding on.[50] Sergeant Warble lay on his back, which was now "on the wall of the hangar," terrified that every time she rolled, *Portland* would not come back upright. He was sure the only reason the ship did keep returning to the vertical was that Captain Bibby had made ballast, a decision he later said saved his life.[51]

When the door buckled, the soldiers in that hangar, desperately hanging on just because of the rolls, suddenly found themselves crushed back against the walls and overwhelmed by seawater rushing everywhere. Now each swell of the ocean threw bunks, furniture, personal items, and people all about. Several men crashed through the canvas that had held them in their bunks but now surrendered to the power of unleashed nature. One of them was Sergeant Warble, who broke his knee and injured his back slamming to the deck after a few bounces off walls. Looking up from the floor, which was then far from horizontal, he saw some shelving that had been used to store the men's life jackets, all now being worn, of course. Warble thought that that ledge might be his sanctuary. Somehow, despite the agonizing pain of his injuries, he climbed up the wall, which was often close to horizontal, and got to that spot. There he wedged himself so he could not fall out, and watched his past life project itself in front of him.[52]

Sergeant T. Lancian of Everett, Massachusetts, who had been wounded in the Battle of the Bulge, said that what happened in *Portland*'s hangar was more terrifying than any of his war experiences.[53] That may not have been an overstatement, because *Portland*'s Navigator, Commander A.D. Jackson, later told the press that the water which rushed through the hangar demolishing bunks and pinning men under wreckage, had hit the room with the force of a "ten-ton truck."[54]

Things were happening fast. At 2155, on hearing that the hangar door had collapsed, the ship's First Lieutenant, in charge of damage control, immediately went to investigate. At 2202, amidst the trouble he was having trying to keep the ship afloat, the Officer of the Deck passed the word for all Army medical personnel to report to sick bay. At 2205, the Captain learned that two soldiers had been washed out of the hangar and were trapped in the starboard catapult. He immediately brought the ship around to a heading that might make their rescue possible.[55]

The new heading was not, however, good to the ship itself. Afterward Commander Jackson told a reporter, "We knew that it would be at the probable sacrifice of the ship's forecastle."[56] And indeed it was. Ten minutes after coming around, at 2215, the ship was hit by a terrible wave that destroyed the SK radar antenna, which was located almost at the *highest* point on the ship. Ten minutes after that another huge swell broke over the bow, tearing away stanchions and deck plating forward of the superstructure and even crushing some bulkheads below decks. Men in the damage-control parties, those heroes of wartime, went to work shoring up the damaged compartments.[57]

Afterward it was discovered that the smashing of the bow caused the area forward of the chain locker to be twisted to port about two feet![58] The boat davits on the starboard side were ripped right off with Motor Whaleboat #1 still attached. Fortunately the crew was able to lash the wreckage to the well deck in yet another piece of heroic labor in the teeth of the storm.[59]

Throughout the disaster, Sweet Pea distinguished herself as she had during the war. Captain Bibby realized that terror was sweeping through his crew and passengers. As events became increasingly perilous, he made a quick speech over the ship's public address system that calmed a lot of fearful men. Bibby's controlled voice restored their confidence when he said, "This is the Captain. The ship has sustained damage, but is in no immediate danger. Damage-control parties are taking measures to put things right. I have ordered all hatches to be secured. For your information, this ship is designed so that, if it turns upside down the turrets will fall off and she will right herself. That is all."[60]

*"The turrets will fall off and she will right herself."* What a great little white lie! The recently discovered sunken wreck of the German battleship *Bismarck* showed that the turrets would indeed fall off, and *Bismarck* did come to rest on her bottom. But that *Portland* would right herself while still afloat was doubtful at best. And yet his promise worked. Many of the soldiers told reporters later that this speech reassured them and from then on throughout the disaster they were never worried the ship would sink.[61]

Crew members worked to amplify the confidence the Captain's remarks had stimulated. When Lieutenant Kliks was asked by an injured soldier if the ship could founder, he responded without thought, "Hell no—the Japs could not put us down and the storm is not going to, either." A toughened sergeant got his two cents worth in, as well. Badly injured himself, he nevertheless shouted at the soldiers who continued to complain about the situation, "Shut up. The Navy is doing all they can. Keep out of their way and hang on."[62] J.J. Horace simply lied to a frightened soldier who asked whether the ship was going to make it. Although Horace was himself frightened as the inclinometer approached forty-five degrees, he told the man that this kind of storm happened a lot and that it was nothing to worry about.[63]

The sailors gave credit to Captain Bibby for his shiphandling excellence, too. Many of these men had seen "Tex" Settle outmaneuver kamikazes, and now they admired Lowe Bibby's competition with an Atlantic hurricane. Moreover, *Portland* had dealt with so many unexpected crises during the war that even the skeleton crew still on board was quick to adjust to this new emergency, sometimes at great personal risk. For example, during the storm, two sailors rushed out to help the two soldiers who had been swept out of the hangar and trapped in the starboard catapult, where they might be washed overboard. A third *Portland* man, pressed up against a bulkhead, assisted by giving useful directions to the four men about what direction to go and where to reach for grips. Although Captain Bibby had changed course to make this rescue possible, the fifth man was repeatedly battered by the waves, but he stayed there helping out. It took about a half-hour, but in the end all were saved.[64]

Emergency repairs were accomplished even while the ship was being tossed about by the storm. The firerooms had to be pumped out so the boilers would continue to operate and the men would not drown. Electricians lowered submersible pumps into the flooded spaces. The pumps kept the depth somewhat manageable until they burnt out and electricians had to rewind them to keep them in action. Merely wrestling those heavy, three-foot pumps with their bulky cords and hoses up and down into and out of a darkened and flooded boiler room while the ship was rolling and heaving took great courage.[65] Likewise, Herman Ferguson and a shipfitter named McGill won the admiration of many when they shored up a hole in the bow with jacks and managed to spot-weld a seam good enough to get the ship through the storm. They worked in knee-deep water and suffered some serious jolts from the electric welder, but they worked on.[66]

This was wearying toil, and it went on for days as the ship tried to find a way out of the storm. When J.J. Horace went back to his compartment to get a couple hours sleep after working for more than twenty-four hours straight, he found a soldier in his bunk trying to sleep but bouncing helplessly as the ship pitched and rolled. The soldier got out for Horace, who promised to show him how to sleep in the bunk the way the sailors did. When he awoke a short time later, Horace demonstrated the sailor's trick of locking one's hands and feet into the webbing and canvas, and the now-stabilized soldier was grateful for the lesson.[67]

Sweet Pea had picked up so many adrift sailors in various battles around the Pacific that she had great experience in taking care of injured men. Her crew was no less heroic in the Atlantic storm. Ship's Cook 1/c John Siri broke three ribs while helping soldiers get out from the wreckage in the hangar bay, and Seaman 1/c William Womack received a bad head wound that had to be sutured.[68] The diminished numbers in the medical department had their hands full. There were only five doctors, including three from the Army who happened to be on board, to handle the more than fifty injured men.[69] The doctors called for help, and when the bridge asked that anyone with experience in first aid report to sick bay, many of *Portland*'s crew did.[70]

Some mistakes were made. Because the triage crew thought others were hurt worse than Sergeant Warble, he was put on a cot lashed to a weight-bearing stanchion in the passageway outside sick bay. He was supposed to await treatment from doctors and corpsmen who were busy dealing with apparently more serious injuries. But injured and cold from his long exposure, Warble went into shock. He began to shake uncontrollably, and it took three sailors to hold him down and get him stabilized. From then on he got very close attention. The corpsmen gave him first aid for his leg and back, and a *Portland* sailor was with him nearly all the time thereafter, checking to be sure that he did not go back into shock.[71]

The workers in sick bay did not have an easy time of it. *Portland* was still being pounded by the storm, so merely standing in place was not possible. One hand had to be used just to hold on, no matter what important job the other hand might be doing. One time the ship's chaplain, Rev. Charles Iley, was helping another officer administer morphine to a seriously injured soldier. Iley observed to his shipmate that neither of them was wearing a life jacket. The other officer just shrugged and said a life jacket "wouldn't be a damn bit of use out there tonight." Iley shrugged and they went on with their work.[72]

In the disaster, one significant change came over *Portland*'s sick bay routine. An Army major visited one of his injured soldiers, and a Navy corpsman began a conversation in a loud voice to put the officer on the spot:

> "HEY, MAJOR, DON'T YOU GUYS HAVE SOME
> WHISKEY UP IN YOUR ROOMS?"
> "Uh. Well, yes."
> "WHY DON'T YOU GET IT DOWN HERE WHERE IT
> CAN DO SOME GOOD?"

It was against regulations to drink any form of alcohol on board any Navy ship, although officers in their unpoliced staterooms frequently violated these rules. But on this hellish occasion plenty of "medicinal" booze flowed into Sweet Pea's sick bay for the injured men. The whiskey relaxed them after what had been a horrible day and got them through what would probably have been an intolerable night.[73]

Someone must have reported to the Captain that not one of the Army men on board was seasick during all this pitching and rolling. He laughed with the troops a few days later, saying, "I know why. Y'all were too damned scared to be sea-sick!"[74] It was not true, though, for the crowds of nauseous soldiers at the crew's head resembled lines where hundreds of sailors once queued up to get paid.[75] Nor was it any joke that three soldiers were killed when the ocean rushed into the hangar berthing space. Sergeant Louis S. Osurics of Steelton, Pennsylvania, broke his back in the collapse of his bunk and then drowned when he was unable to escape the flooding in the hangar, and Sergeant Noah L. Daniels of Amity, Arkansas, fractured his skull and drowned. A third sergeant reported missing was J.M. Lewis of Springfield, Colorado.[76] It was believed that he was crushed and swept away in the huge wave that broke down the hangar door.[77] Fifty-four men were treated for injuries—fifty-two soldier-passengers and two sailors from Sweet Pea's crew—bringing the total casualties to fifty-seven, counting the three who died.[78]

The motor pool of the 104th Cavalry Regiment had suffered no casualties in the war against Germany but was badly bloodied by the ravages of the Atlantic Ocean, more than seven months after the fighting in Europe had ended.[79]

Even while the storm was raging, a few sailors were ordered to retrieve the dead bodies from the hangar. This was the worst working party they had ever endured. Sergeant Daniels had been smashed into an air vent in such a way that his head was laid open, with brain tissue all over the inside of the vent. The working party was ordered to collect all of the human remains, so the men had to pick up the gelatinous mess, a chore that made some of their stomachs turn. The sickened sailors were ordered away, lest their vomit contaminate the remains. All was handled with great delicacy because, as J.J. Horace remembered, everyone felt sorry for the poor man who had come through the war safely only to be killed like this on his way home.[80]

*Portland* plodded painfully on to the Azores. She had lost track of *Washington* during the storm and was simply unable on the 18th to close on a radar contact that may have been the battleship.[81] In the two days it took to make port, the crew and embarked passengers were forced to eat bologna sandwiches three times a day, since cooking was impossible.[82] More injuries were suffered during that time, as men continued to slip and fall on the slick interior decks, receiving cuts and bruises that had to be treated in sick bay. Conditions were so perilous that one man was injured even after Sweet Pea anchored in Horta Bay, Azores, before going to a pier at Ponta Delgada.[83]

On arrival in the Portuguese islands, twenty-two injured men, sixteen of them in stretchers, were taken to a British military hospital, where they remained for a few days.[84] One of the *Portland*'s doctors reported "at least a dozen compound fractures [and] eight spinal fractures with extensive paralysis." These twenty-two seriously hurt soldiers were flown home in hospital planes as soon as arrangements could be made.[85]

Friends and families of the ship's crew suffered, too. The *New York Times* had an electronic news reader on the face of its building overlooking Times Square. On December 18, 1945, Ted Waller and George Pritchard, two *Portland* men who had been given leave in order to make space for the Army passengers, were walking down Broadway when the lights on the *Times* building reported "USS PORTLAND LOST AT SEA."

The two sailors had had several beers while on liberty, but on reading this news they immediately sobered up. They rushed back to the pier where they were temporarily stationed to report for whatever duty had to be done. The two men were horrified when the tragic message was confirmed by the officer who checked them in.[86]

The erroneous story had probably been initiated by men on other ships who lost sight of Sweet Pea as she was battered by the storm.[87] Others of the ship's crew left behind in New York also cut their liberties short to report back early.[88] Many in the United States with friends and loved ones on the ship heard the report that the ship had foundered and were devastated by the news.[89] For two days, people in the United States believed that the cruiser had gone down in the hurricane with her passengers and crew.[90] Finally, when the ship pulled into the Azores, men were allowed to send telegrams that they were safe, which was the first good news the folks back home had received since the *Times* published its error.[91]

While the damage was inspected in the Azores, some of the sailors went ashore and bought as much whiskey as they could locate and brought it back to the ship, where they found a ready market and high prices for the contraband.[92] The damage to the ship proved too extensive for the Azorean shipyard facilities to deal with, and Captain Bibby then did an unusual thing. He asked the crew—but not the troops—to *vote* on whether to await repairs or to try to sail Sweet Pea home in her now dreadful condition. Not surprisingly, the sailors chose to head for the United States "as is," hoping to get there for Christmas.[93]

She did not make it in time for the holiday. In mangled condition to begin with, she had to sail several hundred extra miles on a voyage normally a little more than two thousand miles in order to avoid sea conditions that might worsen the damage already done. Steaming mainly at twelve to thirteen knots, and getting up to a maximum of only sixteen, it took *Portland* nearly seven days to make the trip.[94] The damage left her sailing without some navigational equipment usually available, although her after gyro-compass had been knocked back *into* commission by the storm's buffeting.[95]

When she arrived in New York, Sweet Pea was not only badly damaged, she *looked* badly damaged. The davits were bent, spray shields on the gun tubs were bent down like tissue paper, the aircraft hanger was smashed, pieces of her mast were gone, and the radar antenna was drooping over the superstructure. She was nevertheless greeted as the hero she was. Fireboats sprayed their water cannons into the air, and sailors on board recalled that celebrities Bob Hope and Perry Como were on the tugs to welcome her.[96] Some of the festivities were no doubt routine for Operation Magic Carpet and were not intended just for the damaged but still proud *Portland.* The *New York Times* reported that a total of twenty thousand men had returned from the European Theater to land in New York on that day. Nevertheless, when *Portland* dropped off the 983 Army passengers that she had brought home safely, the newspaper reported the story of the storm, identifying the ship as one with "few equals on the roster of naval units as an experienced warship."[97] Indeed, and proven once again.

USS *Portland* lives on in the memory of the soldiers who made that trip. At least one is a walking—well, *limping*—monument to the cruiser. Claude Warble spent three months in rehabilitation at the Army hospital in Butler, Pennsylvania, not far from his home in Hummelstown. His wife came to Butler, lived in the YWCA, and visited him every day he was there. The first day at the hospital she endured a miserable experience. Because she had no idea how badly her husband had been hurt, she was filled with anxiety as she was steered to his room. Her heart nearly stopped when she saw there a burn victim in bandages from head to toe, with small holes for his eyes and mouth. She sat patiently but tearfully while he slept. Finally he awoke and Mrs. Warble saw that he had brown eyes, while she knew that her husband's eyes were blue. Someone had sent her to the wrong room. Sergeant Warble himself nevertheless left the hospital on crutches and never fully recovered from the smashed knee and spinal injuries. In fact, despite the profound gratitude he feels for all the sailors who treated him so well both before and after the storm, he still calls his difficulty in walking "my Portland limp."[98]

It seems worth noting as just one of those peculiar coincidences that make history so interesting that there was an earlier storm that would have been remembered by some who watched the wounded cruiser come home. Almost fifty years earlier, on November 26, 1898, a powerful gale brought a surprise blizzard to New York City, only ten years after the horrible Blizzard of '88. The 1898 storm destroyed 150 vessels off New England and New York and killed about 450 people. Included in those losses were all two hundred souls on the 291-foot paddle steamer

*Portland,* which went down not far from the city after her Captain wrongly thought he could outrun the storm. That natural disaster has always been known as "the Portland Gale."[99] The 1945 cyclone, which brewed up about a decade before tropical storms were given names, should perhaps be called "the Portland Hurricane."

Despite the recent bad luck, the crew had yet another lovely liberty time in New York City, this one coinciding with New Year's Eve. Malcolm Marks and another man went ashore that night but found Times Square far too much of a hassle. So they jumped on the first subway train and arbitrarily got off fifteen minutes later. They had landed in the Bronx, a short walk from a little bar. Inside, after their eyes had adapted to the dim light, they saw off in a corner a party composed of about fifteen Navy WAVES and no men. The women were stationed nearby but had little contact with any men in the line of duty, so they were as happy to see the two *Portland* gobs as vice versa. Years later, Marks regretted that he was on the ship for only a few more days and then left to be discharged in Texas.[100] In a similar but somewhat less happy episode, two officers, Barney Kliks and Bill Collinson, went to a nightclub where they met two women. But Kliks was so exhausted from working the ship across the Atlantic that he fell asleep with his head on the table. On waking, he found that his partner was gone but the women remained. So he had to take them home a very long way in the wrong direction from the ship, and then of course return back across the whole distance again.[101]

## TAPS

The 1945 hurricane brought a swift end to *Portland*'s glorious career. In New York, a Navy survey and inspection team found Sweet Pea unseaworthy![102] After a cross-Atlantic trip in that very same condition, this judgment speaks volumes about the skill of Captain Bibby and that courageous skeleton crew.

Although admittedly sad, such an end to the life of a great ship seems somehow fitting. From the beginning, when she worked to rescue survivors from a downed blimp, throughout a tough war when she fought in nearly all the important battles, to the end when she was honored to accept the enemy surrender at his island stronghold, she had gone into harm's way on scores of occasions and had always come away the winner. When she finally was defeated, it was not by an enemy fleet but by the irresistible forces of nature. And yet even then her crew performed remarkably well, heroically rescuing hundreds from perilous conditions, caring for the injured, and sailing the ship home for her final interment.

What lay ahead for *Portland* was the scrap pile. She left New York on January 8, 1946, and moored the next day in a cruiser cluster at Pier Baker in the Reserve Basin at the Philadelphia Navy Yard.[103] On January 17, after only six weeks and a couple of days in command, Lowe Bibby was named CO of battleship *New York,* a definite promotion for his good work with Sweet Pea. The Navy did not send an officer in the rank of captain to replace Bibby, but instead turned the ship over to her Executive Officer, Commander Homer H. Nielsen.[104] He served only until April 1, when he was relieved by Commander Ellsworth Smith, who held the title of both Commanding Officer and Executive Officer until the end.[105]

At Philadelphia, *Portland* was stripped of still-usable parts, and decommissioned on July 12, 1946.[106] Thirteen years later, on March 1, 1959, her name was struck from the Navy List. On October 6, 1959, she was sold for scrap to Union Minerals and Alloys Corporation.[107] Finally, the grand old cruiser was demolished in Panama City, Florida.[108]

# 16

# LEGACIES

There may be only two things now left of the physical ship. First is a display in Portland, Maine.[1] A retired Navy Captain named Arthur Forrestall, whose hometown was South Portland, led a team of civic-minded people, none of whom had served on *Portland,* to acquire the after mast and the bridge shielding during the scrapping in Florida. They mounted these remains in a park overlooking the bay as a memorial to the crew, especially those who gave their lives when serving in *Portland* during the war.[2]

The second artifact that survives is Sweet Pea's wardroom silver service set. It had been given to the ship by the city in 1933 despite its large cost during the Depression and the controversy over it during the waning days of Prohibition. When *Portland* was decommissioned, the silver set remained in the hands of the Navy until it was returned to the city in 1957. For a while it was kept in the museum of the Maine Historical Society in Portland.[3] But it found a happier place more recently, as the story will show.

Other memorials to Sweet Pea exist elsewhere. In the late 1990s, a few of her veterans entered into negotiations with the managers of USS *Yorktown* (CV-10), a museum ship in Charleston, South Carolina. This was the second *Yorktown,* another carrier named after the one lost at Midway where *Portland* rescued so many of her men.[4] Sweet Pea operated with the newer *Yorktown,* too, after she reached the fleet in 1943.[5] As a result of these historic connections, the managers of museum

*Yorktown* have allowed a model of *Portland* to be on display in what the carrier calls the Cruiser Room.[6] The model now has artifacts and mementos from other cruisers to keep it company.

## LSD-37

Besides winning the Navy Unit Commendation, being picked as the site of the Truk surrender, and having her artifacts displayed in Portland and Charleston, Sweet Pea was further honored when a later U.S. warship was named after her. The 13,700-ton Dock Landing Ship (LSD) Number 37 is USS *Portland.* LSDs are large amphibious warfare ships. They carry smaller landing craft in well-decks that can be flooded so that the boats can simply swim out and head to the beaches. LSDs also deploy helicopters for vertical envelopment during an invasion. The big ships have sufficient shops and personnel to maintain and repair embarked craft and other small vessels.[7]

USS *Portland* (LSD-37) was commissioned on October 3, 1970, and has operated in the Atlantic Fleet ever since. The fact that she bears the name proudly and that her crew is conscious of the original ship's history is clear from the plaque on her quarterdeck and the statement of "heritage" that appears on her website. The plaque says that she is the "second Naval ship to bear the name. The first USS PORTLAND (CA-33). . . ." and goes on briefly to tell about the cruiser. The LSD's website statement, referring to the older ship, concludes, "Today's Portland carries on in this same standard of pride, duty and service in honor of her predecessor."[8]

One physical connection between the two ships is the silver service set. It was so controversial in 1933 that it nearly failed to be installed in the cruiser. But placing it aboard the LSD was an easy matter. It is now part of the equipment in the officers' wardroom on the newer *Portland,* where it was proudly noted by the older men who visited her in 1988. In this little way, then, part of the old Sweet Pea is still on station.[9]

The veterans of the old cruiser connected with the LSD almost as soon as they organized their group in 1985. They scheduled their 1988 reunion in Norfolk, Virginia, because the new *Portland* was home-ported there. In preparation, they created an "adopt-a-sailor" program, by which a volunteering veteran would be linked with a serving sailor. While in Norfolk, the veterans were hosted on board the LSD by its crew, and they reciprocated by inviting the "adopted sailors" to the cruiser's reunion banquet. Six officers, six chiefs, and eighteen sailors from the LSD attended. The veterans hoped that they had "started a relationship between the CA-33 crew and the LSD-37 crew that [would] become stronger in the years ahead."[10] Indeed it did.

The Commanding Officer of the LSD wrote to the old *Portland* hands later that year to report on what the new ship had done since the two groups had been together.[11] As the new ship prepared in 1990 for the Gulf War, the veterans sent a ten-foot banner signed by everyone at that year's reunion, with "their prayers and best wishes."[12] Thereafter, correspondence between the veterans' organization and the new ship's men became regular.[13] Once in a while members of the two crews would meet each other unexpectedly. Lieutenant Lee Touchsberry of the LSD, for example, walked into a shop in West Branch, Iowa, wearing his ship's ballcap. Imagine his surprise when the woman behind the counter said that her husband had served in CA-33. The officer from the new ship told the older sailor about the cruiser's reunion association, and former Chief Petty Officer Jay Montgomery happily joined up.[14]

The best part of this emotional relationship that spanned the decades and generations may be the thrill the cruiser men felt knowing that the sailors on the LSD referred to their ship as "Sweet Pea."[15]

## PRIDE

So long as any of the men who served in USS *Portland* (CA-33) survive, the pride they felt will endure. Even during the war the men knew they were part of something special. When Lieutenant (jg) David Bloom finally reported after chasing the ship around the South Seas for several months in 1942, he was told that coming to the *Portland* was like getting a promotion. He thought it a joke until within only a few days he began to realize that "the people on the *Portland* were proud of her and her record, and always expected above average performance as a matter of course." Bloom had never been on a cruiser before, so he knew that he could not say the attitude was unique to Sweet Pea. But the longer he served in *Portland,* the more certain he was that she possessed that pride "far more than most other ships."[16]

When men departed Sweet Pea, they knew they were leaving a great warship. For example, Pete Cole and a few other sailors detached when

*Portland* was at Majuro in 1944. Cole said that it was "like watching your home burn down." Although all were going to the States, leave, and new assignments, none of the men "felt like jumping with joy."[17]

The pride had good reason. A man who served in *Portland* for the entire war would be authorized to wear these awards:

American Campaign Medal

Asiatic Pacific Campaign Medal with sixteen stars

World War II Victory Medal

Navy Unit Commendation Ribbon

Philippine Liberation Ribbon with two bronze stars

Philippine Presidential Unit Citation.[18]

Those medals were just for being there and do not include awards for personal gallantry and bravery, which *Portland*'s men won at Guadalcanal and in other actions.

It must be admitted that a few veterans of the ship were not so happy in their memories. Charles Ala said that "life on board wasn't enjoyable. I was twenty-five and being cooped up was awful." He got off the ship in Sydney when he had the chance to stay with the Australian girl he ultimately married.[19] Henry Hight never forgave Executive Officer Turk Wirth for his harshness. These men served the ship and their country honorably, and their dislike for her has reason. But they are exceptions. Almost all who served in that great ship loved it to the end of their lives. Even Hight made a point of attending many *Portland* reunions.[20]

## REUNIONS

Ah, yes, the *reunions*. In 1947, about thirty-five veterans of the ship gathered in Louisville, Kentucky. When *Portland* had been at Okinawa in the last days of the war, eighty-eight men in the crew put up $20 apiece and promised to meet in Louisville two years into the future. Those who came met at the Brown Hotel, had a banquet, and then went to nightclubs, swimming pools, *nightclubs,* restaurants, and NIGHTCLUBS.[21] They were all very young then. One of them got married the week before and made the reunion his honeymoon! The group had a tremendous time, telling their still-fresh sea stories to the women and each other. The only dark spot on that first reunion came at the end when the man holding the unspent remainder of the kitty left Louisville with a few hundred dollars and was never seen again.[22]

But eight years later, in 1955, a few from the Midwest met in St. Louis, and they repeated the event a year later. In 1958 a larger group, this time from all over the United States, met in Chicago. There were a few more gatherings from time to time until the early 1980s, when the reunions became annual affairs.[23] In 1985 the "U.S.S. PORTLAND Reunion Association" was officially created. But the association did more than just organize the reunions. For one thing, it produced a newsletter three or four times a year. The publication included sailors' memories, excerpts from wartime diaries, reprints of wartime documents, information about shipmates living and dead, and other precious materials.

But the reunions did remain the *raison d'être* of the association. According to the American Legion, more than ten thousand reunions of veterans from various units and wars are held every year, so *Portland* was not unusual in having them.[24] Nevertheless, they were raucous events, even as the men and their women got older. One hundred fifty-one former crewmen went to San Diego in 1989, and one hundred fifty-six to Portland, Maine, in 1991, to cite just the two held at the geographic extremes of the country.[25] Clearly, Sweet Pea's men would travel long distances to share their heritage.

Why would so many go every single year to such far away places for a ship's reunion? The association says:

> Shipmates became friends nourished by the day to day activities of living, working, playing, fighting, suffering and celebrating together. There were good and bad days, great and boring times and times where we were both scared and brave. We depended upon each other to get a job done—needed each other to survive battles and boredom. . . .
>
> We later kept in touch with a few of our friends but lost track of many others that we try to remember when we think about those Navy years. Our memories are not always shared with people we now love and live with and they just might be tired of hearing those old sea stories that are so important to [us].
>
> A reunion offers you that chance to remember . . . plus

that wonderful opportunity of making new friends with those former crew members who can so proudly say that "I SERVED ABOARD THE U.S.S. PORTLAND CA-33."[26]

These words are the company line. But the men agree. Pete Cole once wrote that reunions put the lie to the old saying that "you can't go home again." "I come away from each," said Cole, "with a feeling of completion, fulfillment and contentment."[27] In 2001 it was amazing that about sixty men and their companions found their way to Colorado Springs even though the event began on September 11, and most of those who planned to come in the next several days were prohibited from doing so because the airports were closed.[28] The phones jangled all day with calls from veterans distraught that the terrorists' first victory was to keep them away from the reunion, although nearly all of them had gone just the year before. Even under these circumstances, though, many got to Colorado Springs by one means or another over the next few days.

The reunion sites are picked usually because they have some special interest for the veterans. There was the one in Norfolk where they visited the new *Portland,* as noted before. In 1993 they met in San Antonio, not far from the Nimitz Museum in Texas, which of course they visited. The museum staff treated them to a movie on the surrender at Truk in which many of them found their younger selves darting across the screen. They were given the opportunity to place in the garden there a memorial to all who served in *Portland* during the war.[29] In 1994 they met in Charleston, South Carolina, bringing the plaque that had been given to Mary Elizabeth Brooks when she launched the ship in 1933. It was placed in the Cruiser Room on the museum ship *Yorktown.*[30]

The greatest of all the reunions occurred in 1991, when the veterans went back to Portland. In preparation for this meeting, the association created a book entitled *History of Ships Called Portland,* which included twenty-four pages of history, twenty-two pages of photos, and eight pages of rosters.[31] The association hoped that LSD-37 would be able to come to the event, but she was occupied in the Gulf War that cropped up that year.[32]

Nevertheless, the association and the city joined to dedicate a permanent memorial at Fort Allen Park. It took six buses to carry all the men and their guests to the ceremony.[33] The nearby Brunswick Naval Air Station provided a color guard, a chaplain, and a rifle squad for the ceremony, and the city hung out a welcome in signal flags featuring the ship's call sign, NACB.[34] Alas, the city fathers left out the M in "WELCOME," but most of the former sailors just smiled at the error and appreciated the sentiment.[35]

The group took a trip to L.L. Bean while it was in Maine, a very popular excursion.[36] And it received a letter from then-President George Bush, who probably signed many of these letters every day, but who nevertheless pleased Sweet Pea's veterans by saying, "As a former Navy pilot during World War II, I am delighted to send my warmest greetings to those who served on USS PORTLAND CA-33 as you gather in Portland for your reunion. . . . The record of USS PORTLAND CA-33 was one of courage, honor, and distinguished service. . . . I join you in honoring the memory of your comrades who are no longer with you. They, like you, will never be forgotten."[37]

Membership in the association peaked in the late 1990s, when its officers counted 497 dues-payers, but they expected the number to decrease in the future.[38] Almost every issue of the newsletter included a section listing new members, and another section listing those who had recently died.[39] The deaths became more numerous as time passed. For example, one issue in 1988 listed seventeen new members and only two who had passed away. A 1989 issue named fourteen new members with only three who had died.[40] But in 2000, the association held a memorial service for twenty-three men who had died in the past year, while only seven had joined.[41] It was that way with all World War II veterans in the new century. Virtually all these men were born before 1925, most of them before 1920, so the survivors had reached ages greater than the average life expectancy of the average American man. The actuarial tables said that more than half the men and women who served in World War II had already gone.

In recognition of that fact, and perhaps understanding that making a major trip has become too physically demanding for most of the aging veterans, the association announced that the 2003 reunion in Branson, Missouri, would be the last. Branson was "rated as one of the top cities in the country for hosting military reunions." The town also called itself the "Live Entertainment Capital of the World."[42] As a result, the guys would have one more blast, perhaps more like the 1947 gathering at Louisville than anyone could imagine. It had not happened as this book went to print.

At the Branson reunion, the "tontine" will be opened. In 1988, Raye Shumate donated a bottle of Makers Mark Kentucky sipping whiskey, to be opened and shared by those members who would come to the final reunion of the association.[43] It was called the tontine from a system created in seventeenth-century Florence. An Italian banker there got subscribers to pay a sum into a fund called *tontina,* which grew over time and was supposed to be collected by the last surviving original investor. The source does not say if that last investor actually collected.[44] But we can have few doubts that *Portland*'s last reunion will sip Shumate's whiskey. In 1989 Charles Moy, one of Sweet Pea's former sailors, had a beautiful display case built for storing the tontine. It has been brought to most of the reunions since, and passed on from one keeper to another over that time.[45] Sad to say, only fifteen years after its creation, that bottle will be opened and the contents drunk at Branson in 2003.

## LOVE

In addition to their pride in *Portland,* the *love* these men had for their ship was palpable. Even allowing for some understandable inflation of past gallantry over the years, it was clear from even a short time with these veterans that their experience in *Portland* would be high on any list they might compile of great events in their lives. Some of them still had pieces of uniforms. Chuck Martin had an old flat hat with the ship's name on it, the way it was before the uniform style changed for security reasons during the war.[46] Many had old pictures. Willie Partridge had some snapshots of himself and his buddies taken in the Stork Club, and the cigar given to him when he was the pointer for the 40mm mount that shot down the first kamikaze to attack the ship off the Philippines.[47] David Gatrall, one of the gunnery officers, lived only twenty-five years after the war, but a photo of *Portland* adorned one of the walls of his home for that entire time and at least twenty-five more after his death.[48] Dozens of entries in the guest log at the ship's website began with words like, "My father was so proud of his service on the USS *Portland* that. . . ."[49]

The association had produced and sold souvenirs like caps, wrist watches, ship's bells, patches, oil paintings of the ship, and CA-33 license plates.[50] It also had produced and/or promoted privately published books about the ship, which can be found in the bibliography.

One thing that certainly never changed after the war was the affection the men had for Tex Settle. Even in retirement, he and they maintained contact. That's a remarkable thing for a man like Settle, who graduated from the Naval Academy in 1919 when midshipmen were taught about the unbridgeable chasm between officers and enlisted and even between officers of superior rank and their juniors.[51] But Settle wrote lovingly to the officers and men of *Portland.*

In 1960, Dave Babcock contacted the former skipper to thank him for saving the lives of the *Portland* crew by avoiding suicide-plane attacks. Settle diverted credit anyone would give him, replying, "The *Portland*'s fine crew and previous Captains were responsible for her splendid performance throughout the war. I was fortunate in 'inheriting' a ship and ship's company second to none. It is my deepest satisfaction to believe that we 'kept her that way' during my command. There was never a finer or more gallant a man-of-war's fighting team than the *Portland's.*"[52] The effect, of course, was to endear him even further to the men whom he had extolled while minimizing his own contribution. Along the same lines was a letter he wrote several years later to former officer Barney Kliks, in which he said, "While later flag billets were broader in scope, my skippership of *Portland* was the peak of my naval career. To command in wartime that splendid ship and her finest-of-all ship's companies was the best break an officer could have aspired to."[53] When these two excerpts of Settle's letters were published on the same page in the late 1990s, Sweet Pea's veterans around the country were moved in ways that only a member of the crew could recognize.

Admiral T.G.W. Settle died on April 28, 1980. But his widow attended the 1991 reunion in Portland where those killed during the war were honored at Fort Allen Park. Several of the former crew spent precious moments with Mrs. Settle. One day at that reunion she gave Kliks the binoculars her husband had used as the CO of *Portland.* Barney was overwhelmed by the gift, calling the glasses his "proudest possession." Two years later when the reunion was held in San Antonio, he presented them to the Nimitz Museum, where they will be part of the holdings forever.[54]

These men knew the world had changed since they helped to save the Pacific for democracy by liberating it from the ravages of Japanese militarism, but that has made their own accomplishments seem all the greater to them. As the editor of the *Newsletter,* Ted Waller, wounded in *Portland* at Guadalcanal, once wrote:

We were born before T.V., penicillin, polio shots, frozen
foods, Xerox, plastic contact lenses, Frisbees and the Pill. We
were before radar, credit cards, split atoms, laser beams and
ballpoint pens.
    We got married first and then lived together. Closets were
for clothes and not for "coming out of." Having a meaningful
relationship meant getting along with our cousins. We thought
fast food was what you ate during Lent. Outer space was the
back of the local movie theater and time sharing meant
togetherness. We were before house husbands, gay rights,
computer dating, day-care centers, group therapy and nursing
homes. We never heard of FM radio, VCRs, computers,
artificial hearts or guys wearing earrings. Back then "Made in
Japan" meant junk, and "making out" referred to how you did
on your exam. Pizza, McDonalds and instant coffee were
unheard of but you could go to the "5 and dime" and buy
things for 5 and 10 cents.[55]

In contrast, Joe Stables wrote a sardonic account about a television
story that said an aircraft carrier was leaving San Diego for an extended
deployment, during which the sacrificing crew would be away from
saddened families and other loved ones. Stables pointed out, however,
that the ship had email, prepaid phone cards, and twenty channels on the
ship's television system, twenty-four hours a day, seven days a week.
"Ah, the hardships of the modern Navy!!" he joked to his former
shipmates, who often went without mail from home for weeks at a time
during the Pacific War.[56]
    Sweet Pea's veterans had good reason to be proud. Anyone can see
now why the Honolulu newspaper wrote what it did when *Portland*
pulled into Pearl Harbor in 1945: "She is known throughout the navy as
the ship that remained at sea for 20 weeks without time for maintenance
and repair while engaged in advanced areas with enemy air, surface and
sub-surface opposition. Without adequate replenishment of stores and
provisions, the PORTLAND nevertheless maintained her battle fitness
during this period and participated in the Leyte landings, the Battle of
Surigao Straits, the Philippine carrier air strikes, Leyte Gulf, Mindoro
landings, Lingayen Patrol and Army support, Corregidor landings and
[in]numberable air actions with the enemy."[57]

That account was correct but had only part of the story. Sweet Pea was the only ship at all three of the great battles in the early days of the war when Japan might have won. She was the only heavy cruiser in history that twice faced enemy battleships in nighttime engagements, not only surviving to tell the tale but winning both battles. She rescued thousands of men from sunken ships. She carried out missions here, there, and everywhere, winning more battle stars than all but one cruiser. Of course, no one who served in *Portland* was happy about not being awarded battle stars for Tarawa 1942 and Aleutians 1943.[58]

This was some great ship and some great crew! The essence of the matter may live in Joe Arbour's beguilingly emotional quatrain:

> How, you might ask, can a grown man love
> Ten thousand tons of steel?
> Well, you had to have served on the *Portland,* friend,
> To know just how we feel.[59]

If USS *Portland* (CA-33) was not the greatest heavy cruiser of them all, let someone else try to make the case.

# NOTES

## PREFACE

1. Ewing, iv.
2. Some would be: Newcomb, *Abandon Ship*; Lech, *All the Drowned Sailors*; Kurzman, *Fatal Voyage*; and Helm, *Ordeal by Sea.*
3. For just a sample, see Stafford, *The Big E*; Kerminsky, *"Mighty Mo"*; Roscoe, *United States Destroyer Operations in World War II*; and Roscoe, *United States Submarine Operations in World War II.*
4. Reprinted in Stables, *We Remember,* 94.

## 1. THE SHIP

1. Terzibaschitsch, 7.
2. Fahey, Victory edition, 4.
3. Ibid., 9.
4. Ibid., 19–20.
5. Musicant, 15.
6. Ibid., xiii.
7. http://www.hazegray.org/danfs/cruisers.
8. Ewing, 67.
9. http://www.hazegray.org/danfs/cruisers. The carriers were *Lexington* and *Saratoga,* both of which appear later in this history.
10. Fahey, Two-Ocean edition, 14.
11. Ill-fated *Indianapolis* was CA-35. Hull Number 34, in between the two, was assigned to USS *Astoria,* which belonged to the *Northampton* class.
12. *Portland* website; USS *Portland,* Ship's Logs (hereafter cited as Log), July 9, 1933. The logs from 1933 to 1941 are archived at National Archives I on Pennsylvania Avenue in Washington, D.C., and the logs from 1941 to 1946 are at National Archives II on Adelphi Road in College Park, Maryland.
13. Hammel, *Guadalcanal: Decision at Sea,* 460.
14. Terzibaschitsch, 82; Friedman, 473.
15. Friedman, 150.
16. *Newsletter* (Oct. 1994), 4.
17. David Bloom in ibid. (Nov. 1998), 5. Bloom lists nine firings: three during the battle of Santa Cruz, one at Guadalcanal, four by friendly PT boats at Tulagi, and one accidental firing at Samoa. But this history will show there may have been more.

18. Olsen 2.

19. Ibid.

20. Swars letter, Wolf, Morton 2; Fynan 2.

21. Al Lucas in Stables, *We Remember,* 7.

22. Hubert Johnson in Stables, *We Remember II,* 61.

23. Ibid.

24. Ibid.

25. Bart Babcock in Stables, *We Remember,* 9.

26. Berle Brents in ibid.

27. For only one example, see Log, April 6, 1933.

28. Hicks; and USS *Portland,* Action Report (hereafter cited as Action Report), 1 March 1944, about expectations at Kwajalein, for example.

29. H.B. Benge in Stables, *We Remember II,* 4.

30. Holbrook, 4.

31. *Portland (Maine) Press Herald,* Oct. 27, 1944, unpaged, in *Newsletter* (3d Qtr 1990), 6.

32. Holbrook, 3.

33. *Portland (Maine) Press Herald,* Oct. 27, 1944, unpaged, in *Newsletter* (3d Qtr 1990), 6.

34. *Portland* website.

35. List of Officers, Log, Feb. 1933.

36. Benge in *Newsletter* (Oct. 1994), 6.

37. List of Officers, Log, Feb. 1933.

38. Ibid.

39. Log, Feb. and March 1933.

40. Ibid., Nov. 23, 1937.

41. Ibid., Nov. 26, 27, 1937.

42. Ibid., Feb. and March 1933.

43. Ibid., April 4, 1933.

44. Ibid. Readers will perhaps recall that the ancient Hanseatic port city of Danzig was detached from Germany by the Versailles Treaty of 1919 and made an open city chiefly so that otherwise landlocked Poland could have access to the world's oceans.

45. Ibid., April 4, 5, 1933.

46. Benge in Stables, *We Remember II,* 5, says "a few bodies" were recovered. He was the Captain's orderly and was in a position to see such collections. But the ship's logs say nothing about retrieved bodies, and they would have since they do mention wreckage. Another account of the early hours of the operation is in *New York Times,* April 5, 1933, 1:4–8.

47. Ezra Johnson in Stables, *We Remember II,* 10; William White in *Newsletter* (4th Qtr 1990), 4.

48. Log, April 6, 1933.

49. Ibid., April 7, 1933.

50. Ibid., April 19, 1933.

51. On April 18, for example, various vessels came by to deliver wreckage. Ibid.

52. Benge in Stables, *We Remember II,* 5.

53. *Newsletter* (Dec. 1988), 3.

54. Log, June 4, 1933.

55. For example, Dale Figgins and William Naylor in *Newsletter* (Feb. 1989), 3; and the *Newsletter*'s editor's comment about a story in *Collier's* magazine, in ibid. (June–July 1989), 4.

56. Stables, *We Remember II,* 11.

57. *Newsletter* (Feb. 1989), 3.

58. Editor Ted Waller thought so in ibid. (June–July 1989), 4.

59. Ibid. (Feb. 1989), 3.

60. Al Stauffer in ibid. (Oct. 1988), 3; and in ibid. (Feb. 1989), 3.

## 2. Before the War

1. Log, May 4–11, 1933.

2. Ibid.

3. Ibid., May 26–28, 1933.

4. In 1963–1964, the author was a junior officer on a destroyer homeported in Long Beach. While there were many ships and squadrons there, the major fleet commands, training facilities, and schools were all in San Diego.

5. Log, June 10, 1933.

6. Ibid., June 24, 1934.

7. Holbrook, 12.

8. Al Lucas in Stables, *We Remember II,* 16. The easygoing Captain is not identified in the source. If 1939 is correct, it was either John W. Lewis or Howard H. Crosby, since Crosby relieved Lewis on June 28, 1939. List of Officers, Log, June 1939.

9. *Portland* website; Lassen interview; Riehl interview; Allred.

10. The ship's logs throughout the decade show this pattern clearly.

11. Log, Jan. 5, 22, 1934. See almost any of the daily log entries throughout January, February, and March in all of these years.

12. Ibid., April 12 and 24, May 6, 10, and 31, Oct. 5 and 24, and Nov. 10, 1934, set the outlines of these movements.

13. Omar Smith, *Newsletter* (2d Qtr 1991, 2d issue), 4 (two different issues of the *Newsletter* are dated "2d Quarter"; "2d issue" herein means the source is the second one). Smith's memory told him the trip to Midway was in 1934, but he was off by a year; Log, May 11, 1935.

14. Log, May 11, June 14, June 28, July 12, Aug. 12, 1935.

15. Ibid., May 26, June 19, Aug. 8, Oct. 2, 1936.

16. Log, Oct. 24, 26, 1937.

17. Naylor in *Newsletter* (Feb. 1989), 3.

18. Log, Oct. 19, 20, 21, 1937.

19. In NROTC in 1961, the author was taught celestial navigation using what was always called "Dutton" as a textbook.

20. Figgins in *Newsletter* (Feb. 1989), 3.

21. Log, Nov. 29, 30, 1937. Dutton's Executive Officer, Commander Robert English, became temporary CO of *Portland* when Dutton died. The ship's logs for the next several days were signed by him as "Commanding Officer." As Commander, Pacific Fleet Submarine Force until he died in a plane crash in 1943, English directed the boats that did so much to destroy the Japanese Empire. Blair, 223, 366.

Dutton had taken command of *Portland* only five days after the departure of the outgoing Executive Officer, then-Commander Daniel J. Callaghan, another officer who would become famous in the Pacific War, winning a Medal of Honor, and about whom much more later.

22. Ibid., Nov. 30, 1937. The board of investigation met for only an hour and seven minutes. Nothing about its conclusions was published in the logs, and the life of the cruiser went immediately back to normal.

23. *Newsletter* (Feb. 1989), 3.

24. Log, Dec. 2, 1937. The ship's log notes without amplification that Rear Admiral J.D. Wainwright was an hour late for the service. One wonders who he was and why he was tardy.

25. Holbrook, 13. This story is presented as it was given in Holbrook's book without source citation, but something about it is awry. *Portland* did transit the Canal in April 1934, but in company with Cruiser Division Four, which took twelve days—certainly no speed run—to move from Long Beach to Balboa, because it trained all the way down. Perhaps the event was in some other year, but this writer found nothing in the ship's logs.

26. This description of the ship is taken from a photo in Stables, *We Remember*, 84–85.

27. Log, June 19, Aug. 8, Oct. 2, 1936, set the outlines of these movements.

28. Stables, *We Remember*, 4–5.

29. Pete Cole in *Newsletter* (June 1997), 4.

30. *Portland* website.

31. The four members of the president's entourage in Sweet Pea are identified in the ship's log only as: P.M. Hart, D.B. Whiteside, E.L. Roddan, F.A. Storm; Log, Oct. 2, 1935. They do not appear in the indices of any of the five FDR biographies in the author's personal library.

32. Log, Oct. 2–17, 1935.

33. Ibid., Oct. 19–22, 1935. "S.O.P.A." means "Senior Officer Present Afloat," or the commander of whatever ships are present. In this case, of course, it was the Commander-in-Chief, Franklin D. Roosevelt.

34. Holbrook, 29. Again, there is something awry about this report in Holbrook. The ship's log indicates that *Portland* was in Southern California during early July 1937 when the Earhart plane disappeared.

35. Bart Babcock in *Newsletter* (June 1997), 3. The ship's log gives the position as "in the vicinity of" 21–12N Latitude, 135–16W Longitude.

36. Log, Aug. 22, 1941.

37. Babcock in *Newsletter* (June 1997), 3.

38. Logs for April, May, June, July, and Aug. 1941.

39. Ibid., Nov. 14 and Dec. 6, 1940.

40. Charles Tennant in Stables, *We Remember II,* 35. Tennant says there were three cruisers in total, but the ship's log counts *Chicago, Brooklyn,* and *Savannah,* besides *Portland.*

41. Willard Losh in Stables, *We Remember,* 10; *Newsletter* (1st Qtr 1990), 6.

42. The first time was in May 1936. *Portland* website.

43. Log, March 6, 1941. Captain Van Hook's name was *not* part of the tomfoolery.

44. Ibid.

45. Losh in Stables, *We Remember,* 10.

46. Log, March 6, 1941.

47. At the veterans' reunion in 2001, the author saw more than a dozen of the shellback cards, well worn by then but all shown proudly by one man after another.

48. Bart Babcock in Stables, *We Remember,* 20. Babcock wrote that the crossing was on March 10, although the ship's log has it occurring on the 15th.

49. The author made a round-trip across the date line every year in 1963–1967, but is even now a pollywog.

50. Log, March 9, 12, 19, 1941.

51. *Newsletter* (1st Qtr 1990), 6.

52. Ibid.

53. Allred, Reehl 9, for example; William Speer in Stables, *We Remember II,* 33–34.

54. Speer in Stables, *We Remember II,* 33–34.

55. Ibid.

56. Paul Faries in Stables, *We Remember,* 20.

57. Tennant in Stables, *We Remember II,* 36.

58. *Newsletter* (July 1994), 2; Faries in Stables, *We Remember,* 20. The ship's logs for Oct. 13, 15, and 16 confirm the departure date given in the text. But there is nothing more about this trip because *Portland*'s logs for the period November 1, 1940–June 30, 1942, were lost during the war. See Burhans letter to CINCPACFLT, Oct. 19, 1943.

59. Tennant in Stables, *We Remember II,* 36.

60. *Newsletter* (May 1995), 8.

61. Log, Nov. 26, 1941.

62. Zich, 60.

## 3. Pearl Harbor

1. The war game was called Fleet Problem XVIII; Log, May 5–20, 1937.

2. Terzibaschitsch, 84; Ewing, 26; Hight interview.

3. *Newsletter* (1st Qtr 1990), 3. According to Haldorson, the other ships were *Chicago, Astoria, Porter, Drayton, Flusser, Lamson,* and *Mahan.*

4. Lawrence Kotula in Stables, *We Remember,* 23. The source was originally a story in the *Sioux City (Iowa) Journal,* Dec. 7, 1991.

5. Lucas in Stables, *We Remember,* 23; and in *Newsletter* (1st Qtr 1992), 4.

6. Paul Walker in Stables, *We Remember II,* 38.

7. Geriak 1.

8. Lassen interview.

9. Walker in Stables, *We Remember II,* 38.

10. Vernon Cruise in *Newsletter* (April 2000), 3.

11. Jim Young in Stables, *We Remember II,* 149.

12. Jim Engibous in ibid., 137–38.

13. Ibid., 153; Fahey, Two-Ocean edition, 36.

14. Engibous in Stables, *We Remember II,* 137–38.

15. Young in ibid., 141–42. Gunner's Mate Reehl said the catapult used a 5-inch projectile, while aviator Young said a 6-inch shell was used.

16. Engibous and others in Stables, *We Remember II,* 146.

17. Young in ibid., 143, 145.

18. Walker in ibid., 38; Kotula in Stables, *We Remember,* 23.

19. *Newsletter* (Nov. 1998), 4.

20. John Reimer in Stables, *We Remember II,* 40.

21. The men assigned to care for them were Petty Officers E.K. Booth and A.M. Memph, plus unrated men L.R. DeYoung, W.M. Koine, G. McKellip, S.A. McKirahan, T.E. McLain, John Reimer, P.S. Robinson, and G.A. Sullivan. Reimer's copy of the ship's log for Dec. 5, 1941, in ibid., 39.

22. Ibid.

23. Reimer in Stables, *We Remember II,* 41.

24. Ibid.

25. Ibid.

26. *Newsletter* (April 2002), 3.

27. Reimer in Stables, *We Remember II,* 41.

28. Ibid.

29. Ibid., 42.

30. "Guestbook" at the *Portland* website.

31. Kay Wilhelm in *Newsletter* (Oct. 2000), 4.

32. Prange, 645.

33. *Newsletter* (Oct. 2000), 4.

34. Ibid. (July 2000), 4.

35. Stables, *We Remember II,* 42.

36. Ibid., 42–43.

37. Babcock in *Newsletter* (March 1997), 5.

38. Dolezal interview; Babcock in *Newsletter* (March 1997), 5.

39. Lassen interview; Kotula in Stables, *We Remember,* 23–24.

40. *Newsletter* (April 2000), 2.

41. Interviews with Peugh and Banks. Incidentally, Ray Pugh enlisted in 1938 as a recruit, was promoted through all the enlisted ranks to chief petty officer, then was made warrant officer and chief warrant officer, and was finally commissioned as an ensign. He then served through all the officer ranks up to commander.

42. *Newsletter* (Oct. 2000), 4.

43. Ibid. (July 2000), 4.

## 4. Early Days

1. Spector, 158.

2. Stables's list is in *Newsletter* (Oct. 1996), 2. All of the ships on that list that survived the war were scrapped at various times after it.

3. For the record, they were *Houston* (CA-30), sunk at Java Sea; *Astoria* (CA-34), *Quincy* (CA-39), and *Vincennes* (CA-44), sunk at Savo Island; *Northhampton* (CA-26), sunk at Tassafaronga; *Chicago* (CA-29), sunk at Rennel Island; and *Indianapolis* (CA-35), sunk by submarine en route the Philippines in 1945.

4. Again for the record, they were *Minneapolis* (CA-36), *New Orleans* (CA-32), and *Pensacola* (CA-24), severely damaged at Tassafaronga; *Chester* (CA-27), *Portland* (CA-33) and *San Francisco* (CA-38), severely damaged off Guadalcanal; and *Louisville* (CA-28), severely damaged by kamikaze in the Philippines.

5. At Cape Esperance in October 1942, and near the Komandorski Islands in March 1943.

6. Ted Kostik diary in *Newsletter* (Dec. 1992), 2.

7. Ibid.

8. Walker in Stables, *We Remember II,* 38.

9. Log, Jan. 1, 3, 7, 8, 10, 16, 1942.

10. Ted Kostik diary in *Newsletter* (May 1993), 4.

11. *The Pilot* (April 28, 1944), 4.

12. *Newsletter* (3d Qtr 1990), 3; ibid. (4th Qtr 1990), 4.

13. Ibid. (2d Qtr 1992), 3.

14. Sidney Shiffman in *Newsletter* (Aug. 1998), 4.

15. Chester Martinczak in ibid. (April 1998), 2.

16. Stables, *We Remember,* 9–10.

17. *Newsletter* (Sept. 7, 1944), 4.

18. *Port Beam* (May 5, 1944), 5.

19. Thomas Holmes in *Newsletter* (July 1996), 5.

20. *Port Beam* (Sept. 7, 1944), 4.

21. *Newsletter* (Oct. 2000), 6.

22. Log, Jan. 11, 1942.

23. Kostik diary in *Newsletter* (Dec. 1992), 2; Henry Hight in ibid. (April 2000), 2.

24. Kostik diary in ibid. (May 1993), 4.

25. Holbrook, 109.

26. Ibid.

27. Henry Hight in *Newsletter* (April 2000), 2; Holbrook, 109.

28. Pietrok interview. The 1.1-inch round was 28mm in diameter; Terzibaschitsch, 309.

29. Willie Partridge in Stables, *We Remember,* 85.

30. Terzibaschitsch, 309.

31. Speer 2.

32. Ibid.

33. Grace, 127; Terzibaschitsch, 313.

34. Terzibaschitsch, 313.

35. Ibid., 26.

36. Hight in *Newsletter* (April 2000), 2.

37. Friedman, 154, 313.

38. Ala, "My Experiences in W.W. II," 1.

39. USS *Portland,* War Diary (hereafter cited as War Diary), March 3 and April 1, 2, 1942. In Stables, *We Remember,* 24, Kotula says that during this period, the ship conducted raids on Japanese-held islands. But the War Diary makes no mention of any such actions, and it seems doubtful whether there was time to escort Convoy 2034, get to Noumea on April 1, and still shell Japanese outposts.

40. War Diary, April 20, 27, 1942; Losh in Stables, *We Remember,* 28.

# 5. Turning Points

1. For the twenty-one Allied ships at Coral Sea, see Dull, 130. For the twenty-eight American ships at Midway, fifteen of which were also at Coral Sea, see ibid., 141. For the thirteen American ships in the Night Cruiser Action that was early in the Naval Battle of Guadalcanal, see Hammel, *Guadalcanal: Decision at Sea,* 110. For

the six American ships in the Night Battleship Action that was later in the Naval Battle of Guadalcanal, see ibid., 455.

2. Frank, 22–25.

3. Spector, 158.

4. Kenneth Joy in Stables, *We Remember II,* 44; Kostik diary in *Newsletter* (July 1993), 2; Frank Teague in ibid. (Nov. 1995), 7; Smith, *Midway,* 23.

5. Holbrook, 114.

6. Smith, *Midway,* 23; Kostik diary in *Newsletter* (July 1993), 2.

7. List of Officers, Log, May 1942; Smith, *Midway,* 42. Smith was the commander of the cruiser-destroyer screen at both Coral Sea and Midway. Although he tells us about Perlman's destroyer experience and that it was Fletcher who made the call, he does not give us Fletcher's precise thinking. What appears here is just my guess.

8. Grant Nelson in *Newsletter* (March 1997), 4.

9. A good brief account of Coral Sea is in Potter and Nimitz, 662–67.

10. Potter and Nimitz, 665.

11. Action Report, May 12, 1942. William Manchester points out that Allied geographers knew so little about the waters around New Guinea that this battle actually took place in the Solomon Sea. *American Caesar,* 278. This account will stick with the standard terminology.

12. War Diary, May 8, 1942.

13. Action Report, May 12, 1942.

14. Henry Hight in *Newsletter* (April 2000), 2.

15. Ted Kostik diary in ibid. (Oct. 1993), 7; and ibid. (Jan. 1994), 5.

16. Potter and Nimitz, 667.

17. War Diary, May 8, 1942.

18. Reehl 3.

19. Geriak 1.

20. Reehl 3.

21. Reehl 2; Reehl 16; Reehl 19.

22. Johnson in Stables, *We Remember II,* 36.

23. War Diary, May 8, 1942.

24. Geriak 2.

25. *Portland* website.

26. War Diary, May 8, 1942.

27. Ala, "My Experiences in W.W. II," 2.

28. Peterson interview.

29. Walker in Stables, *We Remember II,* 39.

30. Kostik diary in *Newsletter* (Oct. 1993), 7.

31. Losh in Stables, *We Remember,* 28.

32. Ibid. *Portland*'s logs for the period in question have been lost; Burhans letter to CINCPACFLT.

33. Rich Pedroncelli in the "Guestbook" at the *Portland* website.

34. *Newsletter* (Jan. 1999), 4.

35. Ibid. (Nov. 1998), 1.

36. Lassen interview.

37. War Diary, April 20, 1942.

38. Reehl 2.

39. Smith, *Midway,* 53.

40. Ibid.

41. Ibid., 52–53.
42. Potter, 87; Buell, 123.
43. Spector, 168–69, 74.
44. Kostik diary in *Newsletter* (Jan. 1994), 5.
45. Reehl 3.
46. For the ambush of Yamamoto's plane, see, among other sources, Kennedy, 563, and Spector, 230, 453–54.
47. The literature on Midway is extensive, and readers are invited to see similar analyses in almost any volume of it.
48. An excellent account of the Imperial Navy's calamity is Fuchida and Okumiya, *Midway,* but the general bibliography on Midway is virtually endless.
49. *Newsletter* (1st Qtr 1990), 5.
50. Action Report, June 11, 1942, Enclosure A.
51. *Newsletter* (1st Qtr 1990), 5.
52. Action Report, June 11, 1942.
53. Geriak 2.
54. Bo Lash in Stables, *We Remember,* 30; Ted Kostik diary in *Newsletter* (Jan. 1994), 5; War Diary, June 4, 1942. The first mention of the effectiveness of Shanklin's "barrage" is in the Executive Officer's Enclosure to the Action Report, June 11, 1942, which covered Midway. But Shanklin himself wrote about the theory only later, in the Action Report, August 24, 1942, on the Battle of the Eastern Solomons.
55. War Diary, June 4, 1942.
56. Action Report, June 11, 1942.
57. War Diary, June 4, 1942.
58. Holbrook, 140–41. Again, Holbrook gives no sources for his information, and the War Diary, June 4, 1942, does not give a count of the *Yorktown* survivors delivered to *Portland,* although the ship's modern website says "several hundred."
59. Linzey, 74–75, 109.
60. "Guestbook" at the *Portland* website.
61. Ballard, 130.
62. War Diary, June 6, 1942.
63. *Newsletter* (July 2000), 3.
64. Ibid.
65. Ibid.
66. Ibid.
67. Lord, 274–75.
68. *Newsletter* (July 1999), 3. An oil painting by John Greaves depicts Lieutenant (jg) Ralph "Kaiser" Wilhelm and ARM1/c Fred Dyer in this mission. It can be seen on the Internet at <http://centeryinter.net/midway/greaves/soc.html>.
69. Kostik diary in *Newsletter* (Jan. 1994), 5.
70. Reehl 16.
71. Wolf; Bloom in *Newsletter* (April 1998), 5.

## 6. Guadalcanal

1. The literature on War Plan Orange is extensive, but a brief and clear statement of the plan can be found in Blair, 46.

2. Frank, 285.

3. Ibid., 25.

4. Spector, 156–57, 185; Hammel, *Guadalcanal: Decision at Sea,* 16–20.

5. Hammel, *Guadalcanal: Starvation Island,* 11–12. Another concise description of Japanese intentions and reasons for selecting Guadalcanal can be found in Frank, 31.

6. Potter and Nimitz, 691; Steinberg, 20–22.

7. There are innumerable sources on the decision to fight at Guadalcanal. Readers looking for a wonderfully concise description of all the politics can find it in Frank, 10–14.

8. Frank, 616.

9. Reehl 16.

10. Spector, 191–92.

11. Ibid., 186–87.

12. Hammel, *Guadalcanal: Decision at Sea,* 429.

13. Potter and Nimitz, 691; Hammel, *Guadalcanal: Starvation Island,* 24.

14. Hammel, *Guadalcanal: Starvation Island,* 28.

15. War Diary, Aug. 7, 1942.

16. Bloom in *Newsletter* (April 1998), 5.

17. War Diary, Aug. 7, 1942.

18. Johnson in Stables, *We Remember,* 31.

19. Potter and Nimitz, 692.

20. War Diary, Aug. 8, 1942.

21. Spector, 195.

22. Griffith, 69.

23. Lassen interview.

24. Spector, 194–95.

25. Grace, 5.

26. The six battles were Savo Island (August 9), Eastern Solomons (August 24), Cape Esperance (October 11–12), the Naval Battle of Guadalcanal (November 12–15), Tassafaronga (November 30), and Rennell Island (January 30). This list does not include the unnamed calamity on September 14 caused by an IJN submarine that, with a single spread of torpedoes, sank carrier *Wasp* and a destroyer and knocked battleship *North Carolina* out of the war for months.

27. Steinberg, 30.

28. War Diary, Aug. 24, 1942.

29. Action Report, Aug. 24, 1942.

30. War Diary, Aug. 24, 1942.

31. Frank, 602; Steinberg, 30–32.

32. Lundstrom, 171. The judgment on Fletcher expressed in the text is mine.

33. Gunnery Officer's Enclosure, Action Report, Aug. 24, 1942.

34. Ibid.

35. Ibid.

36. The letter is reprinted in *Newsletter* (Feb. 1989), 4.

37. War Diary, Sept. 12, 1942.

38. Ibid., Oct. 9, 1943.

39. *Newsletter* (April 1998), 5.

40. *Portland* website.

41. Parrish, 479, 4–5, 376.

42. Gregg, 54.

43. Reehl 8.

44. The *Indianapolis* tragedy has spawned a small industry of publications. For example, see Newcomb, *Abandon Ship*; Lech, *All the Drowned Sailors*; Kurzman, *Fatal Voyage*; and Helm, *Ordeal by Sea.*

45. Quoted in McGurn, 6:3.

46. Tisdale had been aboard as Commander Cruisers, Task Force 16, since July 4, 1942. War Diary, July 4, 1942.

47. Ibid., Oct. 9, 13, 14, 1942.

48. Action Report, Oct. 17, 1942.

49. War Diary, Oct. 15, 1942.

50. Bloom in *Newsletter* (April 1998), 5.

51. West in ibid. (Oct. 1996), 5.

52. Ibid.

53. War Diary, Oct. 15, 1942.

54. Ibid., Oct. 16, 1942.

55. Ibid., Oct. 15, 23, 1942; Bloom in *Newsletter* (April 1998), 6.

56. Reehl 5; West in *Newsletter* (Oct. 1996), 5.

57. Leroy Rudder in *Newsletter* (July 1996), 4.

58. Bloom in *Newsletter* (April 1998), 6.

59. Action Report, Oct. 30, 1942.

60. Ibid.

61. Johnson in Stables, *We Remember,* 33.

62. Captain DuBose's remark, Action Report, Oct. 30, 1942.

63. *Newsletter* (2d Qtr 1991, 2d issue), 3.

64. Action Report, Oct. 30, 1942.

65. Ibid.

66. War Diary, Oct. 26, 1942.

67. Action Report, Oct. 30, 1942.

68. Ibid.

69. Ibid.

70. Ibid.

71. Turk Wirth in Stables, *We Remember II,* 54.

72. Action Report, Oct. 30, 1942.

73. Ibid.; Johnson in Stables, *We Remember,* 33.

74. Robert Braswell in *Newsletter* (2d Qtr 1992), 2.

75. Holbrook, 168.

76. *Newsletter* (Nov. 1998), 5.

77. Ibid. (April 1998), 6.

78. Lundstrom, 425. The quotation is from Lundstrom and may or may not be Halsey's.

79. Frank, 603.

## 7. Night Cruiser Action, November 13, 1942.

1. McGurn, 6:2.

2. Spector, 197. There were Army, Navy and Marine planes and pilots in the "Cactus Air Force."

3. Hammel, *Guadalcanal: Decision at Sea,* 48–50, 104–5.

4. Johnson in *Newsletter* (June–July 1989), 6.

5. War Diary, Oct. 30, 1942.

6. Ibid., Oct. 31 and Nov. 1, 1942; Potter and Nimitz, 702.

7. Frank, 430; War Diary, Nov. 8, 1942.

8. The details of Turner's maneuvers are given in Frank, 431.

9. War Diary, Nov. 12, 1942.

10. Johnson in Stables, *We Remember,* 35.

11. Hammel, *Guadalcanal: Decision at Sea,* 79; Reehl 6.

12. Action Report, Nov. 18, 1942.

13. Bloom in *Newsletter* (April 1998), 6.

14. Johnson in Stables, *We Remember,* 35; Action Report, Nov. 18, 1942.

15. War Diary, Nov. 12, 1942.

16. Frank, 432.

17. Action Report, Nov. 18, 1942.

18. Hammel, *Guadalcanal: Decision at Sea,* 313–14; Grace, 122.

19. Johnson in Stables, *We Remember,* 35.

20. Edward Smith in Stables, *We Remember,* 33.

21. Lawrence Joers in ibid., 32. Doctor Joers recalled that this event took place during the Battle of the Eastern Solomons on August 24. But in the same breath, he recounted the anti-aircraft use of the 8-inch guns, which happened only at Guadalcanal. Smith, moreover, cited in the preceding footnote, kept a dated copy of the ship's log for the day in question: November 12, 1942.

22. Johnson in Stables, *We Remember,* 35.

23. Spector, 209–11.

24. Frank, 433.

25. An excellent and detailed description of the Naval Battle of Guadalcanal appears in Hammel, *Guadalcanal: Decision at Sea,* which this account follows closely, especially Hammel's chapters 12 through 34, and the map on p. xii.

26. War Diary, Nov. 10, 1942.

27. These were USS *Atlanta* and USS *Juneau,* each of which carried sixteen 5-inch/38-caliber guns in eight twin mounts; Fahey, Victory edition, 18.

28. *Newsletter* (4th Qtr 1992), 2; List of Officers, Logs, Feb. 1936–June 1937.

29. Frank, 433.

30. War Diary, Nov. 11, 1942. Halsey made a poor choice in selecting his chief of staff, too; Potter, *Nimitz,* 87; Buell, 123, 126.

31. Grace, 45.

32. Hammel, *Guadalcanal: Decision at Sea,* 106; Koburger, 54.

33. Frank, 433.

34. The PPI, Planned Position Indicator, radarscope is the type we are all familiar with today: a round bird's-eye view of the scene with the observer's own position in the center of the screen, and a sweep that "paints" targets discovered by the radar. It was a new concept in November 1942. Before then, most radars displayed only those targets down a single bearing from the antenna, so that an operator had to stop sweeping in order to focus on any one blip.

35. Historian Holbrook, actually a member of *San Francisco*'s crew during this engagement, defends all of the admiral's decisions during it, especially on pages 181 and 185n. But most other historians, including this one, find Callaghan's decisions generally faulty.

36. Frank, 435.

37. Kennedy, 550–52.

38. Hammel, *Guadalcanal: Decision at Sea,* 118, 8–9. For brief accounts of the Battle of Savo Island, see Potter, *Nimitz,* 183; Koburger, 35–40.

39. Please recall that, in overview, this text follows that in Hammel, *Guadalcanal: Decision at Sea,* chapters 12 through 34, and the map on p. xii. A different analysis of what had befallen the Japanese formation before the moment of contact is given in Frank, 438.

40. Grace, 64.

41. Potter and Nimitz, 704.

42. Grace, 53.

43. Potter and Nimitz, 704.

44. Hammel, *Guadalcanal: Decision at Sea,* 128–29.

45. Ibid., 111. Grace, 47, says *Portland* had the SG surface search radar during this battle, but it was not installed until 1943 at Mare Island.

46. Hammel, *Guadalcanal: Decision at Sea,* 191. Frank, 438, may be even clearer in condemning the American admiral's decision, saying "Callaghan achieved not a cross but a collision."

47. Hammel, *Guadalcanal: Starvation Island,* 32.

48. Clifford Dunn in Stables, *We Remember,* 38.

49. *Newsletter* (4th Qtr 1990), 4.

50. Ala, "My Experiences in W.W. II," 2.

51. Johnson in Stables, *We Remember,* 26.

52. Dolezal interview.

53. Reehl 6; Dolezal interview.

54. Reehl 16.

55. Gibson interview.

56. Johnson in Stables, *We Remember,* 36.

57. Hammel, *Guadalcanal: Decision at Sea,* 192.

58. Ibid. 193; War Diary, Nov. 13, 1942.

59. War Diary, Nov. 13, 1942.

60. Reehl 6; Johnson in Stables, *We Remember,* 35.

61. Navships 35 (424), 4.

62. War Diary, Nov. 13, 1942.

63. Hammel, *Guadalcanal: Decision at Sea,* 193.

64. War Diary, November 13, 1942.

65. Ewing, 26; Stables 2; Hammel, *Guadalcanal: Decision at Sea,* 198; Grace, 81.

66. War Diary, Nov. 13, 1942.

67. Ibid.

68. Ibid.; Johnson in Stables, *We Remember,* 36.

69. Hammel, *Guadalcanal: Decision at Sea,* 194.

70. Grace, 79.

71. Hammel, *Guadalcanal: Decision at Sea,* 194. On Howard, see Fern Brooks in *Newsletter* (July 2000), 4. On the times, Grace, 79, says the torpedo struck about 0156, and the *Portland* website says 0158. The times given in Grace's book vary by five to ten minutes from those given in Hammel, *Guadalcanal: Decision at Sea.* Naval clocks differed notoriously from ship to ship. This account tries to stay with Hammel, *Guadalcanal: Decision at Sea,* but sometimes corrections have been made to illustrate which events came first and which later.

72. Hammel, *Guadalcanal: Decision at Sea,* 195.

73. Grace, 80, 185, Hammel, *Guadalcanal: Decision at Sea,* 192–93. Hammel, *Guadalcanal: Decision at Sea,* 236, says *Yudachi*'s torpedoes missed *Portland,* but that the Japanese destroyer reloaded and later hit the ill-fated *Juneau.* That analysis defies the known facts, so this account goes with Grace and the *Portland* website, both of which cite "Official Damage Reports." Navships 35 (424), 7, does not identify the enemy that fired the torpedo.

74. Navships 35 (424), 7.

75. War Diary, Nov. 13, 1942.

76. Wolf.

77. Bloom in *Newsletter* (Aug. 1998), 5.

78. Grace, 80.

79. Dunn in Stables, *We Remember,* 38.

80. *Newsletter* (1st Qtr 1992), 4.

81. Johnson in Stables, *We Remember,* 36; Waller 6.

82. Bond.

83. Stables, *We Remember II,* 55.

84. Dunn in *Newsletter* (2d Qtr 1992), 4; Hammel, *Guadalcanal: Decision at Sea,* 195.

85. Speer 2.

86. Peterson interview; Hight interview. Radioman Hight left *Portland* shortly afterward but won a Presidential Unit Citation for his service on USS *Kalinin Bay,* one of the tiny escort carriers that helped drive away the Japanese battleships off Samar in October 1944.

87. Hammel, *Guadalcanal: Decision at Sea,* 195–96.

88. Dolezal interview.

89. Hammel, *Guadalcanal: Decision at Sea,* 196–97.

90. Navships 35 (424), Plate III.

91. Vince Pietrok in Stables, *We Remember,* 39.

92. Navships 35 (424), Plate II.

93. Reehl 5; War Diary, Oct. 31, Nov. 10, 1942.

94. Wirth in Stables, *We Remember II,* 55.

95. Hight interview.

96. Hammel, *Guadalcanal: Decision at Sea,* 195–96; Gibson interview; Grace, 126–27. For several paragraphs, Hammel gives accounts of the dead and wounded. Gibson's account of staying by his gun is typical of what the sailors say they did, and confirms Hammel's account. Grace shows how damage control parties, engine personnel, and corpsmen kept working.

97. Bentley letter; Pietrok interview.

98. Hight interview; Choate 3; Speer 1.

99. Grace, 136.

100. *Portland* website. For just one example of an individual's thinking, see Dan Nixon in the "Guestbook" at the *Portland* website.

101. Stables, *We Remember II,* 56, 66.

102. Holbrook, 190.

103. Wirth in Stables, *We Remember II,* 56.

104. Frank Teague in Stables, *We Remember,* 40.

105. A.J. Arnold in Stables, *We Remember II,* 60.

106. *Newsletter* (April 2001), 3.

107. Ibid.

108. Arnold in Stables, *We Remember II,* 61.

109. Navships 35 (424), Plate III.

110. Ibid., 1–2.

111. *Newsletter* (Dec. 1988), 3.

112. War Diary, Nov. 13, 1942. The battleship's name is pronounced "hee-AYE" by *Portland* veterans.

113. Stables, *We Remember,* 56.

114. *Portland* website.

115. Hammel, *Guadalcanal: Decision at Sea,* 197–98; Grace, 81.

116. Spector, 212; Nimitz and Potter, 704.

117. War Diary, Nov. 13, 1942.

118. Johnson in *Newsletter* (Dec. 1988), 3.

119. War Diary, Nov. 13, 1942; Pietrok in Stables, *We Remember,* 39; Dolezal interview.

120. Bloom in *Newsletter* (Aug. 1998), 5.

121. Hammel, *Guadalcanal: Decision at Sea,* 302. 313.

122. Ibid., 301.

123. Frank, 452.

124. War Diary, Nov. 13, 1942.

125. Grace, 136.

126. Dan Nixon in the "Guestbook" at the *Portland* website; Johnson in Stables, *We Remember,* 37; Geriak 1.

127. Grace, 110.

128. Ibid.

129. Spector, 212.

130. Ibid., 213.

# 8. Repairs

1. Frank, 440; Grace, 79, 110.

2. War Diary, Nov. 13, 1942.

3. Bloom in *Newsletter* (Aug. 1998), 5.

4. Hammel, *Guadalcanal: Decision at Sea,* 324–27.

5. Frank, 456–57, weighs all sides of the issue but leaves the reader uncertain about his own conclusion.

6. War Diary, Nov. 13, 1942. The first time mentioned, the small craft was called "YC-236," but all other times "YC-239."

7. Grace, 138.

8. War Diary, Nov. 13, 1942.

9. Ibid.

10. *Bobolink* had been in commission since 1919. She would be re-designated as an auxiliary minesweeper in 1944. Fahey, Victory edition, 65.

11. Log, June 17, 1933.

12. Two examples are: Log, Dec. 4, 1934, and Oct. 31, 1940.

13. Grace, 143–46.

14. Ibid., 142.

15. Frank Teague in *Newsletter* (3d Qtr 1990), 3.

16. War Diary, Nov. 13, 1942.

17. Peterson interview.

18. *Newsletter* (June–July 1989), 1.

19. Ibid. (3d Qtr 1990), 3.

20. Wirth in Stables, *We Remember II,* 57.

21. Pietrok interview.

22. Hammel, *Guadalcanal: Decision at Sea,* 313–14.

23. Johnson in Stables, *We Remember,* 37; Grace, 147–48.

24. Wirth in Stables, *We Remember II,* 57.

25. Lundstrom, 502.

26. Johnson in Stables, *We Remember,* 37.

27. Ibid.; Ala, "My Experiences in W.W. II," 4; Leroy Riehl interview.

28. Bloom in *Newsletter* (Nov. 1998), 5.

29. Reehl 16.

30. Ibid.

31. Hammel, *Guadalcanal: Decision at Sea,* 428–29.

32. Stables, *We Remember II,* 65.

33. ComSoPac endorsement to USS *Portland,* Action Report, Nov. 21, 1942.

34. Ibid., 177.

35. Grace, 133; *Portland* website.

36. Potter and Nimitz, 737n. The Sixth Fleet has operated in the Mediterranean since about 1950. Its carrier formation is Task Force 67; <http://globalsecurity.org/military/agency/navy/fairmed.htm>.

37. Grace, 179–82.

38. Hight interview; Dolezal interview; Merryman interview; Wirth in Stables, *We Remember II,* 59; Bloom in *Newsletter* (Nov. 1998), 5.

39. Frank, 443 and footnote 443–44.

40. Grace, 178. The other Medals of Honor were awarded to two lieutenant commanders, the senior officers left on *San Francisco* after the bridge was hit, who did heroic work in getting the ship out of the trouble she was in; Frank, 489. But their trouble was nothing compared to what faced Laurence DuBose and *Portland*; all they had to do was sail away with *Helena.*

41. *Newsletter* (July 1993), 4.

42. Teague in Stables, *We Remember,* 40.

43. Stables, *We Remember,* 38.

44. Edens email.

45. Frank Haskell in *Newsletter* (2d Qtr 1991, 2d issue), 4.

46. Holbrook, 196. Holbrook continues the error by misspelling Gober's name.

47. Speer 1.

48. Waller 1.

49. Let the record show that *Portland*'s men who gave their lives in the service of their country were Joseph B. Allen, S2/c; Glyde H. Bragg, PhM3/c; Charles M. Compton, CPhM; Gerald Ferro, SC2/c; Harry O. Fitzsimmons, S2/c; Joseph R. Gober, MM1/c; Leslie J. Helm, PhM3/c; Riley C. Hook, Pfc; Erwin W. Hotcamp, AS; Jimmie Johnson, OC2/c; Donald D. Joyce, AS; Maynard G. Lokken, S1/c; Robert Mattix, S1/c; Franklin R. Osborne, Matt1/c; Charles G. Parker, EM2/c; Hayes E. Robertson Jr., S2/c; George A. Sullivan, SF3/c; and Lt. Robert H. Williams (MC); inside back cover of Stables, *We Remember II.*

A rumor went around the ship that George Sullivan was related to the five

Sullivan brothers—one of them named George, too—who became national heroes when they were lost later that day in USS *Juneau,* but no one could confirm it; Al Lucas in Stables, *We Remember II,* 15.

50. Allen, Bragg, Fitzsimmons, Holtkamp, Hook, Osborne, Sullivan, and Williams. Undated memo for the ship's files, Box 76, Archives II.

51. Ibid.

52. Series of letters, Commanding Officer *Portland* to Secretary of the Navy, Jan. 1943, Box 76, Archives II.

53. Johnson in Stables, *We Remember,* 38.

54. Stables, *We Remember II,* inside back cover.

55. Clifford Dunn in *Newsletter* (2d Qtr 1992), 4.

56. Johnson in Stables, *We Remember,* 38.

57. Speer 2.

58. Again, let the record show that these *Portland* men were wounded in action: J. Alexander Sea1/c; T.H. Anderson AMM2/c; J.B. Farnsworth CM3/3; T.P. Johnson BM2/c; E.G. Knottingham AS; J.A. Landry AS; H.J. Lowe AS; R.G. Ostlund Sea2/c; J.L. Pagel Sea2/c; O.E. Parking AS; [??] Prosieur CM1/c; J.R. Reimer Cox; R.F. Scanlon Sea1/c; R.T. Slaughter Sea2/c; J.T. Stelly P2/c; D.G. Sullivan Sea 1/c; Cdr. T.R. Wirth; Holbrook 197. This list does not include the name of Ted Waller, who was awarded a Purple Heart for the shrapnel wounds he received in this battle; Waller 3. But Waller's name was R.T. Slaughter in those days; Waller 9. See also *Newsletter* (1st Qtr 1992), 3.

59. *Newsletter* (1st Qtr 1992), 3.

60. Stables, *We Remember II,* 57. Wirth did not explain why he was charged for the X-ray, a most unusual occurrence at a naval medical facility.

61. Stables, *We Remember,* 104.

62. *Port Beam* (May 24, 1944), 4.

63. Linderman, 188–92.

64. One gedunk stand worker whose name survives in the sources was Ross Zimmerling; Stables, *We Remember II,* 43.

65. Stables, *We Remember,* 104.

66. A.R. Bentley and Sam Perdue in *Newsletter* (1st Qtr 1990), 4.

67. Ibid. Chief Bentley remembers that the torpedo itself passed through the gedunk stand, but the evidence presented in the text shows that his memory is flawed on that count.

68. Navships 35 (424), 12.

69. Ibid., 5.

70. Wirth in Stables, *We Remember II,* 58.

71. Ibid.

72. Reehl 6.

73. Stables, *We Remember II,* 39.

74. Stables, *We Remember,* 33.

75. Ibid., 45.

76. Al Lucas in ibid., 44.

77. Haskell in *Newsletter* (2d Qtr 1991, 2d issue), 4.

78. Holbrook, 201; War Diary, Nov. 18, 1942.

79. War Diary, Nov. 22, 1942.

80. Speer 1.

81. War Diary, Nov. 22, 1942. Bloom in *Newsletter* (Nov. 1998), 5, says the

second destroyer was *Southard,* not *Zane,* and that the tug was *Bobolink,* but the War Diary has the correct data.

82. Fahey, Two-Ocean edition, 41.
83. Haskell in *Newsletter* (2d Qtr 1991, 2d issue), 2; War Diary, Nov. 22, 1942.
84. Bloom in *Newsletter* (Nov. 1998), 5.
85. Grace, 179; Terzibaschitsch, 84.
86. War Diary, Nov. 24, 1942.
87. Reehl 9; Peterson interview.
88. Navships 35 (424), 7.
89. Bloom in *Newsletter* (Nov. 1998), 5.
90. Wolf.
91. E.g., Reehl 9.
92. War Diary, Nov. 30, 1942.
93. Bloom in *Newsletter* (Nov. 1998), 5.
94. Ibid.; War Diary, Dec. 1, 1942.
95. Johnson in Stables, *We Remember,* 46.
96. Bloom in *Newsletter* (Nov. 1998), 5.
97. Fahey, Two-Ocean edition, 10–11.
98. Johnson in Stables, *We Remember,* 46–48.
99. Reehl 9.
100. Johnson in Stables, *We Remember,* 46.
101. Reehl 9.
102. Riehl interview. Leroy Riehl and Bill Reehl spell their last names differently.
103. Gibson interview.
104. Ala, "My Experiences in W.W. II," 2; *Newsletter* (Jan. 1994), 4.
105. Pietrok interview.
106. Reehl 11.
107. Johnson in Stables, *We Remember,* 46.
108. Reehl 11.
109. *World Book,* 539.
110. *Port Beam* (Aug. 30, 1944), 1.
111. Foster Cole in Stables, *We Remember,* 65.
112. Handwritten, undated memo for the file in Box 76, Archives II.
113. Riehl interview.
114. Ala, "My Experiences in W.W. II," 5.
115. Reehl 11.
116. Reehl 9.
117. Ibid.
118. Ibid.
119. Ibid.
120. War Diary, Feb. 12, 1943.
121. Ibid., Feb. 14, 1943.
122. Ibid., Feb. 13–17, 1943.
123. Ibid., Feb. 17–March 1, 1943.
124. Bloom in *Newsletter* (Nov. 1998), 5.
125. Johnson in Stables, *We Remember,* 48.
126. Hight interview.

127. Johnson in *Newsletter* (June–July 1989), 6.
128. Bloom in ibid. (Nov. 1998), 5.
129. *Portland* website.
130. *Newsletter* (2d Qtr 1991, 2d issue), 3.
131. Ibid. (4th Qtr 1990), 3.
132. Bloom in ibid. (Nov. 1998), 5.
133. Terzibaschitsch, 23.
134. Ibid., 84; Reehl 9.
135. List of Officers, War Diary, May 1943.
136. Merryman interview.
137. Riehl interview; Reehl 9.
138. Holbrook, 110.
139. Riehl interview. In his interview, Dolezal said similar things.
140. Johnson in Stables, *We Remember,* 50.
141. *Newsletter* (4th Qtr 1990), 3; Reehl 9.
142. *Newsletter* (Jan. 1999), 1.
143. Ibid. (July 1996), 4.
144. McGurn, 5:2.
145. Holbrook, 206.
146. *Newsletter* (2d Qtr 1991, 1st issue), 4.
147. Hicks 1.

# 9. Central Pacific

1. Spector, 57.
2. War Diary, May 21–31, 1943.
3. Reehl 9.
4. Johnson in Stables, *We Remember,* 50.
5. This description of the ship is based on many photographs that exist. For just one example, see Stables, *We Remember,* 103.
6. Friedman, 152, includes a drawing from this bird's-eye view.
7. War Diary, June 1, 1943.
8. Art Lindholm in *Newsletter* (4th Qtr 1990), 4; List of Officers, War Diary, May 1943.
9. Blair, 418.
10. Waller 1.
11. Terzibaschitsch, 84; *Portland* website.
12. For a few examples, see War Diary, June 15, July 20; ComBatDivTwo Action Report (Aug. 24, 1943) for Aug. 15–16, 1943, Box 561, Archives II.
13. Bloom in *Newsletter* (Jan. 1999), 5.
14. Reehl 10.
15. *Newsletter* (June 1997), 2.
16. This event is given various names: "The Battle of the Pips," "The Battle of the Great Sitkin Blip," "The Battle of Sitkin Pip," and perhaps others; Holbrook, 208; Bloom in *Newsletter* (Jan. 1999), 5; War Diary, July 26, 1943.
17. Bloom in *Newsletter* (Jan. 1999), 5.
18. War Diary, July 26, 1943.
19. Action Report, July 28, 1943. See also Confidential letter from CO

*Portland* to CincPacFlt, July 28, 1943, filed with the War Diary in Box 1342 at Archives II, which makes virtually an identical report.

20. Bloom in *Newsletter* (Jan. 1999), 5.

21. Action Report, July 28, 1943. The 8-inch rounds are counted in Holbrook, 209; the battleships fired 418 14-inch, and the cruisers 487 8-inch.

22. Harold Johnson, in Stables, *We Remember,* 51.

23. Pete Cole in Stables, *We Remember,* 53.

24. Confidential letter from CO *Portland* to CincPacFlt, July 28, 1943, filed with the War Diary in Box 1342 at Archives II; Action Report, July 28, 1943.

25. Ibid.

26. Action Report, July 28, 1943.

27. W.E. Guitar, "Orders for the Day . . . 15 November 1943," in *Newsletter* (2d Qtr 1990), 6.

28. Cole in *Newsletter* (1st Qtr 1990), 3.

29. Merryman interview.

30. *Newsletter* (Jan. 1999), 5. A new explanation cropped up recently: the pips were migratory birds; Mac Metcalfe, "Recalling Kiska, the battle that never was," [Juneau] *Empire* (Sept. 17, 2003), C1.

31. Milton Poulos in Stables, *We Remember II,* 74.

32. Leroy Berlin diary in *Newsletter* (Oct. 1997), 6.

33. Bloom in *Newsletter* (Jan. 1999), 5.

34. War Diary, Sept. 23, 1943.

35. Terzibaschitsch, 5.

36. War Diary, Oct. 1, 1943.

37. Bloom in *Newsletter* (Jan. 1999), 6.

38. Berlin diary in *Newsletter* (Oct. 1997), 6.

39. Reehl 5.

40. Arbour tape.

41. Reehl 8.

42. Reehl 9.

43. Bloom in *Newsletter* (Jan. 1999), 6.

44. Arbour tape.

45. Ibid.

46. Steinberg, 105; Spector, 257–58.

47. War Diary, Oct. 21, 22, Nov. 2, 1943; Arbour tape.

48. An excellent recent history is Alexander. An older but briefer account is Baldwin. Please see bibliography for full titles.

49. Reehl 10; Bloom in *Newsletter* (Jan. 1999), 6.

50. Contemporary documents call it "Bititu," which must have been an earlier spelling of the island's name; War Diary, Nov. 20, 1943; Action Report, Dec. 1, 1943.

51. Bloom in *Newsletter* (Jan. 1999), 6.

52. Alexander, 235–36.

53. War Diary, Nov. 20, 1943.

54. Reehl 10.

55. Bill Speer in ibid. (Oct. 1996), 4.

56. Andy Pappas in ibid. (July 2001), 4.

57. Vince McNamara diary in *Newsletter* (Oct. 2000), 5.

58. Action Report, Dec. 9, 1943.

59. Ibid.

61. Bloom in *Newsletter* (Jan. 1999), 6.

62. Action Report, Jan. 23, 1944.

63. Reehl 12; Bloom in *Newsletter* (Jan. 1999), 6.

64. War Diary, Feb. 2, 1944.

65. Reehl 12; Action Report, March 1, 1944.

66. Arbour tape.

67. Action Report, March 1, 1944.

68. Ibid.

69. Ibid.

70. McNamara diary in *Newsletter* (Oct. 2000), 6.

71. Ibid.

72. Ibid.

73. Memo for the ship's file, Jan. 31, 1945, "concerning finding of death," Box 76, Archives II.

74. Action Report, March 1, 1944; on the mattress, War Diary, Feb. 23, 1944.

75. Memo for the ship's file, Jan. 31, 1945, "concerning finding of death," Box 76, Archives II.

76. McNamara diary in *Newsletter* (Oct. 2000), 6; A.L. Putnam in Stables, *We Remember II,* 155.

77. Action Report, March 1, 1944.

78. Ralph Wilhelm in Stables, *We Remember II,* 151.

79. *Newsletter* (Oct. 2000), 6.

80. Waller 5.

81. Stables, *We Remember II,* inside back cover.

82. Bloom in *Newsletter* (Jan. 1999), 6; Dolezal interview. Bloom said the battleship was *New Mexico,* but the ship's log says *Colorado*; War Diary, Feb. 19, 1944.

83. Bloom in *Newsletter* (April 1999), 4.

84. Confidential letter from CO *Portland* to CincPacFlt, July 28, 1943, filed with the War Diary in Box 1342 at Archives II.

85. Action Report, Dec. 9, 1943.

86. First endorsement on ibid.

87. War Diary, May 6, 1943; List of Officers, War Diary, May 1943.

88. Bloom in *Newsletter* (April 1999), 4. One wonders if this visit may have been a model for the similar fictional event in Herman Wouk's *The Caine Mutiny,* 360–66. Unlike *Portland*'s officers, those in the novel got cold feet on the flagship and aborted their visit to report on Captain Queeg.

89. War Diary (Feb. 20, 1944). Doctor friends of the author cannot decipher the diagnosis, and the Navy's Bureau of Medicine and Surgery does not respond to inquiries. One guess is that it could be the redundant "Diagnosis Unknown."

90. Ibid.

91. Guitar signed the Combat Action Report of 1 March 1944, as Commanding Officer.

92. War Diary, Feb. 21, 1944.

93. Bloom in *Newsletter* (April 1999), 4.

94. Dolezal interview.

95. Morton 2.

96. Bloom in *Newsletter* (April 1999), 4.

97. U.S. Naval Academy, *Register of Alumni,* 82.

98. Reehl 12.
99. War Diary, Feb. 23, 1944.
100. Ibid., March 2, 1944.
101. Bloom in *Newsletter* (April 1999), 4.
102. Ancell, 609.
103. Charles Iley in Stables, *We Remember,* 107.
104. http://www3.uakron.edu/archival/arnstein/usrigid.htm. Settle's picture, taken when he was a young man in the office of inspector, appears in this source.
105. Ancell, 609.
106. Poulos in Stables, *We Remember II,* 77.
107. War Diary, March 2, 1944. Chandler was in the Class of 1915 at Annapolis, Settle 1919; Morison, vol. 13, xii; Ancell, 609.
108. War Diary, March 3, 1944.
109. Morton 3; Reehl 2; Hicks 1.
110. Reehl 16; Dolezal interview; Partridge interview.
111. Holbrook, 251.
112. Zee Loftin in *Newsletter* (March 1997), 6.
113. Action Report, May 3, 1944.
114. Ibid., Sept. 29, 1944.
115. Ibid.
116. McNamara in Stables, *We Remember,* 81.
117. Loftin in *Newsletter* (March 1997), 5.
118. Ray Bertrand in Stables, *We Remember II,* 96.
119. Arbour tape.
120. Ancel, 609.
121. Spector, 285.
122. Reehl 12.
123. Bloom in *Newsletter* (Jan. 1999), 6.
124. Berlin diary in ibid. (Oct. 1997), 7.
125. Reehl 12; *Portland* website.
126. Berlin diary in *Newsletter* (Oct. 1997), 7.
127. Bloom in *Newsletter* (April 1999), 4.
128. Ibid.

# 10. Mid-1944

1. Berlin diary in *Newsletter* (Oct. 1997), 7; Bloom in ibid. (April 1999), 4.
2. The newspaper is described in this chapter.
3. *Port Beam* (May 19, 1944), 3.
4. Holbrook, 231.
5. Terzibaschitsch, 24.
6. Bloom in *Newsletter* (April 1999), 4.
7. Reehl 12.
8. Choate 3.
9. Holbrook, 232.
10. Choate 1.
11. Choate 2.
12. Choate 3.

13. Bloom in *Newsletter* (July 1999), 2.

14. Ibid.

15. *Newsletter* (Jan. 1998), 2.

16. Holbrook, 233.

17. *Port Beam* (undated, but probably Sept. 1944), 8.

18. *The Pilot* (April 28, 1944), 5. The original text says "wild the crew," an obvious typographical error corrected here.

19. *Newsletter* (Oct. 2000), 6.

20. See the bibliography for the issues the author was able to find. Note 22 below suggests that there may have been others, though.

21. *Port Beam* (May 5, 1944), 1.

22. Ibid., 2; Stables, *We Remember II,* 66. McDannold's claim to have been editor-in-chief is evidence that there were issues of *Port Beam* other than those the author has found, because McDannold's name does not appear on any of those mastheads.

23. *Port Beam* (Aug. 30, 1944), 1.

24. *The Pilot* (April 28, 1944), 5; *Port Beam* (Aug. 30, 1944), 1.

25. *The Pilot* (April 28, 1944), 1.

26. *Port Beam* (May 24, 1944), 1–2; ibid. (May 5, 1944), 1; ibid. (Sept. 7, 1944), 2.

27. "The Lucky Bag" changed its name to "On the Beam" after a few issues.

28. *Port Beam* (May 19, 1944), 3.

29. Ibid. (May 5, 1944), 5; ibid. (May 19, 1944), 3.

30. Ibid. (May 5, 1944), 5.

31. Ibid., 4.

32. Ibid. (May 19, 1944), 8.

33. Ibid. (undated, probably Sept. 1944), 7.

34. Ibid. (May 19, 1944), 8.

35. Chuck Martin interview.

36. *Port Beam* (May 5, 1944), 8.

37. Ibid. (Sept. 7, 1944), 3.

38. Arbour kit.

39. *The Pilot* (April 28, 1944), 5.

40. *Port Beam* (undated, probably Sept. 1944), 7.

41. Ibid. (May 5, 1944), 8; ibid. (undated, probably Sept. 1944), 7; ibid. (Sept. 7, 1944), 3.

42. Partridge interview.

43. Blackie Oliver in Stables, *We Remember II,* 71.

44. *Port Beam* (Aug. 30, 1944), 2.

45. *Newsletter* (Oct. 1989), 4.

46. Bloom in *Newsletter* (July 1999), 2.

47. *Port Beam* (Aug. 30, 1944), 2.

48. Spector, 419–20.

49. Reehl 12.

50. Action Report, Sept. 29, 1944.

51. Ibid.

52. Ibid.

53. Ibid.

54. Berlin diary in *Newsletter* (Jan. 1998), 2.

55. Spector, 420–21.

56. Sternberg, 177.

57. Action Report, Sept. 29, 1944.

58. Partridge in Stables, *We Remember,* 76; Action Report, Sept. 29, 1944.

59. *Newsletter* (Jan. 2001), 5.

60. Clay Ridgely, "My Life at Sea," in *Newsletter* (April 2002), 6.

61. Chuck Martin interview.

62. Miles 2.

63. Johns.

64. Partridge interview.

65. Choate 2.

66. Dennis Mannion, former U.S. Marine, in a lecture given annually at Choate Rosemary Hall, Wallingford, Connecticut, c. 1981–c. 1999.

67. Hicks 1.

68. Miles 2.

69. Choate 2.

70. Berlin diary in *Newsletter* (Jan. 1998), 2; Floyd Marcy in Stables, *We Remember II,* 100.

71. Bloom in *Newsletter* (Oct. 1999), 2.

72. Ibid.; Reehl 12.

73. Bloom in *Newsletter* (July 1999), 2.

74. Action Report, Sept. 29, 1944.

75. Ibid.

76. Reehl 12.

## 11. Life on Board

1. Choate 2; Allred; Morton 3; Hight interview; Partridge interview; Geriak 1; Reehl 1; Goff interview; Hicks 1; Gibson interview; Reehl 1; Mahala in the "Guestbook" at the *Portland* website.

2. Reehl 1.

3. Mahala 1; Allred; Valdes 2.

4. Miles 2.

5. Arbour tape.

6. *Newsletter* (Jan. 1994), 2.

7. For example, Gibson, Dolezal, and Reehl went to Great Lakes, Illinois; while Choate, Allred, and Hight went to San Diego, California.

8. Morton 3; Hicks 1; Fynan 1.

9. Lassen interview.

10. Reehl 2; Stables interview.

11. Morton 2; Spector, 537.

12. Perhaps the most famous was the fight the ship's crew gave fires and other destruction caused by an overwhelming air attack on USS *Franklin,* an aircraft carrier plastered off the coast of Japan in March 1945. About a third of her crew was killed, but the rest sailed the carrier home under her own power.

13. Bentley; *Port Beam* (May 5, 1944), 1; Hight interview; Peterson interview.

14. Hicks 1.

15. Reehl 11.

15. Reehl 11.

16. Ibid.; Reehl 15; Dolezal interview; Partridge interview.

17. Arbour tape. Arbour was actually in F Division, the fire-control crew, which *aimed* the guns, but his career illustrates what the men in the deck divisions did, too.

18. Reehl 2; Partridge interview; Hicks 1.

19. Fynan 1.

20. Dolezal interview.

21. Hicks 1.

22. Valdes 1.

23. Stables, *We Remember,* 9–10.

24. Dolezal interview.

25. Valdes 1.

26. Lassen interview.

27. *Newsletter* (1st Qtr 1990), 4.

28. Goff interview. In the more recent Navy, it would take a young man four or more years to climb to SK1, which Goff made in twelve months.

29. Stables, *We Remember II,* 66.

30. Morton 3.

31. Partridge interview.

32. Reehl 12.

33. Reehl 13–14.

34. Fynan 1.

35. Valdes 1.

36. *Port Beam* (May 19, 1944), 5. The names of some of the musicians are badly garbled in the copy of the newspaper studied by the author. The first names of the chaplain and band leader Thomas are not given.

37. Photo in Stables, *We Remember,* 73.

38. Dolezal interview; Bentley; Fynan 1.

39. Hicks 1.

40. Chuck Martin interview.

41. Banks interview; Peugh interview.

42. Arbour tape.

43. Holbrook, 38.

44. Ibid., 237.

45. *The Pilot* (April 28, 1944), 3.

46. McNamara diary in *Newsletter* (Jan. 2001), 5.

47. *Port Beam* (Sept. 7, 1944), 3.

48. *Newsletter* (Oct. 1994), 6.

49. Hicks 1; Merryman interview.

50. Allred.

51. Hicks 1; Reehl 16; Miles 1; Dolezal interview.

52. Partridge interview.

53. Merryman interview; Dolezal interview; Partridge interview.

54. Arbour tape.

55. Reehl 3.

56. Partridge interview.

57. Allred.

58. Sam Perdue in Stables, *We Remember,* 22.

59. *Newsletter* (2d Qtr 1991, 2nd issue), 3; Waller 4.

61. Dewey Stimson in ibid. (Aug. 1998), 2.

62. Geriak 1.

63. Reehl 3.

64. Action Report, April 20, 1945.

65. The following are some of the menus that have come to light: Christmas 1938, in *Newsletter* (Dec. 1988), 3; Christmas 1940, in *Newsletter* (1st Qtr 1991), 1; Christmas 1943, in Choate kit; Ship's Birthday 1944, in Arbour kit.

66. *Newsletter* (Aug. 1998), 2.

67. Stables, *We Remember II,* 73, 79.

68. Reehl 3.

69. Peterson interview; Hicks 3.

70. Choate 2.

71. Miles 2.

72. Choate 1.

73. Dolezal interview.

74. Miles 2.

75. Waller 1–2.

76. Commanding Officer, USS *Portland,* letter to the Bureau of Naval Personnel, 8 May 1945, in Box 76, Archives II.

77. Commanding Officer, USS *Portland,* letter to the Bureau of Medicine and Surgery, May 19, 1945, in Box 76, Archives II.

78. Walter Martin interview.

## 12. Leyte Gulf

1. Reehl 12.

2. *Portland* website.

3. Hight interview.

4. Morton 2; Miles 2.

5. Action Report, Oct. 25, 1944.

6. Perhaps the best account of this, the most gigantic naval fight of all time, is Thomas J. Cutler, *The Battle of Leyte Gulf: 23–26 October 1944* (New York, 1994).

7. Bates, vol. 7, pt. 2, 735.

8. Ibid., vol. 5, pt. 1, 240a; Potter and Nimitz, 785; Cutler, 417.

9. *Mississippi,* the other battleship at Surigao Strait, was not at Pearl Harbor on December 7, 1941; Bates, vol. 5, pt. 1, 240a. Also sunk or damaged on December 7 but not at Surigao were *Arizona, Nevada,* and *Oklahoma. Nevada* was at work in the European theater. *Oklahoma* was righted and raised from the bottom at Pearl Harbor but accidentally sank again in 1947 while being towed to the scrap-yard in California. As everyone probably knows, *Arizona* is still on station.

10. Bates, vol. 5, pt. 1, 240a; Potter and Nimitz, 785–86.

11. Diary in *Newsletter* (Jan. 2001), 6.

12. Bloom in *Newsletter* (Oct. 1999), 2.

13. McNamara diary in *Newsletter* (July 1994), 2.

14. Poulos in Stables, *We Remember II,* 76; Action Report, Oct. 28, 1944; Bloom in *Newsletter* (Oct. 1999), 2.

15. Action Report, Oct. 28, 1944; Bloom in *Newsletter* (Oct. 1999), 2. The enemy battleship is named in Potter and Nimitz, 786.

16. McNamara diary in *Newsletter* (Jan. 2001), 6.

17. Morton 3.

18. Merryman interview; Morton 2.

19. Choate 3.

20. Action Report, Oct. 28, 1944.

21. Miles 2.

22. Partridge in Stables, *We Remember,* 77.

23. McNamara diary in *Newsletter* (July 1994), 2.

24. Action Report, Oct. 28, 1944.

25. Ibid.

26. McNamara in Stables, *We Remember II,* 87.

27. Action Report, Oct. 28, 1944.

28. Bloom in *Newsletter* (Jan. 2000), 3.

29. Ibid.; Bates, vol. 5, pt. 1, 213.

30. For the heroism of the underdog Americans in the Battle off Samar, see Cutler, chapter 18.

31. *Port Beam* (Nov. 3, 1944), 3.

32. McNamara in Stables, *We Remember II,* 89.

33. Don Martin in Stables, *We Remember,* 67.

34. Miles 2; Cutler, 272–73.

35. Partridge interview.

36. McNamara diary in *Newsletter* (Jan. 2001), 6.

37. Partridge interview; Reehl 12. The plane was probably a "Val" dive-bomber, which had fixed landing gear.

38. Partridge interview.

39. McNamara diary in *Newsletter* (Jan. 2001), 6.

40. Partridge interview; Dolezal interview; Merryman interview.

41. Reehl 16.

42. Partridge interview.

43. Miles 2.

44. Log, Jan. 6, 1945.

45. H.F. Fountain in *Newsletter* (July 2000), 2.

46. Action Report, Jan. 11, 1945.

47. Ibid.

48. Bloom in *Newsletter* (Jan. 2000), 4.

49. McNamara diary in *Newsletter* (Dec. 1994), 3. *Portland* was with two other admirals when they died: Daniel Callaghan and Norman Scott at Guadalcanal. Chandler's death is given in detail, with some erroneous dates, in Morison, vol. 13, xii–xiii, a volume that the author dedicated to the admiral. Perhaps the only other flag officer who was killed in action in the Pacific War was Rear Admiral Isaac Kidd, who remains on station in *Arizona* at Pearl Harbor.

50. War Diary, Jan. 6, 1945.

51. Fountain in *Newsletter* (July 2000), 2.

52. Ibid.

53. Partridge in Stables, *We Remember,* 78–79.

54. *Newsletter* (Jan. 2001), 6.

55. Ibid. (Aug. 1998), 2.

56. Stables, *We Remember,* 78–79.

57. Dewey Stimson in *Newsletter* (Aug. 1998), 2.

58. Martin in *Newsletter* (Oct 1988), 4.
59. McNamara in Stables, *We Remember II,* 90.
60. Choate 2.
61. Partridge interview; Action Report, Jan. 11, 1945.
62. ComBatDivTwo endorsement to USS *Portland,* Action Report, Jan. 11, 1945.
63. Morison, vol. 13, 103–9.
64. Reehl 14.
65. Partridge interview.
66. Berlin diary in *Newsletter* (Aug. 1998), 3.
67. Action Report, Jan. 11, 1945.
68. Ibid., Fourth Endorsement.
69. Berlin diary in *Newsletter* (Aug. 1998), 3.
70. Partridge in Stables, *We Remember,* 77.
71. Choate 2.
72. *Newsletter* (July 2000), 2.
73. Spector, 539, 535.
74. Kennedy, 833.
75. Reehl 13.
76. Spector, 539.
77. Partridge interview.
78. McNamara diary in *Newsletter* (Dec. 1994), 3.
79. Ibid. (Jan. 2001), 6.
80. Guitar, "Orders for the Day . . . 15 November 1943" in *Newsletter* (2d Qtr 1990), 6; and explained to the author by Ted Waller, Waller 4.
81. *Newsletter* (Feb. 1995), 5.
82. Paul Hupf in Stables, *We Remember II,* 109.
83. McNamara diary in *Newsletter* (Jan. 2001), 6.
84. Action Report, Dec. 21, 1944; McNamara in Stables, *We Remember II,* 89.
85. Reehl 12.
86. *Newsletter* (April 1998), 4.
87. Ibid.
88. Berlin diary in *Newsletter* (April 1998), 4.

# 13. 1945

1. During the author's naval career, an unrep always attracted large numbers of spectators from the ships involved. The system was so routine in World War II that no mention of it found its way into the sources for this book. For an excellent and brief overview of the Navy's Pacific logistics, see Potter and Nimitz, 642–45.
2. On the general question of the importance of mail to American servicemen during the war, see Linderman, 302–5.
3. Berlin diary in *Newsletter* (April 1998), 4.
4. Wolf.
5. Choate 3.
6. Reehl 14.
7. Stables, *We Remember,* 53–54.
8. Reehl 14.

9. Choate 3.

10. Berlin diary in *Newsletter* (April 1998), 4.

11. Linderman, 192.

12. McNamara diary in *Newsletter* (Oct. 2000), 6.

13. Miles 2.

14. Choate 2.

15. Spector, 268.

16. Wheeler, 8.

17. *Port Beam* (Nov. 3, 1944), 1.

18. *Newsletter* (Aug. 1998), 3.

19. Riehl interview.

20. Choate 2.

21. *Port Beam* (May 19, 1944), 8.

22. Linderman, 189.

23. McNamara in Stables, *We Remember,* 74.

24. Linderman, 189.

25. Reehl 14.

26. Stimson in *Newsletter* (Aug. 1998), 2.

27. *Newsletter* (Oct. 1997), 2.

28. Johnson in Stables, *We Remember,* 31.

29. Stables, *We Remember II,* 98.

30. Stables, *We Remember,* 59–60.

31. "Cal" Sunderland in *Newsletter* (May 1995), 6.

32. Berlin diary in *Newsletter* (April 1998), 4.

33. McNamara in Stables, *We Remember II,* 90.

34. Poulos in Stables, *We Remember II,* 79.

35. Partridge in Stables, *We Remember,* 79.

36. Putnam in Stables, *We Remember II,* 157.

37. Action Report, Feb. 17, 1945.

38. Spector, 525.

39. Action Report, Feb. 17, 1945.

40. Morton 2.

41. McNamara in Stables, *We Remember,* 72.

42. *Newsletter* (Oct. 2001), 4.

43. Spector, 326.

44. Berlin diary in *Newsletter* (Aug. 1998), 3.

45. Bloom in *Newsletter* (April 2000), 5. A lieutenant in C Division, Bloom actually omitted Eniwetok, although he had the count right.

46. *World Book* (1946), 5879.

47. Wheeler, 98.

48. Ibid., 135.

49. Action Report, April 20, 1945.

50. Berlin diary in *Newsletter* (Aug. 1998), 3; see slightly different versions of this event in Stables, *We Remember,* 79–81, and *Newsletter* (April 2000), 5.

51. Stables, *We Remember,* 74.

52. Morison, vol. 14, 117.

53. Stables, *We Remember,* 74.

54. Ibid.

55. Marcy in Stables, *We Remember II,* 111–14.

56. Stables, *We Remember II,* 162.
57. This tin can was probably USS *Longshaw*; Morison, vol. 14, 247.
58. Bloom in *Newsletter* (April 2000), 5; Morison's history does not describe this second grounded destroyer.
59. Morton 3.
60. Bloom in *Newsletter* (April 2000), 5.
61. Stables, *We Remember,* 110.
62. Action Report, April 20, 1945.
63. Berlin diary in *Newsletter* (Aug. 1998), 3.
64. Hupf in *Newsletter* (1st Qtr 1990), 4.
65. Action Report, April 20, 1945.
66. Ibid.
67. Bloom in *Newsletter* (April 2000), 5.
68. Ibid.
69. Partridge in Stables, *We Remember,* 81.
70. Action Report, April 20, 1945.
71. George Loock in *Newsletter* (Nov. 1998), 2.
72. List of Officers, Log, July 1945.
73. Holbrook, 251.
74. Reehl 13.
75. Log, Aug. 3, 1945.

# 14. War's End

1. Choate 3; Lech, 4.
2. Reehl 13.
3. Choate 2.
4. Choate 1; Reehl 16; Hicks 1.
5. Hicks 1; Miles 2.
6. Miles 2.
7. Reehl 13.
8. http://www.history.navy.mil/photos/events/wwii-pac/japansur/js-10.htm.
9. *Portland* website.
10. http://www.thorfinn.net/history.html.
11. Miller, 342–43.
12. Ibid.
13. *Portland* website; Hicks kit; Reehl 12.
14. Partridge interview; Reehl 16.
15. War Diary, Aug. 31, 1945.
16. Bertrand [Berlin] diary in *Newsletter* (Aug. 1998), 4. Although the headline at this source says it is "By Ray Bertrand," editor Ted Waller wrote in a handwritten note on the author's copy that the source is actually the diary of Leroy Berlin, correctly cited on the previous page in the *Newsletter*. Notes herein will cite the source as Bertrand [Berlin] diary in *Newsletter* (Aug. 1998).
17. Choate 1.
18. War Diary, Sept. 1–2, 1945. In *Newsletter* (Aug. 1995), 3, Sweet Pea pilot Jim Young wrote that there was only one destroyer to escort *Portland,* and that *Osmus* and *Stack* joined just as the task unit reached Truk.

19. Bertrand [Berlin] diary in *Newsletter* (Aug. 1998), 4.

20. War Diary, Aug. 28, 1945.

21. Ibid., Sept. 1, 1945.

22. Partridge interview.

23. *Newsletter* (Aug. 1995), 3.

24. War Diary, Sept. 2, 1945. The general's name is spelled "Mugikura" on the *Portland* website; http://www.history.navy.mil/photos/events/wwii-pac/japansur/js-10g.htm. The spelling in the text is taken from War Diary, Sept. 2, 1945.

25. War Diary, Sept. 2, 1945.

26. Reehl 13.

27. War Diary, Sept. 2, 1945.

28. Partridge interview.

29. Choate 1.

30. Hicks 1.

31. Allred; Partridge interview.

32. http://www.history.navy.mil/photos/events/wwii-pac/japansur/js-10.htm.

33. The photographs of the event show how ashamed the Japanese were, despite Hicks's thought that the admiral was actually glad. http://www.history.navy.mil/photos/events/wwii-pac/japansur/js-10.htm.

34. Partridge interview.

35. Log, Sept. 2–3, 1945.

36. Partridge interview.

37. Chuck Martin interview; Partridge interview; Choate 1; Miles 2; Reehl 16.

38. Morton 2; *Newsletter* (Jan. 1996), 1.

39. *Newsletter* (Aug. 1995), 3.

40. Letter from the mayor of Portland in *Newsletter* (Feb. 1995), 2. The official name of the museum is "The National Museum of the Pacific War," but since it began as the "Nimitz Museum," that name has lingered in public usage and even at its own website; http://www.nimitz-museum.com/.

41. Bertrand [Berlin] diary in *Newsletter* (April 1998), 3.

42. Wolf; List of Officers, War Diary, Nov. 1942.

43. Stables, *We Remember II,* 120.

44. Bertrand [Berlin] diary in *Newsletter* (Aug. 1998), 4. The source does not say how the length was calculated. When carrier *Enterprise* made the same trip her homeward-bound pennant was 578 feet long, one foot for every day she had been away from the United States; Stafford, 500. The *Portland* had been away more than 960 days during the war. Perhaps the length was calculated at one foot in length for each member of the crew still on board, although that number was not recorded.

45. Undated, unidentified newspaper clipping in Stables, *We Remember,* 94. The story itself suggests that the newspaper was Hawaiian and written about the time *Portland* reached Pearl Harbor.

46. Log, Sept. 25, 1945; Bertrand [Berlin] diary in *Newsletter* (Aug. 1998), 4.

47. *Newsletter* (Nov. 1998), 2.

48. Log, Oct. 2, 1945.

49. Bertrand [Berlin] diary in *Newsletter* (Aug. 1998), 4.

50. Morton 2.

51. Miles 2.

52. Stables, *We Remember II,* 131.

53. Reehl says the liberty was in Cristobal. Most other sources say it was in the

larger city of Colon, including Malcolm Marks, cited in the text, who spelled it "Cologne." The towns are on opposite sides of the Canal's Atlantic opening, so some sailors may have gone to one and some to the other.

54. Log, Oct. 9–11, 1945.
55. Ibid., Oct. 13, 1945.
56. Bertrand [Berlin] diary in *Newsletter* (Aug. 1998), 4.
57. Choate 1.
58. *Newsletter* (Nov. 1998), 2.
59. Bertrand [Berlin] diary in *Newsletter* (Aug. 1998), 4.
60. Log, Oct. 17, 1945.
61. Choate 1.
62. Hicks 1.
63. "The Fleet's In," *Life,* Nov. 5, 1945.
64. Miles 2.
65. Log, Oct. 21, 23, 1945.
66. Reehl 13; Morton 3.
67. Morton 3.
68. *Newsletter* (March 1997), 8.
69. Holbrook, 255–56.
70. Log, Oct. 25, 1945.
71. Ibid.
72. Bertrand [Berlin] diary in *Newsletter* (Aug. 1998), 4.
73. Morton 2.
74. Reehl 13.
75. Hicks 1.
76. Log, Oct. 26, 1945.
77. Ibid., Oct. 28, 1945.

## 15. The Final Mission

1. Log, Oct. 31, 1945.
2. Miles 2; Bill Perrault in *Newsletter* (Nov. 1998), 4; Log, Nov. 7, 1945.
3. Log, Nov. 2, 3, 1945.
4. Log, Oct. 23, 24, 25, 28, Nov. 3, 7, 1945.
5. Valdes 1.
6. Warble 1.
7. Valdes 3.
8. Reehl 14.
9. Log, Nov. 18, 1945.
10. Fountain in Stables, *We Remember,* 95; and Fountain in Stables, *We Remember II,* 123.
11. Martin in Stables, *We Remember,* 96.
12. Log, Nov. 21, 22, 23, 1945.
13. Ibid., Nov. 29, 1945.
14. Ibid., Dec. 1, 1945.
15. List of Officers, ibid., Dec. 1945.
16. Reehl 13.
17. Log, Dec. 13, 1945.

18. Thomas Holmes in *Newsletter* (Oct. 1996), 4.

19. Log, Dec. 13, 14, 1945.

20. Fountain in Stables, *We Remember,* 102.

21. Warble 1.

22. Warble 1 and 2.

23. Reehl 14.

24. Warble 1.

25. Log, Dec. 14, 1945.

26. Reehl 13.

27. Ibid.

28. Martin in Stables, *We Remember,* 96.

29. Braswell in Stables, *We Remember,* 97.

30. Log, Dec. 16, 1945.

31. Ibid.

32. Warble 1.

33. Barney Kliks in *Newsletter* (3d Qtr 1991), 4; Log, Dec. 17, 1945.

34. Warble 1.

35. Log, Dec. 17, 1945.

36. Ibid.

37. Herman Ferguson in Stables, *We Remember II,* 129.

38. Chris Horace in the "Guestbook" at the *Portland* website.

39. Morton 3.

40. Kliks in *Newsletter* (3d Qtr 1991), 4.

41. Ibid.

42. Warble 1.

43. Ibid.

44. Bob Braswell clipping in *Newsletter* (1st Qtr 1991), 4. The original source, reprinted in its entirety in the *Newsletter,* was an unidentified and unpaged story from a New York daily newspaper sent in by Braswell, but originally written the day *Portland* finally made it to New York.

45. Warble 2.

46. Horace.

47. Reehl 13.

48. Not in order to disguise the identities: Warble 1; Reehl 13; Roberts interview.

49. Log, Dec. 17, 1945.

50. *Portland* website; Braswell clipping in *Newsletter* (1st Qtr 1991), 4.

51. Warble 1.

52. Ibid.

53. *New York Daily News,* undated story reprinted in Stables, *We Remember,* 99.

54. Braswell clipping in *Newsletter* (1st Qtr 1991), 4.

55. Log, Dec. 17, 1945.

56. *New York Times* (Dec. 12, 1945), 8:2.

57. Log, Dec. 17, 1945.

58. Ferguson in Stables, *We Remember II,* 130.

59. Log, Dec. 17, 1945.

60. Fred Patton, clipping from the *Glenns Falls (New York) Post-Star* (April 23, 1996), unpaged, in *Newsletter* (July 1996), 6. Patton was a soldier-passenger on the ship during the storm.

61. Both the Braswell and Patton clippings mention how the fears of the troops were quieted by Libby's calm presentation.

62. *Newsletter* (3d Qtr 1991), 4.

63. Horace.

64. Warble 1. Former Sergeant Warble recalled that this heroic fifth man was washed overboard, but in fact no members of *Portland*'s crew were lost in the storm.

65. Ed Glatzel in *Newsletter* (May 1993), 2; Stables, *We Remember II,* 167.

66. Stables, *We Remember II,* 167; Herman Ferguson in ibid, 130.

67. Horace.

68. Log, Dec. 17, 1945.

69. Barney Kliks, letter to his parents, Dec. 19, 1945, reprinted in Stables, *We Remember II,* 129; Thomas Holmes in *Newsletter* (June 1997), 3; Log, Dec. 21, 1945.

70. Kliks in *Newsletter* (3d Qtr 1991), 4.

71. Warble 1.

72. Stables, *We Remember,* 102.

73. Warble 1.

74. Warble 2.

75. Albert Bowman in Stables, *We Remember II,* 126.

76. Log, Dec. 17, 1945.

77. *New York Times,* Dec. 12, 1945, 8:2.

78. Log, Dec. 17, 1945.

79. Warble 2.

80. Horace.

81. Log, Dec. 18, 1945.

82. Ancharski.

83. Log, Dec. 18–21, 1945.

84. Ibid., Dec. 21, 1945; Warble 1.

85. Thomas Holmes in *Newsletter* (June 1997), 3.

86. Waller in Stables, *We Remember,* 98–99.

87. Ibid.

88. Reehl 13; *Portland* website.

89. Roberts interview; Chuck Martin interview.

90. *New York Times,* Dec. 29, 1945, 8:2.

91. Kliks in *Newsletter* (3d Qtr 1991), 4.

92. Hunter Brown in *Newsletter* (4th Qtr 1992), 2. Brown was a civilian sailor on a tanker that was severely damaged in the storm and also found refuge in the Azores.

93. Horace in the "Guestbook" at the *Portland* website.

94. Log, Dec. 22–28, 1945.

95. Ibid., Dec. 22, 1945; Morton 4; Warble 1.

96. Horace in the "Guestbook" at the *Portland* website.

97. *New York Times,* Dec. 12, 1945, 8:2.

98. Warble 1.

99. Larson, *Isaac's Storm,* 76.

100. Stables, *We Remember II,* 132.

101. Ibid., 124–25.

102. *Portland* website.

103. Log, Jan. 8, 9, 1945.

104. Ibid., Jan. 17, 1946.
105. List of Officers, ibid., May 1946.
106. Terzibaschitsch, 84.
107. *Portland* website; Ewing, 26.
108. *Newsletter* (4th Qtr 1991), 5.

## 16. LEGACIES

1. Grace, 177.
2. *Newsletter* (4th Qtr 1991), 3. Holbrook, 258, says it is the "main mast." But the statement in *Newsletter* (4th Qtr 1991), 3, is from a review of the 1991 reunion at the site, and it specifies "after mast."
3. Holbrook, 258.
4. *Yorktown* was named *Bon Homme Richard* while under construction, but her name was changed when CV-5 went down. Fahey, Two-Ocean edition, 10.
5. McNamara diary in *Newsletter* (Oct. 2000), 6.
6. Partridge interview.
7. Fahey, Victory edition, 78.
8. *Portland* website.
9. *Newsletter* (June 1988), 2, 4.
10. Ibid., 4.
11. Ibid. (Dec. 1988), 2.
12. Ibid. (4th Qtr 1990), 5.
13. See, e.g., ibid. (2nd Qtr 1992), 5; ibid. (April 1998), 1; ibid. (April 2001), 2.
14. Ibid. (Oct. 1989), 2.
15. Ibid. (June 1988), 4.
16. Ibid. (April 1998), 5.
17. Stables, *We Remember II,* 65.
18. *Newsletter* (Oct. 1989), 2.
19. Ala 2.
20. Hight interview.
21. Story from the *Louisville (Kentucky) Courier Journal,* June 20, 1947, in *Newsletter* (Feb. 1995), 4.
22. Chuck Martin interview.
23. A history of the reunions through 1991 is given at *Newsletter* (2d Qtr 1992), 5.
24. *Newsletter* (1st Qtr 1991), 2. The site is called VETNET http://www.theveteran.net/vet/, but it may have changed its character since 1991.
25. *Newsletter* (June–July 1989) 1; ibid. (4th Qtr 1991), 3.
26. Ibid. (Jan. 1993), 3.
27. Ibid. (2d Qtr 1991, 2d issue), 3.
28. Ibid. (Oct. 2001), 5.
29. Ibid. (Oct. 1993), 3.
30. Ibid. (Oct. 1994), 1; ibid. (May 1993), 3.
31. Ibid. (2d Qtr 1991, 2d issue), 1.
32. Ibid. (2d Qtr 1991, 2d issue), 2; but ibid. (3rd Qtr 1991), 1.
33. Ibid. (4th Qtr 1991), 3.
34. Ibid. (3d Qtr 1991), 1.
35. Ibid. (May 1993), 2.

36. Ibid. (2d Qtr 1991, 1st issue), 5; Waller 4.

37. Ibid. (4th Qtr 1991), 6.

38. Ibid. (Jan. 1999), 1.

39. For just one example, see ibid. (July 2001), 1. There is a similar notation in nearly every issue.

40. Ibid. (Oct. 1988), 2; ibid. (June–July 1989), 1.

41. Ibid. (Oct. 2000), 4.

42. Ibid. (April 2002), 1.

43. Ibid. (June 1988), 2.

44. <http://www.worldwidewords.org/weirdwords/ww-ton1.htm>.

45. *Newsletter* (June–July 1989), 3.

46. Chuck Martin interview.

47. Partridge interview.

48. "Guestbook" at the *Portland* website.

49. Ibid.

50. *Newsletter* (4th Qtr 1991), 1; ibid. (July 1996), 4.

51. A brief biography of Settle appears in Ancell, 609.

52. Stables, *We Remember,* 107. The author has corrected two meaningless typographical errors that appeared in the reprinting of this letter in the Stables book.

53. Ibid. An unwarranted comma was deleted.

54. Stables, *We Remember II,* 135.

55. *Newsletter* (May 1993), 3.

56. Ibid. (Dec. 1996), 2.

57. Reprinted in Stables, *We Remember,* 94.

58. *Portland* did not win a battle star for her support of the recapture of the Aleutians or for her one-ship attack on Tarawa in October 1942. Dolezal interview; Reehl 5; *Portland* website. Only two ships won more battle stars than *Portland*'s sixteen: USS *Enterprise* (CV-6) with eighteen, and USS *San Francisco* (CA-38) with seventeen; Ewing, 26, 40.

59. Arbour kit.

# BIBLIOGRAPHY

## OFFICIAL NAVY DOCUMENTS

BATRON TWO and BATDIV TWO. World War II Diaries. Box 561, in RG38, Records of the Office of the Chief of Naval Operations at National Archives II, 8601 Adelphi Road, College Park, Maryland.

Burhans, A.D. Letter to CINCPACFLT, 19 October 1943. Box 1342, in RG38, Records of the Office of the Chief of Naval Operations at National Archives II, 8601 Adelphi Road, College Park, Maryland.

CINCPAC. World War II Diaries, September 27, 1942–October 24, 1942, vol. 1. Box 15, in RG38, Records of the Office of the Chief of Naval Operations at National Archives II, 8601 Adelphi Road, College Park, Maryland.

———. World War II Diaries, October 24, 1942, vol. 2. Box 16, in RG38, Records of the Office of the Chief of Naval Operations at National Archives II, 8601 Adelphi Road, College Park, Maryland.

Navships 35 (424), *War Damage Report 35*. Box 1328, in RG38, Records of the Office of the Chief of Naval Operations at National Archives II, 8601 Adelphi Road, College Park, Maryland.

USS *Portland*. Ship's Logs for 1933 (beginning Feb. 23), 1934, 1935, 1936, 1937, 1938, 1939, and 1940. National Archives I, 700 Pennsylvania Ave., Washington, D.C.

USS *Portland*. Ship's Logs for January 1, 1941–October 31, 1941, September 3, 1945–July 12, 1946. Boxes 1328, 1329, and 1342, in RG38, Records of the Office of the Chief of Naval Operations at National Archives II, 8601 Adelphi Road, College Park, Maryland. See Burhans letter, above, which states that some of the logs were lost in action.

USS *Portland*. War Diaries and Action Reports for July 1, 1942–December 31, 1942; May 1, 1943–September 2, 1945. Boxes 1328, 1329, and 1342, in RG38, Records of the Office of the Chief of Naval Operations at National Archives II, 8601 Adelphi Road, College Park, Maryland. See Burhans letter, above, which states that some of the logs were lost in action.

Various Commanders. World War II Diaries.
1) Marianas to Mar Gil Area, Apr. 4, 1945. Box 62 in RG38, Records of the Office of the Chief of Naval Operations at National Archives II, 8601 Adelphi Road, College Park, Maryland.
2) Mar Gil Area, Oct. 15, 1945 to North Pac Aug 26, 1943. Box 65 in RG38,

Records of the Office of the Chief of Naval Operations at National Archives II, 8601 Adelphi Road, College Park, Maryland.
3) TF 51.17.3 to TF 51.20. Box 185 in RG38, Records of the Office of the Chief of Naval Operations at National Archives II, 8601 Adelphi Road, College Park, Maryland.
4) TF 53 8-10-44 Copy DF Vol. 2 to TF 53.1.3. Box 199 in RG38, Records of the Office of the Chief of Naval Operations at National Archives II, 8601 Adelphi Road, College Park, Maryland.

### INTERVIEWS

*All interviews were tape-recorded at Colorado Springs, Colorado, on September 13, 2001.*

Banks, J.C. (former MM2/c)
Couch, Paul (former S1/c)
Dolezal, Bob (former BM1/c)
Gibson, Herb (former SK2/c)
Goff, Tom (former SK1/c)
Hight, Henry (former RM1/c)
Lassen, Jack (former RM2c)
Martin, Chuck (former S1/c)
Martin, Walter (former PH3/c)
Merryman, Dean (former S1/c)
Partridge, Willie (former Cox)
Pearson, Henry (former SK2/c)
Peterson, Eldon H. (former S1/c)
Pietrok, Vince (former Cox)
Pugh, Ray (former MMCPO)
Pynes, Lindsey (former SK3/c)
Riehl, Leroy (former GM2/c)
Roberts, Marshall (former SK1/c)
Stables, Joe (former Cox)

### OTHER MATERIALS FROM FORMER CREW

Ala, Charles William. "My Experiences in W.W. II." I have a copy.
Ala 1. Exchange of emails with Danyell Ericksen Maloney, Oct. 15, 17, 18, 2001.
Ala 2. Tape-recorded answers to my questions, sent Nov. 5, 2001.
Allred. Exchange of emails with John Allred, Jan. 2001.
Ancharski. Exchange of emails with Juanita Warble-Ancharski, June 17, 2001.
Arbour. Phone conversation with Joe Arbour, April 17, 2002.
Arbour kit. A collection of various items sent to me by Joe Arbour, May 2002. Returned to Arbour.
Arbour tape. Tape-recording of Joe Arbour as he read a kind of diary.
Bentley. Letter from Art Bentley, July 6, 2001.
Bond. Exchange of emails with Gail Bond, May 27 and Oct. 14, 2002.
Choate 1. Letter from Chuck Choate, June 29, 2001.
Choate 2–3. Tape recordings from Merle Choate, July 30 and Aug. 15, 2001.

Choate kit. A Christmas menu and some cartoons from the ship's crew, sent by
    Chuck Choate, Oct. 31, 2001.
Craven, Ralph. Remark in USS *Portland* "Guestbook."
Edens. Email from Cathy Edens, May 30, 2002.
Fulmer. Letter from Bayard C. Fulmer, Nov. 24, 2001.
Fynan 1–3. Exchange of emails with John Fynan, Jan. 24 and May 13, 2001, and
    May 14, 2002.
Geriak 1–2. Emails from Eileen Geriak, April 21 and June 6, 2001.
Hicks 1. Phone conversation with Ronald Hicks, July 6, 2001.
Hicks 2. Email from Ronald Hicks's daughter Cindy, Aug. 29, 2001.
Hicks kit. A collection of various items sent by Ronald Hicks.
Hopper. "The History of the U.S.S. PORTLAND From 1933–1946." Unpublished
    paper by Nick Hopper, submitted for credit in Humanities 310, June 18, 2001,
    Devrey College, Phoenix, Ariz. I have a copy.
Horace. Email from Chris Horace, April 2001.
Johns. Exchange of emails with Valerie C. Johns, May 15, 2002.
Mearns. Email from Edward Mearns, April 7, 2002.
Miles 1. Exchange of emails with Pat Miles, May 29, 2001.
Miles 2. Tape-recording from Pat Miles, June 21, 2001.
Mahala. Email from Ted Mahala, April 21, 2001.
Morton 1. Email from Charles Morton, May 29, 2001.
Morton 2. Phone conversation with Charles Morton, June 11, 2001.
Morton 3, 4. Letters from Charles Morton, Aug. 8 and 23, 2001.
Morton 5. Phone conversation with Charles Morton, Aug. 10, 2001.
*Newsletter* of the USS PORTLAND Reunion Association (1988–2002). I used Bill
    Reehl's copies and returned them to him.
Olsen 1. Email from Gordon Olsen, Jan. 7, 2002.
Olsen 2. Email from Gordon Olsen, Feb. 3, 2002.
*Pilot, The.* See *Port Beam.*
*Port Beam.* The ship's newspaper. The first issue was called *The Pilot.* These issues
    were lent to me by Joe Arbour and returned to him: April 28, May 5, May 19,
    May 24, Aug. 30, Sept. 7, undated but probably Sept. 14, Nov. 3, all in 1944.
*Portland* website. http://www.ussportland.org/. Contains a chronology of the ship's
    activities and a "Guestbook" to which interested people can write.
Reehl 1–20. Email exchanges with Bill Reehl. Feb. 2001 through July 2002.
Speer 1. Letter from Bill Speer, Nov. 17, 2001.
Speer 2. Undated letter from Bill Speer with answers to my questions, sent to him on
    Dec. 4, 2001.
Speer 3. Postcard from Bill Speer, Dec. 22, 2001.
Stables, Joe. *We Remember.* Unpublished collection of memories, diaries, etc., of
    the sailors who served in *Portland.* Virtually every member of the Association
    has a copy.
————. *We Remember II: USS Portland CA-33, 1933–1946.* A second collection of
    memories, diaries, etc., of the sailors who served in *Portland.*
Swars, George J. Letter, Oct. 7, 2003.
"USS PORTLAND (CA-33): Truk Surrenders to USS Portland." I have a copy.
Valdes 1–3. Exchange of emails with Fernando Valdes, Oct. 9, 11, 13, 2002.
Waller 1–9. Exchange of emails with Ted Waller, Jan. 2001–Oct. 2002.
Warble 1–2. Emails from Claude Warble through his daughter, June 2001.

## WEBSITES

http://globalsecurity.org/military/agency/navy/fairmed.htm. The modern United States Sixth Fleet in the Mediterranean.

http://www.history.navy.mil/photos/events/wwii-pac/japansur/js-10.htm. Japanese surrenders around the Empire.

http://www.theveteran.net/vet/. List of veterans' reunions.

http://www.thorfinn.net/history.html. A history of Truk.

http://www.worldwidewords.org/weirdwords/ww-ton1.htm. Tontine.

http://www3.uakron.edu/archival/arnstein/usrigid.htm. T.G.W. Settle's correspondence as inspector of naval aircraft, 1930–1932.

## PUBLICATIONS

Alexander, Joseph H. *The Three Days of Tarawa: Utmost Savagery*. Annapolis: Naval Institute Press, 1995.

Ancell, R. Manning, with Christine M. Miller. *The Biographical Dictionary of World War II, Generals and Flag Officers: The U.S. Armed Forces*. Westport, Conn.: Greenwood Press, 1996.

Baldwin, Hanson W. *Battles Lost and Won: Great Campaigns of World War II*. New York: Avon Books, 1968.

Ballard, Robert D., and Rick Archbold. *Return to Midway*. Washington: National Geographic, 1999.

Bates, Richard W. *The Battle for Leyte Gulf, October 1944*. Newport, R.I.: Naval War College, 1953–1957.

Blair, Clay, Jr. *Silent Victory: The U.S. Submarine War Against Japan*. Philadelphia: J.B. Lippincott Company, 1975.

Buell, Thomas B. *The Quiet Warrior: A Biography of Admiral Raymond A. Spruance*. Boston: Little, Brown, 1974.

Cutler, Thomas J. *The Battle of Leyte Gulf: 23–26 October 1944*. New York: Harper Collins, 1994.

Dull, Paul S. *A Battle History of the Imperial Japanese Navy (1941–1945)*. Annapolis: Naval Institute Press, 1978.

Ewing, Steve. *American Cruisers of World War II: A Pictorial Encyclopedia*. Missoula, Minn.: Pictorial Histories Publishing Co., 1984.

Fahey, James C. *The Ships and Aircraft of the United States Fleet*, Two-Ocean Fleet edition. 1941. Reprint, Annapolis: Naval Institute Press, 1976.

———. *The Ships and Aircraft of the United States Fleet*, Victory edition. 1945. Reprint, Annapolis: Naval Institute Press, 1976.

Frank, Richard. *Guadalcanal*. New York: Random House, 1990.

Friedman, Norman. *U.S. Cruisers: An Illustrated Design History*. Annapolis: Naval Institute Press, 1984.

Fuchida, Mitsuo, and Masatake Okumiya. *Midway: The Battle that Doomed Japan, The Japanese Navy's Story*. New York: Ballantine Books, 1955.

Grace, James W. *The Naval Battle of Guadalcanal: Night Action, 13 November 1942*. Annapolis: Naval Institute Press, 1999.

Gregg, Charles T. *Tarawa*. New York: Stein and Day, 1984.

Griffith, Samuel B., II. *The Battle for Guadalcanal.*: The Nautical and Aviation Publishing Company of America, 1979.

Hammel, Eric. *Guadalcanal: Decision at Sea: The Naval Battle of Guadalcanal, November 13–15, 1942.* New York: Crown, 1988.

———. *Guadalcanal: Starvation Island.* New York: Crown, 1987.

Helm, Thomas. *Ordeal by Sea.* New York: Signet, 2001.

Holbrook, Heber A. *The History and Times of the U.S.S. Portland.* Dixon, Calif.: Pacific Ship and Shore, 1990.

Kennedy, David M. *Freedom from Fear: The American People in Depression and War, 1929–1945.* New York: Oxford Univ. Press, 1999.

Kerminsky, Bob. *"Mighty Mo": USS Missouri, a Navy Legend.* Washington, D.C.: Navy Office of Information, 1995.

Koburger, Charles W., Jr. *Pacific Turning Point: The Solomons Campaign, 1942–1943.* Westport, Conn.: Praeger, 1995.

Kurzman, Dan. *Fatal Voyage.* New York: Athenaeum, 1990.

Larson, Erik. *Isaac's Storm: A Man, a Time, and the Deadliest Hurricane in History.* New York: Crown, 1999.

Lech, Raymond B. *All the Drowned Sailors.* New York: Military Heritage Press, 1982.

*Life,* Nov. 5, 1945.

Linderman, Gerald F. *The World Within War: America's Combat Experience in World War II.* New York: The Free Press, 1997.

Linzey, Stanford E. *God Was at Midway: The Sinking of the USS Yorktown (CV-5) and the Battles of the Coral Sea and Midway.* San Diego: Black Forest Press, 1996.

Lord, Walter. *Incredible Victory.* New York: Harper and Row, 1967.

Lundstrom, John B. *The First Team and the Guadalcanal Campaign: Naval Fighter Combat from August to November 1942.* Annapolis: Naval Institute Press, 1994.

Manchester, William. *American Caesar: Douglas MacArthur, 1880–1964.* Boston: Little, Brown, 1978.

McGurn, Barrett. "Log of the Sweet P." *Yank: The Army Weekly* (Jan. 5, 1945). Photocopy in *Newsletter* (June 1988), 5–6.

Miller, Edward S. *War Plan Orange: The U.S. Strategy to Defeat Japan, 1897–1945.* Annapolis: Naval Institute Press, 1991.

Morison, Samuel Eliot. *History of United States Naval Operations in World War II.* Vol. 4, *Coral Sea, Midway and Submarine Action, May 1942–August 1942.* Boston: Little, Brown, 1953.

———. *History of United States Naval Operations in World War II.* Vol. 13. *The Liberation of the Philippines: Luzon, Mindinao, the Visayas, 1944–1945.* Boston: Little, Brown, 1959.

———. *History of United States Naval Operations in World War II.* Vol. 14. *Victory in the Pacific, 1945.* Boston: Little, Brown, 1960.

———. *The Two-Ocean War: The Definitive Short History of the United States Navy in World War II.* New York: Ballantine, 1972.

Musicant, Ivan. *U.S. Armored Cruisers: A Design and Operational History.* Annapolis: Naval Institute Press, 1985.

Newcomb, Richard F. *Abandon Ship.* New York: Holt, 1958.

*New York Times,* 1933, 1945.

Parrish, Thomas, ed. *The Simon and Schuster Encyclopedia of World War II.* New York: Simon and Schuster, 1978.

Potter, E.B. *Nimitz.* Annapolis: Naval Institute Press, 1976.

———. *Triumph in the Pacific: The Navy's Struggle against Japan.* Englewood Cliffs, N.J.: Prentice-Hall, 1963.

Potter, E.B., and Chester W. Nimitz. *Sea Power: A Naval History.* Englewood Cliffs, N.J.: Prentice-Hall, 1960.

Prange, Gordon W. *At Dawn We Slept: The Untold Story of Pearl Harbor.* New York: Penguin Books, 1981.

Roscoe, Theodore. *United States Destroyer Operations in World War II.* Annapolis: Naval Institute Press, 1984.

———. *United States Submarine Operations in World War II.* Annapolis: Naval Institute Press, 1984.

Smith, William Ward. *Midway: Turning Point of the Pacific.* New York: Thomas Y. Crowell, 1966.

Spector, Ronald H. *Eagle Against the Sun: The American War with Japan.* New York: The Free Press, 1985.

Stafford, Edward P. *The Big E: The Story of the USS Enterprise.* New York: Dell, 1962.

Steinberg, Rafael. *Island Fighting.* Chicago: Time-Life, 1978.

Stillwell, Paul. *Battleship Arizona: An Illustrated History.* Annapolis: Naval Institute Press, 1991.

Terzibaschitsch, Stefan. *Cruisers of the US Navy, 1922–1962.* Transl. from German by Harold Erenberg. Annapolis: Naval Institute Press, 1988.

U.S. Naval Academy. *Register of Alumni.* Book 1, Classes 1846–1917. USNA Alumni Association, 1996.

Wheeler, Keith. *The Road to Tokyo.* Chicago: Time-Life, 1979.

Willmott, H.P. *The Barrier and the Javelin: Japanese and Allied Pacific Strategies, February to June 1942.* Annapolis: Naval Institute Press, 1983.

*World Book.* Chicago: The Quarrie Corporation, 1946.

Wouk, Herman. *The Caine Mutiny.* New York: Dell paperback, 1951.

Zich, Arthur. *The Rising Sun.* Alexandria, Va.: Time-Life Books, 1977.

# INDEX

Fletcher, Frank Jack, 46, 50-51, 53,
    60, 62
Florida, 98
Foley, James L., 97
Ford Island, 31
Forrestall, Arthur, 226
Fountain, H. F., 181
Frank, Richard, 58
*Franklin,* 260 (n.12)
*Fulton,* 55-56
Fynan, John, 49, 159

Gallagher, Ned, xii
Gatrall, David, 233
Gaylord, Delvan C., 49
gedunks, 105-106
Generous, Diane, Michelle and
    Suzanne, xii
Geriak, John, 48-49, 164
Ghormley, Robert L., 60, 76, 102
Gibson, Herbert, 82, 154
Giffin, R.C., 123
Gilbert Islands, 127-128, 169
Gober, Joseph R., 252 (n.49)
Goff, Tom, 158-159
Great Lakes, 211
*Greer*, x
Guadalcanal, 44, 58-62, 72, 93-94,
    202. *See also Naval Battle of
    Guadalcanal*
Guam, 203-204
*Guam,* 3
Guhl, Eldon, 159
Guitar, Wallace, 133-134
Guthrie, Woodie, x

Haldorson, Ray, 26
Hall, John, 145
Hall, Walter, 39, 157
Halsey, William F., 71, 76-78, 88,
    93, 101-102, 146-147, 191
*Hamman,* 54, 56
Hammel, Eric, 81, 248 (n.25)

Hara, Chichi 201
Hardin, Daniel, 105
Haskell, Frank, 107
Hawaii, 17, 19, 20, 22, 23
Hayes, Frank, 181-182
Healy, 145
Heavy Cruisers
    casualties, 37
    usefulness, 37
Hedberg, 160
Heinolds, 160
*Helena,* 78-79, 93, 95-96
Helm, Leslie J., 252 (n.49)
Henderson Field, 71, 73, 79, 94, 108
Hicks, Ronald, 154-155, 160-162,
    205-206
*Hiei,* 78, 81, 90
Higgins boats (LCVPs), 96
Hight, Henry, 33, 87-89, 154-155,
    250 (n.86)
Hildreth, Horace, 206
Hill, Harry W., 135
Hiroshima, 197-198
*Hiryu,* 53
History Channel, 202
Hitler, Adolf 18, 35
Hoge, Frank, 111
Holbrook, Heber, 117
Hollandia, 137-138, 192
*Honolulu,* 147
Hook, Riley C., 252 (n.49)
Hoover, Gilbert, 95-96
Hope, Bob, 223
Horace, J.J., 214-215, 221
*Hornet,* 51, 58
Horta Bay, Azores, 221-222
Hospital Point, 31
Hotcamp, Erwin W., 252 (n.49)
*Houston,*18-19, 242 (n.3)
Howard, Eugene, 85
Hunt, John, 206
Hupf, Paul, 182